053000

The Structure of Mind in History

THE STRUCTURE
OF MIND IN HISTORY
Five Major Figures
in Psychohistory

Philip Pomper

Columbia University Press
New York
1985

The chart on p. 91 is reprinted from *Childhood and Society,* 2d edition, by Erik H. Erikson, by permission of W.W. Norton & Company, Inc. Copyright 1950, and © 1963 by W.W. Norton & Company, Inc. Further acknowledgment is made to Erik Erikson and to The Hogarth Press for permission to reprint in the United Kingdom.

The chart on p. 108 is reprinted from *Toys and Reasons: Stages in the Ritualization of Experience,* by Erik H. Erikson, by permission of W.W. Norton & Company, Inc. Copyright © 1977 by W.W. Norton & Company, Inc. Further acknowledgment is made to Marion Boyars, Ltd., for permission to reprint in the United Kingdom.

Library of Congress Cataloging in Publication Data

Pomper, Philip.
The structure of mind in history.

Bibliography: p.
Includes index.
1. Psychohistory.   I. Title.
D16.16.P66 1985   901′.9   84-22988
ISBN 0-231-06064-5

COLUMBIA UNIVERSITY PRESS
NEW YORK   GUILDFORD, SURREY
COPYRIGHT © 1985 COLUMBIA UNIVERSITY PRESS
ALL RIGHTS RESERVED
PRINTED IN THE UNITED STATES OF AMERICA

*Clothbound editions of Columbia University Press books are
Smyth-sewn and printed on permanent and durable acid-free paper.*

IN MEMORY OF
Louis O. Mink

There is an intellectual function in us which demands unity, connection, and intelligibility from any material, whether of perception or thought, that it grasps; and it does not hesitate to supply a false one if, as a result of particular circumstances, it is unable to establish a true connection.

Sigmund Freud, *Totem and Taboo*

Man by understanding the way he historicizes may yet overcome certain stereotyped ways in which history repeats itself—ways which man can no longer afford.

Erik H. Erikson, *Gandhi's Truth*

Contents

Acknowledgments   xi

Introduction   xiii

ONE **The Psychohistorical Intelligentsia**   1

TWO **Architectonics of the Unconscious Mind**   21

THREE **Freud**   49

FOUR **Erikson**   81

FIVE **Marcuse and Brown**   115

SIX **Lifton**   143

SEVEN **The Limits of Psychohistory**   167

Notes   177

Index   183

Acknowledgments

I WOULD LIKE to thank a number of people who contributed to the realization of this book. First, my thanks go to Robert J. Lifton, who admitted me into his seminar on psychohistory at Yale more than fifteen years ago, and who has provided both inspiration and help over the years. He bears responsibility neither for the idiosyncrasies of my position nor for the treatment of his own. Second, the intellectual ambience of the journal *History and Theory* strongly affected my overall project. The late Louis O. Mink, to whom this book is dedicated, his fellow editors Richard Vann and Richard Buel, and several other scholars associated with the journal helped me immeasurably. Hayden White especially helped me to define my own position. A number of colleagues at Wesleyan— C. Stewart Gillmor, Oliver W. Holmes, J. Donald Moon, and Jill Morawski—encouraged me to believe that the larger intellectual community, not just psychohistorians, would be interested in architectonics. Third, one of my former teachers, William H. McNeill, who still troubles to read the manuscripts of superannuated students, went through two drafts with a critical eye and provided useful comments and encouragement.

My students in History 380, with laudable intellectual eagerness and alertness, gave me the opportunity to test and refine the central concepts in this book. I owe them a debt of gratitude for their patience as well.

My thanks to Jane Muskatello and Fran Warren for helping to prepare the manuscript. My wife Alice not only helped with the manuscript at all stages, but did her best to reduce the frequency of polysyllabic terms, for which readers should be thankful.

Finally, I am very grateful to my editors at Columbia University Press, Susan Koscielniak and David Diefendorf, for their support and their willingness to publish this book in the form in which it was originally conceived.

Introduction

THE GROWTH in the importance of the idea of the "unconscious," or more accurately, the "unconscious mind," in recent historical thinking might itself be the subject of a lengthy scholarly investigation. The subject of this book, however, is not the history of the idea of the unconscious mind and the circumstances which have made it so important in contemporary historical thought. This is a study of the structural principles used by the foremost theoreticians of psychohistory. A few comments on the different concepts of unconscious mind are in order, however, for the psychoanalytic conception of unconscious mind must be carefully distinguished from other concepts of an unconscious mind. The unconscious mind studied by psychoanalysts and psychohistorians is usually the *dynamic unconscious,* the contents of the mind which are forcibly restrained from entering consciousness. The unconscious, by far the largest part of the mind, is sometimes erroneously identified with the *id* in Freud's tripartite psyche, which consists of an ego, superego, and id. However, in Freud's mature structural theory the ego and superego also have repressed unconscious layers. Furthermore, the unconscious mind described by Freud is formed out of biological inheritances and is not simply a repository of the repressed impulses and wishes of the individual. The evolutionary aspect of Freudian theory is so uncongenial to contemporary historians that a great deal of effort has been spent in an effort to sever the Freudian unconscious mind from its biological roots. Freud's ideas of phylogenetic memory traces and "organic" repression have been abandoned for the most part in favor of a vision of changing forms of repression affecting specific human groups in a great variety of historical cultures. The emphasis has shifted from innate biological forces shaping the unconscious mind and determining much of its contents to the exogenous power of culture and society. Contemporary psychohistorians now see the unconscious mind mainly as the product of external historical forces. Indeed, when the shift from inner to outer, from biology to historical culture, is sufficiently radical, one is left with the notion of historical psychology. This notion, programmatically developed by generations of French historians in the *Annales* tradition, led to the abandonment of the Freudian drive-determined unconscious mind for the culturally coded unconscious group mind or *mentalité* of structuralism and the *épistème* of poststructuralism.

For a large segment of the contemporary intelligentsia, the idea of unconscious codes has become associated with the tyranny of internalized social and cultural forms. Whether the fundamental evil of the social and cultural world is called capitalism, patriachalism, racism, or some other "ism," the contemporary intelligentsia seem to prefer nurture over nature: the idea that not nature but our own historical environments are responsible for the shape and contents of both the conscious and unconscious parts of the human mind. The intelligentsia mission to investigate the unconscious and to discover its origins is a continuation of the revolutionary program of the Enlightenment. The hopes of rationalists have not been defeated by the failures of several generations to achieve rational solutions to political, social, and economic problems. However, the striking failure of twentieth-century revolutions to bring about radical changes in morality and group consciousness made investigation of the unconscious mind all the more important. By delving into the unconscious mind, whether envisioned as a product of biological inheritance or cultural code, the radical intelligentsia believe that they can bring to light the inner products of external oppression and explain why it is so difficult to overthrow the tyrannies which have prevented us from achieving happiness, truth, a universalistic conception of justice, and equality. Thus, Freud became a hero of the left, for he had dramatized for the twentieth-century intelligentsia the importance of the unconscious mind and repression, even though he had presented them in an unacceptable psychobiological theory of the mind.

Students of Freud, the psychoanalytic movement, and psychohistory have long been aware of the political implications of both Freudian orthodoxy and the various revisions of Freud's theory of the human psyche. Philip Rieff, Paul Robinson, and Paul Roazen are perhaps the outstanding students of the politics of the psychoanalytic movement. They and other scholars have produced excellent intellectual biographies of Freud, Erikson (Robert Coles as well as Roazen), and Marcuse (most recently, Barry Katz). Their efforts and those of others—Carl Schorske, Fred Weinstein, Gerald Platt, and Russell Jacoby for example—to understand the cultural and social background of psychoanalysis, generations of psychoanalysts, and individual psychoanalytic thinkers cannot possibly be surveyed adequately here, and any effort to synthesize or revise their work would entail the writing of a voluminous monograph rather than this slim volume.[1] I assume here that a comparative overview of several classic theories and works of psychohistory which subjects them all to the same structural analysis will yield new insights and make psychohistorical theory more accessible to readers who might not otherwise study the vast corpus of psychoanalytic and psychohistorical thought. Readers who expect a survey of the most recent trends in psychohistory will be disappointed, for other than some passing references, there is very little here about the new schools of narcissism or feminist psychoanalytic thought. A further assumption of my study is that Herbert Marcuse and Norman O. Brown prefigured many of these trends and that their major psychohistorical works represent with classical clarity both earlier and later radical positions within psychoanalysis, particularly amalgamations of a theory of the unconscious with left Hegelianism, Marxism, feminism, and poststructuralism.

I hope that my eschewal of monographic density and coverage of all the recent work in psychohistory will be justified by the use of a mode of analysis which has not heretofore been used systematically in psychohistorical study. The closest approach is that of Charles Hampden-Turner in his recently published book, *Maps of the Mind* (1982). It is a compendium of considerable scope but it is not mainly about psychohistory. The aim of my study is to reward the reader with insight into psychoanalytic efforts to provide a map of human history through psychoanalytic penetration of the unconscious mind.

Philip Pomper
Middletown, Connecticut
November 1983

• CHAPTER I •

The Psychohistorical Intelligentsia

T HE INVESTIGATION of the human mind and the efforts of modern minds to discover the structure of history have converged during the last half century in psychohistory. Theories about the characteristics and origin of the human mind vary from the theological to the sociobiological, from biblical creationism to neo-Darwinism. The methods used to investigate it range from introspection and the study of poetry to controlled laboratory experiments on rodents or observation of primates in their natural habitats. We use anything we can in our efforts, including the vast array of artifacts deposited by past cultures and those of an enormous variety of active cultures. We know that at best we can tell a likely story about the human mind—that when we examine the products of human activity we can only infer or imaginatively reconstruct an antecedent mental process.

Occasionally, a creative thinker startles us with an original hypothesis about human mental evolution. For example, in a recent book the psychologist Julian Jaynes presented the hypothesis that auditory hallucinations precipitated by stress were functional during large stretches of history, rather than acutely dysfunctional, as they are in our culture. Jaynes encourages us to imagine a time when human beings did not possess consciousness as we experience it today and when schizoid states of mind (a "bicameral mind") maintained social order. In brief, Jaynes suggests that today's maladapted minds, the minds of schizophrenics, would have been well adapted for life in bicameral civilizations.[1]

I

It is very difficult for a contemporary social scientist to imagine how societies which systematically depended upon schizoid states of mind to preserve themselves functioned. Yet studies of shamanism and of the role of shamans in a great many cultures show how schizoid trances or seizures can play a social role, and psychohistories of modern mass movements show how communities in crisis chose leaders whom we now diagnose as paranoid. Delusional systems embodied in extremist ideologies, products of paranoid states of mind, seem to mobilize communities for heroic efforts or at the very least to sustain their morale during the crises. If we restricted ourselves to the study of "rational" mental activity in the past, as some philosophers of history prescribed, we would be poor investigators of the human condition. In several thousand years, historians may balk at the notion that our theologies and secular ideologies could sustain the achievements of our technological civilization, just as we balk at the hypothesis that large masses of human beings in bicameral civilizations obeyed auditory hallucinations of the voices of their deities and rulers. Given our present reality, in which leaders who control vast technologies are guided by ideologies which seem to be little more than the detritus of earlier delusional systems, we should stand humbly before Jaynes' hypothesis.

Of course, we have other options. We might dispense with concepts of normal and healthy and aim at some neutral posture—some neutral description of mental phenomena. We might suspend our habitual diagnostic and therapeutic outlook and stop prescribing for the dead. It might be just another form of that unfortunate practice of preaching to the dead, which we so strongly condemn in moralistic historians. However, to do either—to eschew judgment or diagnosis—would so limit our discourse that it would be of little interest to serious thinkers about the human condition. In practice, we are all judges and diagnosticians. We would do well to admit it in advance. We try to reconstruct the states of mind motivating the kinds of expression and activity that interest us in our historical studies, and we assume that some kinds of human expression and activity issue from rational or normal mental states and other kinds from irrational or abnormal ones. To be sure, philosophers have shown what a muddle we can make out of such terms, but hardly anyone (in his right mind) today would assume that anyone of us is rational all of the time, in whatever sense that word is used; and only the most dedicated relativist would dispense with a concept of normal.

Some contemporary thinkers believe that we, as a species, have distinctive abnormalities, indeed self-destructive ones. They further assume that time is running out—that we are showing lethal symptoms as a species—and that a correct diagnosis and prescription is crucial for our survival. Freud himself suggested something of this sort in *Civilization and Its Discontents* and other works, where he offered psychoanalysis as a diagnostic method for communal ills, and as a source of therapeutic prescriptions for them. However, he never came forward with a satisfactory method for defining a normal culture, a sound basis for the diagnosis of abnormal cultures, or any ideas about the politics of communal therapy. In his early psychohistorical works he speculated about the origins of human misery in culture. Later, he posed the problem of human misery in even more cosmic terms, as a symptom of the perpetual struggle between life and death instincts, Eros and Thanatos. This problem, as set forth in *Civilization and Its Discontents,* became the starting point for some of the most important works of later psychohistorians. The hypothesis that we are a sick species is no longer novel, even if it is still problematic. Later psychohistorians revised Freud's theory about the causes of human misery and dealt with the issue of the self-destruction of the human species in their own terms.

Not all hypotheses that we are a sick species or approaches to the problem of human self-destruction are psychoanalytic, of course. The best-known popular accounts suggest that evolution and the physiology of the human brain are at the root of the problem. We become increasingly dangerous to ourselves as the newer and technically inventive part of our brain, the neocortex, creates ever more effective instruments of destruction. They can be triggered by older brain structures which are the site of primitive emotions. These are the limbic system, or paleomammalian brain, and the midbrain, or reptilian brain. The approaches based upon brain physiology, while provocative, will not be investigated here, not because they are unworthy of comment but because they have not entered the mainstream of intelligentsia thought. On the other hand, the psychoanalytic approach and psychohistory are well established, if still controversial. Psychoanalysis has undergone the fate of all intelligentsia doctrines. It has been revised, amalgamated with other doctrines, and appropriated by thinkers of right, left, and center. Freudian psychology and Freud's own efforts at psychohistory have inspired a multitude of followers and a huge literature. Several of the most influential members of the psychoanalytic branch of the modern intelligentsia will be examined here, primarily through their best realized and most important works of psychohistory.

At this point, some definitions might be useful. "Intelligentsia" is a familiar term that is often preceded by adjectives, such as "revolutionary," "Marxist," or "Parisian." The adjectives need no clarification, but "intelligentsia" is one of those words about which entire volumes have been written. Only a very brief résumé of the use of the term and a homely definition are offered here. At one time denoting the group of leading figures who embodied the intelligence of a nation, it acquired a more specialized meaning by the late nineteenth century. It usually was reserved for the alienated members of the highly educated stratum of society—those in opposition to the Establishment of their nations. They attracted most attention when they became revolutionaries. However, for our purposes it is sufficient to think of the intelligentsia as those members (please note the plural) of the educated classes who combine advanced or vanguard ideologies with activism. They need not be the authors of ideologies themselves, so long as they make a significant contribution to a growing ideological tradition. Thus, we include in the intelligentsia ideologues, who create vast world views, artists whose imaginative works inspire the ideologues or are inspired by them, and popularizers who spread the ideas to a larger community. For example, studies of the Russian intelligentsia include not only Chernyshevskii, Bakunin, and Lenin, but Dostoevsky, Turgenev, and Chekhov. Sometimes imaginative writers themselves become ideologues, as was the case with Dostoevsky and Tolstoy. The ideologues, those who create the major "isms," are the ones who are considered to be the leaders of the intelligentsia. The theorists are accorded special dignity, even if they are not as effective strategists as their followers in actualizing the theory. They hold up ideals of truth and justice that provide inspiration and guidance to disciples.

The word "ideology" should be defined, for without it the above definition of intelligentsia would be a bit hollow. An ideology is a systematic doctrine which contains developed ideas about evils and miseries that

4

must be overcome and a good that must be pursued and realized, in order for human beings to achieve or maintain their rightful place in a larger
order, whether divine or secular. In modern secular thought, especially
since the nineteenth century, ideologies set forth the conditions in which
the next advancement in human development, if not the ultimate one,
will occur. Most ideologies, even the universalistic ones, have tended to
promote distinct groups and institutions. Despite great changes of ideological idiom, most ideologies can be thought of as expressions of the
belief of a group in its special dignity or mission. Whether the group's
ideologues confer its status and mission in the name of God, Nature, or
History, the outcome is an enhancement of group morale and often, its
mobilization for heroic effort. The actualizers of intelligentsia theories have
been successful precisely because they have been able to translate theoretical abstractions into programs for groups and to recruit leaders in the
name of the ideology. Intellectual historians construct elaborate geneal-
ogies of the great ideologies showing how they merge with newer isms
or how they revert to their earlier forms. The term "generation" is often
used to describe a group of disciples which develops a variation of the
ideology at a given historical moment. Almost every modern ideology has
experienced more than one conflict of generations. So far as psychoanalysis is concerned, Freud's movement suffered from schisms almost immediately, and the current psychohistorical intelligentsia often turn to earlier
heretics (from Freud's point of view, that is) like Otto Rank, Wilhelm
Reich, and Geza Roheim. There are Freudo-Marxists and analysts who
combine unorthodox versions of psychoanalysis with other theories and
use them in conjunction with new historical methods. One can also find
at any given moment in the history of an intelligentsia movement thinkers who try to purify the doctrine and reestablish orthodoxy.

Some intellectual histories locate grand intelligentsia traditions that
stretch back to the pre-Socratics. Others go back even farther, to sha-
manistic traditions and to the anonymous creators of myths. However far
back one goes, and however cunningly one constructs intellectual ge-
nealogies, the ideologies themselves are obviously inspired by immediate
historical contexts. In these new environments, the formidable devils which
haunted past intelligentsia generations dwindle into petty demons, and
new concerns dominate intelligentsia awareness. What gives the intelligentsia their special élan is their engagement with the ultimate ques-

tions—sometimes called the "accursed questions"—the riddles of the human condition, the position, nature, and destiny of the species in the greater scheme of things, indeed the most accursed question of all, is there a greater scheme of things? They tended to ask these questions of the great constructed unities: God (or the gods), Nature, Fate, Mind, and most recently, History. In our era, the intelligentsia still inquire into Nature with great zeal, but Fate has given way to Law and Probability, and God has tended to drop out of the picture. Although Society and Culture are often at the center of intelligentsia discourse, it is usually understood that they are historical in character, for the modern intelligentsia have been most impressed by the historicity of all things, but especially that of the human condition. This has been the case since the early modern period. The French Revolution, the Industrial Revolution, the Hegelian and Marxist theories of history, and Darwin's evolutionary theory were perhaps the most significant turning points for the modern intelligentsia. Efforts to understand the French Revolution yielded a satisfying dialectical vision of history—a vision in which conflict is part of the very structure of historical progress and human development. The Industrial Revolution and its attendant miseries focused the mid-nineteenth century intelligentsia upon the vast inequalities of property and power issuing from a new system of production and new social relationships. Marx and Engels believed and professed that such misery would, in dialectical fashion, provide the stimulus for the next great revolution in human relationships. Darwin's theory of evolution deepened the growing belief of the European intelligentsia that change governed everything and their confidence (bolstered by continuing dramatic progress in the natural sciences) that the human mind might solve the mysteries of change in both nature and history. In 1883, at Marx's funeral, Engels opined that Marx and Darwin had already solved the major puzzles. He said: "Just as Darwin discovered the law of development of organic nature, so Marx discovered the law of development of human history."

Scientific optimism and the intelligentsia belief that change in nature and history signified progressive development made conflict and misery more bearable. All of the misery and destruction in nature and history now had a benign meaning. Nothing was for nought. The laws of nature and history did not signify oppressive limits so much as a promise of development. One could accept cruel evolutionary and dialectical laws, for they guaranteed a better future. Necessity yielded development. Nature's laws were bountiful. The dialectical laws of history would bring universal justice and freedom. To be sure, this did not lead to quietism, for the activist spirit of the intelligentsia encouraged what we usually call "voluntarist" interpretations of law. That is, the most activist segment of the intelligentsia felt that as obedient servants of history's laws they ought to struggle to bring about the next step in human development, which often seemed a bit slow in coming. It was one thing to believe in dialectical laws, and another to be the daily witness of inequality, misery, and injustice.

As the nineteenth century advanced, the hopes of the radical intelligentsia struggled against the seemingly regressive trends of nationalism and imperialism. At each step of the way, at least some members of the radical intelligentsia proved themselves up to the task of incorporating the new miseries and evils into a dialectical framework. But when twentieth century wars and socialist revolutions still failed to give unambiguous signs that vast conflicts and human sacrifice were yielding justice, freedom, and a unified human species, a mood of increasing pessimism entered historical thought. Furthermore, by the mid-twentieth century, not only had scientific and technological progress created the destructive power of nuclear weapons, technology seemed to be yielding diminishing returns. New knowledge about ecology brought with it a new sense of limits, no less sober than the Malthusianism that had been at the basis of the more pessimistic visions of incessant struggle in both the natural and historical worlds.

> Like all other forms of life, humankind remains inextricably entangled in flows of matter and energy that result from eating and being eaten. However clever we have been in finding new niches in that system, the enveloping microparasitic-macroparasitic balances limiting human access to food and energy have not been abolished and never will be.[2]

This image of unconquerable nature, although updated for twentieth-century minds, is familiar enough. Throughout the nineteenth century it appealed to a great variety of thinkers, some interested in supporting the status quo, others promoting visions of new social orders.

7

The hopes of the radical intelligentsia had always been confronted by interpretations of Darwin that justified uneven distributions of wealth, social hierarchies, and monopolies of political power. Despite Marx's own efforts to distinguish human development in history from natural evolution, many socialists, including several of his own followers, tried to steal Darwin from the thinkers of the right who had created social Darwinism. These Darwinian Marxists tried to connect socialism and the victory of the laboring classes to natural selection. In addition, there were radical thinkers who found more cooperation and solidarity in the natural world than struggle and competition. In *Mutual Aid* and other works Prince Kropotkin put forth the theory that history, not nature, was the problem. Accretions of petrified institutions worked against the natural human tendency toward cooperation. He wrote:

> In the practice of mutual aid, which we can retrace to the earliest beginnings of evolution, we thus find the positive and undoubted origin of our ethical conceptions; and we can affirm that in the ethical progress of man, mutual support—not mutual struggle—has had the leading part. In its widest extension, even at the present time, we also see the best guarantee of a still loftier evolution of our race.[3]

The tendency illustrated by this quotation from Kropotkin persists in the contemporary radical intelligentsia, despite the assaults of antinaturalists, who usually associate any idea of innate endowments with social and political conservatism. They fear any suggestion that biology controls human relationships. However, the view that human beings are shaped completely by historical cultures and social structures has been assailed by Noam Chomsky, who remains within Kropotkin's tradition. He shows the dangers implicit in the "empty organism" approach:

> A vision of a future social order is in turn based on a concept of human nature. If in fact man is an indefinitely malleable, completely plastic being, with no innate structures of mind and no intrinsic needs of a cultural or social character, then he is a fit subject for the "shaping of behavior" by the state authority, the corporate manager, the technocrat, or the central committee. Those with some confidence in the human species will hope this is not so and will try to determine the intrinsic human characteristics that provide the framework

for intellectual development, the growth of moral consciousness, cultural achievement, and participation in a free community.[4]

Late-twentieth-century communities have had ample evidence that atrocities can be committed in the name of either God, Nature, or History. When communities are told that they have been selected or judged by a divine being, natural selection, or the dialectic of history, they should suspect that the appeal to higher agencies in such ideological pronouncements signifies in some cases well-intentioned fantasies, and in others, ambition and political manipulation. We should beware of ideologues bearing gifts, even though we cannot fail to appreciate the enormous positive role of ideologies in mobilizing our energies. Our spiritual need for visions of good and evil, and order and chaos, and promises of human salvation, development, and fulfillment cannot be doubted. Who is to blame for the atrocities committed in behalf of either religious revitalization movements or progressive ideologies? Every great doctrine, whether issuing from religious or secular thought, has been implemented by both gentle saints and fierce inquisitors, dreamy intellectuals and bloody-minded despots. It is difficult to assign blame to the doctrines themselves, or to their creators. The human quest for optimistic unifying visions, for new syntheses of the information flowing from more and more disciplines and media, continues unabated. We cannot do without either realism or hope.

Modern intelligentsia thinkers who have incorporated psychoanalysis into theories of human development in history offer a novel position. On the one hand, they recognize the wishful thinking and power motives in past ideologies of human development. On the other hand, they commit themselves to the very same struggle for human development. They have found a way to do this despite Freud's repudiation of the benignity of the agencies in whose name intelligentsia ideologues have traditionally acted: God, Nature, and the dialectic of History. Freud's admonitions against the illusions of religion, his unmasking of the sources of traditional visions of good and evil, tend to thwart both a sense of virtue and any aspiration toward "higher" goals. Furthermore, he showed that the causes of human misery lie in nature itself and are part of the biological inheritance of the species. So much for wise and generous Nature. Finally, he took the position that human misery can never be fully overcome, only mitigated. Ethical systems, whether issuing from religious

9

prophecy or the "scientific" views of the socialist intelligentsia, in Freud's view are part of the problem rather than solutions to human misery, for they fail to get at the root of the problem. Only psychoanalysis does. This radical and sectarian vision—a founder's stubborn vision—challenged thinkers who valued Freud's contribution but who felt the need to commit themselves to movements for social justice and human development.

Not only did Freud deny his followers utopian hopes, his statement of the problem seemingly denied them commitments to religious, social, and political movements which might be used to remedy communal ills. Freud had studied group psychology and had proposed a psychoanalytic explanation of the way in which leaders and ideas bound groups together. He had touched upon the therapeutic functions of religious, social, and political commitments as well as the costs of communal life. But he had exalted the autonomous intellect and believed in the leveling effect of life in groups. The great mass of humanity partook of group psychology and its illusions, and would always do so unless lifted to the level of the enlightened elite. The scientific elite lived without communal faith and hope. Enlightenment without hope for the few and the false consolations of communal illusions for the many—this is hardly an attractive vision. Indeed, it is unacceptable for the intelligentsia, as defined here.

Freud's theory of group psychology made it exceedingly difficult for those who believed that the group is the appropriate locus of treatment for communal ills to cling to much hope for the species as a whole. He hypothesized what the twentieth century illustrated with savage force— that in-group therapy usually involves the persecution of out-groups. Even worse, the twentieth-century intelligentsia has grown increasingly aware of the transitory nature of such therapy. Dispensers of group salvation are saviors pro tem, from a psychoanalytic point of view (therapeutic, that is), and all too often wrathful judges of those who do not accept the new dispensation. With the passage of time, vital faiths lose their full meaning and the attendant therapeutic benefits. To be sure, they may be revitalized in every generation, with varying degrees of success. When revitalization fails, the aged faith becomes a burden—the dead weight of the past with little meaning or inspiration for the living. This is of course truest of all for cultures experiencing rapid change. In them, faith itself becomes problematic. The increased velocity of cultural change and the breakdown of communities have made traditional forms of communal therapy obsolescent. However, the spiritual impoverishment of groups has not been attended by the psychoanalytic enlightenment of the masses, but by endless revivals and recombinations of old faiths, religious and secular. The psychoanalytic intelligentsia are thus faced with a difficult situation. Either they abandon the project of communal therapy or they find within themselves the justification for committing themselves to religious, social, and political movements which psychoanalysis has already unmasked.

Such commitment must look very doubtful to the true believers in movements. How is it possible for a psychoanalytic thinker to justify it? History abounds with seemingly inexplicable alliances—inexplicable from a doctrinal point of view, that is—of church and state, party and church, or savagely opposed parties, each using the other or making peace with the other as a means to some end. But not all such alliances need be cynical and manipulative. Believers often see in seemingly unrelated doctrines versions of their own, or its extension and completion. There may even be a kind of family resemblance among all intelligentsia doctrines. Perhaps self-deception is involved; but perhaps other doctrines do indeed contain kindred insights. Whatever the true reason for the commitment of members of the psychoanalytic intelligentsia to religious, social, and political movements, their therapeutic goals rather than the stated aims of the movement may be uppermost in their minds. They almost certainly diverge in their views from that of true believers in any movement, unless they can achieve a temporary suspension of the disbelief that Freud made part of the psychoanalytic attitude toward church, party, and people.

On the other hand, true believers in other doctrines appropriate the insights of psychoanalysis—and perhaps its mystique—to further their causes. For example, an intelligentsia thinker grounded in Hegelianism or Marxism tends to use psychoanalysis to confirm the power of an historical dialectic. Whereas the therapeutically oriented intelligentsia seek to achieve their concrete (odd though this word may seem here) aims through religious, political, and social movements, the Marxian intelligentsia (for example) use psychoanalytic ideas as an addendum to their theory of history. However, in order to use psychoanalysis they have to revise those aspects of the doctrine that are unfriendly to dialectics and to dismiss Freud's critique of their views or else pass by them silently.

11

These familiar strategies remind us that the most important and durable doctrines in history survived because they spread beyond the group which initiated them and became connected with a great many other isms and group projects. Only philosophers, intellectual historians, and finicky people with developed aesthetic faculties worry very much about the internal consistency of doctrines.

The psychoanalytic intelligentsia belong to the twentieth century and it is still a bit too early even to try to assess their impact. But the use of expert testimony in the politics of our era has already taken psychoanalysis out of the offices of psychiatrists and scholars and into the political arena. For example, during World War II the Office of Strategic Services commissioned a prominent psychiatrist, Walter Langer, to do a study of Adolph Hitler. It was later published under the title *The Mind of Adolph Hitler*.[5] The practice of psychoanalyzing one's political enemies at a distance is not at all uncommon today. Congressional investigating committees now routinely listen to the testimony of experts, some of them outstanding figures in the psychoanalytic intelligentsia, about such things as the psychology of terrorism and the reasons for the mass suicide at Jonestown in 1978. President Carter, who had begun to wonder what had happened to the moral fiber of his fellow citizens, invited Christopher Lasch, the author of *The Culture of Narcissism*,[6] to discuss communal ills and their treatment at Camp David. Such examples suggest that those in political power are interested in both the psychopathology of individuals, whose actions affect large communities, and the diagnosis and treatment of communal ills.

However, the impact of the psychoanalytic intelligentsia in general, and of psychohistorians in particular, upon the larger world of politics will not be studied here. Rather, we will study the strategies of psychohistorians for creating hopeful theories of history out of the materials provided by Freud. The formulation of psychohistorical ideologies is a central aspect of the creativity of the psychohistorical intelligentsia, and this in itself is a formidable task in an age of realism. We will examine the psychohistorical intelligentsia's use of a number of structural principles in their effort to revise Freud's most pessimistic formulations. The works to be analyzed are the most distinguished books in the field, what we usually call "classics." The thinkers to be examined carried with them hopeful visions learned from other intelligentsia traditions quite different from

Freud's. They found the aspects of psychoanalysis which could be joined to hopeful traditions. Prominent among the hopeful traditions are Christianity and Marxism, the very doctrines whose illusions Freud had assailed, even while appreciating Christianity's therapeutic benefits to historical communities and Marxism's contributions to historical understanding. They also found the structural principles most suitable for optimistic or utopian interpretations of human development, taking into account the natural and historical forces shaping the human mind. Finally, they identified historical trends and agencies which would further human development and achieve the long-frustrated goal of the secular intelligentsia, the harmony and unity of the species.

We know from the study of sophisticated theories of history that intelligentsia thinkers who create hopeful theories of history use structural principles together with active principles (agencies) in nature, history, and the human mind, in ways that assure or, at the very least, permit the desired outcome. Psychoanalytic theories of history are quite distinctive, in that they, contrary to the trends of modern historical psychology, emphasize innate biological agencies. Freud postulated two active principles, Eros and Thanatos, the former a biological force for the unification of living things, the latter a disintegrative force. However, he complicated matters for his intelligentsia followers by making both forces unruly and assuming that the conflict between them was as eternal as nature itself. There was no higher agency which might reconcile the antagonists and yield a utopian outcome. Instead, Freud, who tended to see organic life as something on temporary loan from inorganic matter, settled on the Nirvana principle. This principle, a principle of quiescence, resolved the tensions of life by restoring it to an inorganic state—an apparent victory for Thanatos. As shall be seen below, psychohistorians found ways to give Eros, the agency of unification, greater power in human history, if not in the greater scheme of things.

In addition, utopian psychohistorians sought agencies in history which might serve the same goal. These agencies are best thought of as historical vehicles for achieving the victory of Eros, or as superior forces which serve human development by changing the balance of power in favor of Eros. The struggle between Eros and Thanatos and the creative efforts of psychohistorians to make it work out for the best do not, however, exhaust the possibilities. Freud did not introduce the idea of conflict or struggle into modern historiography or into the thinking of the intelligentsia. He simply enriched intelligentsia thought with new agencies of conflict and tested their mettle on natural principles which, in his view, governed human history. Later generations of psychoanalysts retained the idea of conflict, but abandoned Freud's notion that it was a conflict between Eros and Thanatos. Both historical and natural agencies can be assigned a variety of tasks in the struggle for human development in psychohistorical theories. Intelligentsia utopias usually reflect a sense of the historical moment, pressing historical concerns and some current version of the forces for good and evil in the world. As the intellectual vanguard, the intelligentsia are almost by definition in a state of rebellion against prevailing world views. They also tend to be schismatics, forever diverging from the several orthodoxies to which they pay tribute. The schisms within psychohistory involve not only modifications of Freudian orthodoxy, but very major differences in outlook and corresponding variation in the choice of structural principles and historical agencies of progress. To put it simply, psychohistorians diverge in the choice of means by which they seek to achieve goals such as species unity and harmony and individual wholeness and development. Like intelligentsia before them, they continue the quest for a way out of human misery and mutual depredation, and for the key to human self-fulfillment.

The intelligentsia need to construct abstract unities out of vast areas of experience, such as the natural world or the human past, implies not only a drive for cognitive mastery (putting things in Order), but a quest for meaning and purpose (the Good, Salvation) within or against the traditional ethics of their culture. For the secular intelligentsia, Nature and History have taken over attributes that formerly belonged to God. For centuries, Christian philosophers, Hegel prominent among them, labored to sustain God's position as the ground of Being and Order, whether natural or historical. Their rebellious heirs borrowed whatever they found convenient from these theodicies, but dispensed with God himself/herself. Thus, whatever order and meaning the modern secular intelligentsia found in either Nature or History had to be expressed in terms that supported a new kind of ethics—ethics without God, meaning and purpose without a divine scheme of things and human place in it. Darwin shattered the basis for meaning or purpose in nature by removing teleology (for those with the wit to see what he had done) from the biological world. But perhaps history had meaning and purpose. It is at this point that intelligentsia theories of history become relevant, for they assert that history does indeed have meaning and is achieving its purpose: the meaning is benign—human development—and the purpose, maximization of human values associated with human development—justice, freedom, and equality in modern liberal and radical ideologies.

But now a grave difficulty appears—one which is still with us today. Those intelligentsia thinkers who tended to view the historical world as an appendage of the natural world—derivative of it—could assign no more meaning or purpose to human history than they could to nature. In a word, everything was meaningless. Freud sympathized with this point of view. Yet his outlook on the human condition was informed by therapeutic values—the healing of human illness, reduction of human misery, and the maximization of human pleasure. The good life for Freud was the life with less suffering and more pleasure. There was no meaning in human existence beyond this. Freud did, however, have very definite ideas about the best ways to minimize suffering and maximize pleasure, and one can construct his morality from them. A great deal has been written about connections between Freud's cultural heritage and the morality expressed in his theory.[7] He was a Jew who admired his own culture, had distinct biases about different national cultures, showed little inclination for radicalism in politics or social philosophy, and seemed above all a believer that the natural sciences, of which psychoanalysis was a branch, would solve whatever problems were soluble.

There are several difficulties with this naturalistic point of view for the modern intelligentsia. For example, in one neo-Darwinian form, sociobiology, such naturalism assumes that the replication of genes is the only purpose implied in the existence of any species, including the human species. Unless one takes the maximization of the gene pool of the entire species as the purpose to be served, one might infer the war of each against all from neo-Darwinian theory, just as was done with Darwinism. On the other hand, if we do take the entire species as a gene pool in competition with all other gene pools in nature, we tend to affront the modern intelligentsia's ecological sensibility. The modern intelligentsia accept naturalism to this extent: They accept the narrowing of the range of options for human self-fulfillment that is implied by natural limitations and a species-specific biological inheritance inextricably connected with all human achievement. Acceptance of naturalism thus precludes real immortality for human beings, although it does permit the idea of symbolic immortality. The difficulties come when we try to determine the relationship between biological limits and the phenomena of history.

The intelligentsia's sense of human possibilities in history depends upon their estimate of the extent to which our cultures are shaped or programmed by natural limits in general and by our genetic inheritance in particular. Most would agree that the "empty organism" approach is infeasible for the modern intelligentsia. It would be prudent at this point to outline the range of positions that has developed.

The extreme naturalistic position is often labeled "biological determinism" or "naturalistic reductionism." Its proponents argue that our cultures are closely bound to our genetic inheritance. Culture is at best an instrumentality of the genes. It can function as part of a positive feedback system for replicating at an astonishing rate certain successful genes, but it is not an autonomous realm. We are always on a "leash" in our cultural behavior.[8] Thus, human history expresses human nature or, to put it another way, is its appendage.

The position antithetical to the position outlined above can be labeled "historical indeterminism." Proponents of this position argue that the debate about human nature is fruitless, for the only laboratory available to us for studying human behavior is history. We can never observe, analyze, or describe behaviors presumably associated with a genetic endowment without cultural bias entering into our selection of significant "traits." We can only deal with the remarkably diverse, unpredictable, and nonrepetitive phenomena of history.

There are two less extreme positions, one of them labeled "biological potentialism"[9] and the other "historical determinism." Biological potentialists admit the existence of biological limits, but believe that their specification is largely irrelevant to the study of history. Biology simply does not explain diversity and change among historical cultures. Historical determinists believe that the phenomena of human history are distinct from natural phenomena, but unlike historical indeterminists, they posit the existence of historical laws. These can take the form of serial (or dialectical) laws quite unlike those familiar to natural scientists, but they are laws nonetheless.

The positions outlined above permit a great deal of latitude in the efforts of intelligentsia thinkers to relate nature to history. Furthermore, it is one's attitude toward change rather than a mere statement of position that is important. Thus, one can be activist with respect to biological determinism by taking the attitude that nature is "wise" and that we should not meddle with the process of selection determined by the conjoint workings of nature and culture. Activism here takes the form of opposition to misguided intervention. The activist attitude is a well-known feature of intelligentsia thinkers who believe in laws of history. By making the dialectical laws of history progressive, Marx, an historical determinist, encouraged the radical intelligentsia to intervene in their behalf—to hasten the inevitable. Quite clearly, it is difficult for intelligentsia thinkers to assume a neutral posture toward either nature or history.

The words "attitude" or "posture" are unfortunately vague. Were we to engage in a more technical discussion, readers might reasonably expect something like a psychoanalysis of the intelligentsia as a group, or at the very least, psychobiographies of the authors to be studied. Nothing of the sort will be attempted here, but several more aspects of the intelligentsia's orientation (aside from the quest for cognitive mastery, meaning, and purpose) need to be examined. The reader will also note that many of the characteristics described above are hardly unique to the intelligentsia, so it might be worth stating that the intelligentsia distinguish themselves by their systematic effort and creativity. In a sense, they are poets of the human condition, despite the abstruseness of their doctrines. The construction of the great abstract unities cannot be accomplished without the use of distinctively poetic strategies: the representation and familiarization of the natural and historical worlds by way of models, metaphors, and anthropomorphism. This is as true today as it was when primitive peoples saw their own emotions embodied in spirits all around them, or when natural philosophers saw machines everywhere. To use a more modern example, anthropomorphic metaphors lie behind the terms "natural selection" and "the selfish gene." A thinker's attitude toward nature or history is no doubt intimately associated with his choice of metaphors and models, and the tone of his anthropomorphism. The following is a more complicated illustration: Since the Enlightenment of the eighteenth century, intelligentsia thinkers have tended to see history as benign. With this optimistic or hopeful attitude inspiring them, they have constructed history on the model of human development, but more particularly on the model of those aspects of development most prized by them. Philosophers tended to identify historical agencies embodying Reason—and to see historical change as the achievement of higher levels of Reason. They thus imagined History as Reason (or Consciousness) in the process of developing or becoming. An attitude of self-affirmation, one conjectures, preceded the poetic act of transposing to history the philosopher's own special virtues. We might multiply examples, but let the case rest here for the moment.

Anthropomorphism and the use of models and metaphors have long been known to philosophers of history and to a great variety of critical thinkers in different disciplines. Yet their use persists, suggesting that they are closely related to our creativity itself, and our methods for making the unfamiliar familiar. However self-conscious they may be about problems of representing reality, intelligentsia ideologues are still subject to imaginative and linguistic limitations and still rely upon models, metaphors, and anthropomorphism when they try to represent reality. In this respect they are just like the rest of us. The process of familiarization no doubt affects our feelings about one area of human experience by bringing them into contact with ideas, feelings, and attitudes associated with other areas. Our efforts at representation always distort "reality" or depart from it. The strategies of familiarization outlined above are evidently the very stuff of scientific creativity, as well as of poetry. Since the seventeenth century, natural scientists have tried to purge their representations of nature of earlier animistic (and therefore anthropomorphic) features, but at each step of the way some newer anthropomorphic model or metaphor has replaced the old one.

Every intelligentsia generation inherits an immediate tradition, with its dominant models and metaphors for Nature and History. Given the richness of intelligentsia culture in the modern era, there is plenty of room for heresy and for revivals of old traditions, as well as the creation of new ones. For example, the idea of "the healing powers of nature" recurs throughout the history of medicine. By the end of the eighteenth century a great many intelligentsia thinkers had rebelled against the mechanistic world view, but the fight against mechanism persists today. Often, one can only speak of the relative dominance of a metaphor or model. For our purposes, it is important to note the relative dominance of models and metaphors taken from the organic world and from our own mental

life. The modern intelligentsia have thought of history as an organic process—a process of development—since the late eighteenth century.[10]
However, some thinkers, of which Hegel is the most prominent, richly
combine the organic metaphor of development with mental and spiritual
metaphors of logic, creativity, maturation, and healing. History took on
a peculiar combination of organic, mental, and spiritual attributes in his
Phenomenology of Mind. History not only unfolded like an organism, or
an intellectual problem solving itself, it showed features not unlike those
of a conflicted psyche, or a creative spirit—a spirit achieving its creativity
by transcending earlier conflicts in a dialectical process of healing and
maturation. We will have occasion to examine Hegel again. For the present,
it is important to take note of this particular kind of anthropomorphism,
for it is indeed an early version of the kind of anthropomorphism sometimes encountered in psychohistory: endopsychic anthropomorphism, or
the transposition (in this case) to history of human psychological attributes. The word "panpsychism" is sometimes used to convey a more all-
embracing version of endopsychic anthropomorphism.

Freud presented in *Totem and Taboo* his theory of the origins of human
religions and with it a psychoanalytic theory of animism, the primitive
ancestor of modern panpsychism. Whether in its early form, animism, or
in later religious doctrines, in which deities were invested with human
attributes, or in modern theories, in which Mind infuses God, Nature,
and History, this type of anthropomorphism has played and continues to
play an important role in the formation of world views. Although psychoanalysis does not resolve the ancient ontological problem of mind in
the greater scheme of things, and although Freud only relied upon the
insights of earlier thinkers for his understanding of anthropomorphism,
he suggested that one could transpose not only conscious but unconscious mental processes to that greater scheme of things. Whatever their
ontology, and whatever their starting point for constructing the great
unities, intelligentsia thinkers of the modern period have tended to use
endopsychic anthropomorphism. In the following chapter, we will examine how psychohistorians use models, metaphors, structural principles, and particularly, endopsychic anthropomorphism in their quest for
meaning and purpose in history.

19

• CHAPTER II •

Architectonics of the
Unconscious Mind

S IGMUND FREUD made available to the intelligentsia of the twentieth century the idea that much of our behavior is determined by
a mental underworld of unconscious drives. He did so by translating the
idea of the unconscious mind into a modern idiom, the now familiar
Freudian lexicon. Very early in his career as a psychoanalyst Freud determined that he would be a psychologist rather than a physiologist of mind.
The immediate data with which he worked (aside from symptoms and
behavior which could be observed visually) were psychological—the ver-
bal products of conscious mental effort and life in an historical culture.
Furthermore, his case studies, his work with dream symbols, and his prose,
rich with allusions to world literature, suggest less a natural scientist than
a humanist. A kind of struggle over Freud's heritage has been waged in
recent years to determine to which culture he belongs, that of the natural
sciences or that of the humanities. Humanists working with theories of
symbolization, representation, figurative language, narrative, and interpretation find in Freud a kindred spirit. Yet for all of his contribution to
these areas, and for all his allusions to Sophocles, Shakespeare, and Goethe,
Freud saw his intellectual ancestors in figures like Copernicus and Darwin. He identified himself with the natural scientists who had changed
the human self-image by overturning accepted views of the structure of
the universe and our position in it. He claimed that he had completed

the humbling of the human species begun by Copernicus and furthered by Darwin by showing that we were largely governed by unconscious drives rather than by conscious reason. This self-estimate confirms everything we know about Freud's allegiance to the traditions of the natural sciences. Thus, however attractive his work is to humanists, it is no exaggeration to call Freud a "biologist of the mind"[1] in view of his commitment to biological explanations of its origins and development.

The architectonic of the mind constructed by Freud out of naturalistic theories and models and clinical observation reflects his sense of the power of origins, a power exercised mainly through the unconscious part of the mind. It is time to confront the forbidding word "architectonic." Apologies are in order, for manuals of style tell us that the English language is most vigorous and readable when least riddled by multisyllabic words of ancient Mediterranean origin. Aside from the fact that it would be virtually impossible in a study of this sort to do without such words, "architectonic" in particular was chosen in order to avoid using "structural," which would have served equally well. Unfortunately, the word "structural" is too easily associated with the very broad intellectual movement known as "structuralism." In order to dispel any suggestion in the title that this is a work in the structuralist tradition, the word "architectonic" will be used both as an adjective and a noun. "Architectonics" is therefore a plural noun.

Architectonics are principles for structuring processes of development. Five of them will be examined here: the genetic, epigenetic, dialectical, systemic (or cybernetic), and catastrophic principles. The five architectonics are widely used. All five terms will be familiar to students of biology, psychology, and history. However, the architectonics are metaprinciples, in that they operate equally well in a great variety of disciplines. It appears that thinkers in many fields apply the same morphologies to the objects which they investigate. One should add that the objects are often constructed unities—things that do not exist for anyone but those who share a culture's or subculture's perspective. Thus, the idea that there is such a thing as History with a particular morphology would be absolutely incomprehensible to persons who did not have a theory of history. The important point to keep in mind is that the same architectonic might be applied to History, Nature, and Mind, and the development of the sea urchin. It will also be clear that no complex process can be structured exclusively through the use of a single architectonic.

As suggested in the preceding chapter, architectonics can be connected with metaphors and models, and these in turn can be anthropomorphic. Of the five architectonics, the dialectical is most certainly anthropomorphic in its classic form, for it issues from the mind's self-reflection. It is also probably the single most important architectonic for modern intelligentsia utopians, for it is associated with the idea of progress in Hegel and Marx, who are undoubtedly the two most influential philosophers of history in the modern era. The dialectical architectonic therefore deserves special attention. We can use it to illustrate one of the most important points to be made about the architectonics in general: They tend to be associated with attitudes, moods, wishes, and anxieties. No less than our "primitive" ancestors who created mythic structures, we moderns reveal wishes and fears about the structure of things. Thus, Kant expressed dismay at the thought of a universe governed by "gloomy chance." Einstein clung to a more traditional idea of universal laws than his twentieth-century contemporaries because he would not accept the idea that God played dice with the universe. How does the dialectical architectonic express wishes or anxieties?

A prominent philosopher of science and critic of "historicism," Karl Popper, suggested that anxiety about change might be associated with the historicist's strategy for structuring reality. He wrote:

It can hardly be doubted that Hegel's and Marx's historicist philosophies are characteristic products of their time—a time of social change. Like the philosophies of Heraclitus and Plato, and like those of Comte and Mill, Lamarck and Darwin, they are philosophies of change, and they witness to the tremendous and undoubtedly somewhat terrifying impression made by a changing social environment on the minds of those who live in this environment. Plato reacted to this situation by attempting to arrest all change. The more modern social philosophers appear to react very differently, since they accept, and even welcome change; yet this love of change seems to me a little ambivalent. For even though they have given up any hope of arresting change, as historicists they try to predict it, and thus to bring it under rational control; and this certainly looks like an attempt to tame it. Thus, it seems that, to the historicist, change has not entirely lost its terrors.[2]

In this illustration, Popper connects anxiety about social change with a strategy for structuring history. Although it is not certain that Popper would agree, one might substitute "dialectician" for "historicist" in order to pursue the idea of the emotional or attitudinal connections of architectonics. Psychoanalytic thinkers have commented more directly on the psychological background of dialectics. Norman O. Brown, one of the thinkers to be examined in the chapters to follow, had this to say about dialectics:

> We may therefore entertain the hypothesis that formal logic and the law of contradiction are the rules whereby the mind submits to operate under general conditions of repression. As with the concept of time, Kant's categories of rationality would then turn out to be the categories of repression. And conversely, "dialectical" would be the struggle of the mind to circumvent repression and make the unconscious conscious. But by the same token, it would be the struggle of the mind to overcome the split and conflict within itself. It could then be identified with that "synthesizing" tendency in the ego of which Freud spoke, and with that attempt to cure, inside the neurosis itself, on which Freud came finally to place his hope for therapy.[3]

It follows that a dialectical architectonic in history might imply the transposition of an inner struggle for self-healing to history. To put it another way, both Popper and Brown suggest how psychological attitudes or processes can be transposed to history, and how *endopsychic anthropomorphism* underlies the dialectical architectonic.

Another student of dialectics, Robert L. Heilbroner proposes still another way to view dialectics.

> Together, the commonsense organization of data and the obedience to canonical or logical rules of utterance describe a great deal of the activity we call rational discourse. They do not, however, embrace all our mental activities. Another, very important kind is our ability to perform such mental feats as. . . . discerning pat-

terns, resemblances, or other relationships that are not discoverable by common sense or by formally structured logic. . . . Metaphors and images and insights bubble up "from below." . . . I believe that formal dialectics, in all its different forms, is an effort to capture and to reduce to discourse this inventive psychic capacity.[4]

One might infer from Heilbroner's hypothesis that historical dialecticians transpose to history the unconscious creative processes of the human mind. Whether we accept Popper's, Brown's, or Heilbroner's hypothesis is not as important as recognizing that they see in dialectics a formal principle that probably stands for a variety of psychological states and processes. However, it is important to note that Brown and Heilbroner have a positive attitude toward dialectics, even though they have delved into the underworld beneath its formal appearance. For them, the psychological processes underlying dialectics are benign. On the other hand, Popper emphasizes the negative aspects of dialectics and suggests that it is an unsatisfactory response to a state of anxiety or terror—an overreaction to change. This brings us to the crux of the matter.

The architectonics structure continuity and change. In a sense, they represent a given thinker's response to change as a *problem*. In the Western philosophical tradition, the intelligentsia have tended to see change and diversity as problems, and staticity (or equilibrium) and unity (or harmony) as the proper way of the world. If Popper is correct, the intelligentsia's seeming affirmation of change in modern philosophies of history is really a form of whistling in the dark. If Brown and Heilbroner are correct, the use of the dialectic signifies mainly the intelligentsia's faith in benign processes, even though they involve misery and conflict on the one hand and mysterious mental processes on the other. The latter two seem to suggest that spontaneous *unconscious* forces drive us toward health and creativity, and that the dialectical architectonic, paradoxically, is the *formal expression of that spontaneity*. It shows that parts can be synthesized into wholes, that conflicts can be transcended, and that there is an implacable drive for unity.

The idea that a blind underworld of unruly human passions—aggressive impulses and ambitions—served a larger rational scheme of things had existed in European thought before Hegel's idea of the "cunning of reason." The Western intelligentsia have also long believed in the fruit-

25

fulness of conflict and the redemptive value of suffering. Hegel summarized these traditions brilliantly in his vision of history. Although he used the traditional idioms of theology and philosophy, Hegel imagined history as a process and he structured its development dialectically in a way that anticipates the psychoanalytic intelligentsia's theories of history. He made the kinds of connections between mental process and historical development that psychohistorians make in the language of psychoanalysis. If there is a psychology informing Hegel's dialectic and phenomenology of the spirit, then it is reasonable to speculate that the appeal of his vision of history is in some way associated with it—that what appeals in it, in fact, is an intuitive developmental psychology.[5]

Hegel saw essential reality (he being a metaphysician) as objective mind, the product of the activity of Absolute Spirit. By giving the progress of Absolute Spirit in history a dialectical character, he was apparently transposing to it his own psychological history. In a brief but illuminating chapter on Hegel's youthful crisis in his book, *Marx's Fate,* Jerrold Seigel suggests that Hegel's resolution of that crisis during young adulthood strongly affected his later thought. Indeed, his triumph over his own spiritual illness became his model for the dialectic of the Absolute Spirit, for the transformation of the spiritual ills of alienation, isolation, and inversion *(Verkehrung)* into reconciliation and reintegration, harmony and unity. Hegel could only reconcile himself with a world which could be *trusted,* in the end, to achieve what he personally had achieved. That is, all of the conflicts and miseries involved in history had to have positive meaning—they had to be transcended and synthesized into a self-realized wholeness in a process akin to Hegel's self-healing.

An ego psychologist might say that Hegel's optimistic vision of history—his theodicy—was modeled on the ego's powers of synthesis and Hegel's faith in them based upon his own self-healing. Like the human ego, the Absolute Spirit must undergo alienation, conflict, and suffering in order to enrich itself, to achieve full development. With maturity, it is able to survey the process in a spirit of reconciliation, for it is able to see the inevitability of everything that it has suffered. In Hegel's ontology, individual psychology is purely instrumental to the dialectic of the Absolute Spirit. This is simply a restatement of the principle of the "cunning of reason," which states that historical actors unconsciously serve a higher purpose. Hegel's rejection of the importance of individual psychology in history might easily be misread as a repudiation of psychology. Hegel rendered *individual* psychology unimportant by transposing an intuitive developmental psychology to an imagined rational and unitary process of historical development. The psychology is in history as a *whole,* and the architectonic of development is dialectical.

Hegel's demotion of individual genius to an instrumental status in a larger historical process did not appeal to all nineteenth-century philosophers of history. However, the search for a unifying process and collective heroes, or structural agents of progress, became the intelligentsia's preoccupation. These were to replace the great military-political heroes—conquerors and empire builders—who had awed historians. Marx chose an underclass as the agency of progress, and in this respect, his theory of history is structurally homologous with theories that emphasize the underworld as the locus of creative conflict. Odd though it may seem, Marx also chose to retain the dialectical architectonic in a theory that claimed to explain *material* rather than spiritual relationships. This aspect of Marx's theory annoyed Freud, who dismissed it, with dialectics, rather summarily:

> There are assertions contained in Marx's theory which have have struck me as strange; such as that the development of forms of society is a process of natural history, or that the changes in social stratification arise from one another in the manner of a dialectical process. I am far from sure that I understand these assertions aright; nor do they sound to me "materialistic" but, rather, like a precipitate of the obscure Hegelian philosophy in whose school Marx graduated.[6]

The difficulties of transposing to a complex world of "material" relationships the characteristics of a mental or spiritual process need not be reviewed here. The point is, once the Absolute Spirit had been removed by Marx, he had to show somehow that things would work out for the best, in the end. He settled on the familiar oppositions and conflicts of the social world, which issued from economic changes, but eventuated in changes of consciousness in the minds of entire classes. These changes in consciousness would in turn lead to restructurings of society and a more progressive arrangement in all respects. "Matter" would teach human beings to liberate themselves, assuming that the underclass could learn from its suffering, develop the appropriate consciousness, and revolt against the ruling class, which had contributed everything useful that it could to material development, presumably at the expense of the underclass.

Freud was not so hopeful. He had little patience with dialectics in history and was well aware of the central tendencies of human cosmologies. He knew about anthropomorphism, and quoted Hume's plain statement about it in *Totem and Taboo:*

> There is an universal tendency among mankind to conceive all beings like themselves and to transfer to every object those qualities with which they are familiarly acquainted, and of which they are intimately conscious.[7]

Freud added to Hume's observation his own, to the effect that primitive habits of mind persisted in human language, beliefs, and philosophies— a not altogether surprising observation from the man who had founded psychoanalysis on the idea that the child persisted in the man. But Freud himself might have unwittingly provided still another illustration of Hume's point when he created his own theory of history. Like other thinkers in the tradition of the Enlightenment, Freud tended to divide human development and human history into stages and to see parallels between them. Hopefully, at the end of both individual development and historical change one achieved the scientific self-understanding of the human mind. It now grasped itself as the product of natural evolution and cultural change. Yet, paradoxically, everywhere Freud saw the persistence of the early, the primitive. Freud's psychoanalytic theory of the human mind inspired the following vision of history:

> I perceived ever more clearly that the events of human history, the interactions between human nature, cultural development, and the precipitates of primaeval experiences (the most prominent example of which is religion) are no more than a reflection of the dynamic conflicts between the ego, the id, and the superego, which psychoanalysis studies in the individual—are the very same processes repeated upon a wider stage.[8]

The human mind, now with scientific realism, sees that history mirrors the mind's own structures and processes. But such a vision of history recalls one of Freud's earlier statements about animism in *Totem and Taboo:*

Animism came to primitive man naturally and as a matter of course. He knew what things were like in the world, namely just as he felt himself to be. We are thus prepared to find that primitive man transposed the structural conditions of his own mind into the external world; and we may attempt to reverse the process and put back into the human mind what animism teaches as to the nature of things.[9]

Freud believed that the discovery of the *unconscious* part of the mind, the larger part, and its workings gave the psychoanalyst a scientific framework for studying history, for understanding its major structural features, but *we* may question whether the psychohistorian's vision is so far different from animism, or its heir, panpsychism. To put it bluntly, even a scientifically established method of endopsychic exploration did not prohibit endopsychic anthropomorphism. It may be that psychoanalysis applied to the great constructed unities, and in particular, to History, yields new kinds of spirits and demons, heroes and deities, now scientifically labeled (although not in Freud's more down-to-earth German) *id, ego,* and *superego.*

There are many examples of endopsychic anthropomorphism in Western intelligentsia thought. Two of the best known are Plato's *Republic,* in which he made the three chief social functions in the State correspond to the three parts of the individual soul, and Hegel's dialectic of the Absolute Spirit, discussed above. Examples might be multiplied. Suffice it to say here, nations, races, social groups, geographic regions, and genders have traditionally been portrayed as the external agencies of psychological faculties or states, such as Reason and Passion, or Activity and Passivity. In the more sophisticated modern versions, such as Hegel's *Phenomenology of Mind,* psychological development was taken into account. Reason unfolded through time and migrated to new locations. Eventually, traditional faculty psychologies yielded to Freud's new psyche, with its drives, dynamic conflicts, tripartite structure, and vast underworld—the unconscious mind.

Recent scholarship has stressed a point that has been known for years: Freud did not invent the unconscious mind. Rather, he and his followers gave unconscious mental processes and structures the kind of preeminence in the life of the mind that evolutionists had given to natural history compared to recorded history in their view of human development. Facing reality meant, above all, uncovering origins, descending into the abyss of the unconscious mind, and emerging strengthened and better equipped to deal with human misery. The central position of the unconscious mind in psychoanalysis and psychohistory cannot be overemphasized. Sometimes it is seen mainly as the historical environment, which has been internalized and silently controls behavior from within. In Freudian psychohistory, the unconscious mind is also the repository of the evolutionary past, which rises up to control behavior in an immediate historical setting. In different psychohistorical theories, unconscious mind is thought of as a brake upon human development and a threat to human survival and, antithetically, as a reservoir of creative powers, a source of rejuvenation, and if used properly, the key to our next great historical advancement.

We can hypothesize that these different images of the unconscious mind reflect the same kinds of wishes, anxieties, fears, and moods that inspired the creation of earlier human cosmologies. We can also surmise that both the use of metaphors (particularly anthropomorphic ones) to familiarize the great constructed unities, and of a small number of architectonics to structure the processes of development imagined in those unities, reflect what we ordinarily call "poetic" activity. Whether or not those who aspire to science approve of the label "poet" is of little importance. Both self-affirming poets using natural figurative language and scientists using artificial languages give structure to things. It matters little whether they are frankly creating an imaginary world or trying to "discover" the structure of a portion of the "real" world. Thus, we will be examining in several major works of psychohistory the use of poetic strategies for structuring a world of anxiety-producing and hope-inspiring developments into a theory of history expressed in the "scientific" idiom of psychoanalysis.

The Five Architectonics

In a stimulating study of historical thought of the nineteenth century, *Metahistory*, Hayden White proposed that historians "prefigure" an historical field of investigation by means of a limited number of linguistic formal principles. Here we assume that psychohistorians use five architectonics: the genetic, epigenetic, systemic, dialectical, and catastrophic principles. Theoreticians identify the principles that they have consciously placed at the center of their studies. Thus, Freud invokes genetic analysis; Brown, Marcuse, and Lifton identify themselves as dialecticians; and Erikson explicitly refers to the epigenetic structure of individual development. Although this lightens the task for an investigator seeking structural principles, it might be misleading as well, for all of the psychohistorians named above use more than one architectonic. The architectonics overlap or bracket each other, and a given theoretician might not even be aware of the role played by architectonics other than the one consciously chosen. Perhaps we should specify the role of architectonics more precisely.

In their quest for meaning and purpose in history, intelligentsia thinkers invariably use structural principles which serve their goals. Whether we think of the architectonics as law, code, grammar, or logic, they govern the relationships of the phenomena being investigated. Psychohistorians tend to borrow the architectonics of organic systems created by biologists. Over the centuries biologists have created the lexicon of development and elaborated its structural principles. (Freud himself was also attracted to mechanistic models for the psychic "apparatus.") Ordinarily, architectonics govern both dynamic (developmental) and static or homeostatic (dynamic equilibrium) relationships. To put it another way, the constructed unities of psychohistorians are *systematized* according to structural principles governing both development and the states of developed organic systems. One should add that not only development but degeneration concerns psychohistorians. However, thought about the structure of degenerative processes leading to the disintegration of a constructed unity (for example, Culture thought of as a system) has been mainly a stimulus for creative thought about development. Freud's own anxiety about the degeneration of the human species provided a great deal of that stimulus. Let us now begin with Freud's own preferred architectonic and, in keeping with the preceding discussion, suggest some of the attitudes associated with architectonics.

THE GENETIC ARCHITECTONIC

In his own classics of psychohistory, *Totem and Taboo, Group Psychology and the Analysis of the Ego, Civilization and Its Discontents,* and *Moses and Monotheism,* Freud showed how terms invented to describe psychic pro-

31

cesses and structures could be applied to history. He also provided excellent illustrations of the use of the genetic architectonic in psychohistory. Erik Erikson used the term "originology" to describe and to express his disapproval of the central feature of the genetic architectonic—an overvaluation of the power of origins. Freud's sense of the power of origins has been analyzed from different points of view—including the point of view of psychoanalysis itself. Ernest Jones, Freud's disciple and official biographer, speculated about the gloomy outlook associated with Freud's genetic principle, and he proposed that the Old Testament might have been its source:

> Was an ineffaceable mark left on his mind when he learned as a child that God visits the iniquity of the fathers upon the children, to the third and fourth generation? For according to Freud, it was, above all, guilt and fear that were transmitted in this fateful manner.[10]

Jones refers here to Freud's psycho-Lamarckianism, a theory of inherited psychological tendencies based upon phylogenetic memories, which might explain otherwise inexplicable behaviors, such as the tendency to be afraid of one's father. More will be said about Freud's theory of acquired psychological characteristics later. Jones's remark is equally apt with respect to Freud's general gloominess about what evolution had done to human sexuality. The point is, Freud believed that our origins, whether through Darwinian or Lamarckian evolution, had burdened us as a species with unique disabilities, that we were in fact cursed by our origins.

Carl Schorske, one of the students of Freud who had the temerity to reinterpret Freud's own dreams and thereby gain new insight into the stimulus for Freud's career, concluded the following:

> The brilliant, lonely, painful discovery of psychoanalysis, which made it possible for Freud to overcome his Rome neurosis, to kneel at Minerva's ruined temple, and to regularize his academic status was a counterpolitical triumph of the first magnitude. By reducing his own political past and present to an epiphenomenal status in relation to the primal conflict between father and son, Freud gave his fellow liberals an a-historical theory of man and society that would make bearable a political world spun out of orbit and beyond control.[11]

This suggests that Freud's psychoanalytic theory of the origins of political conflict was a rationalization of Freud's own political disappointments and anxieties. Schorske connects Freud's originology, and indeed his psychology, with late nineteenth-century politics rather than with the Old Testament.

Mircea Eliade offered still another interpretation of Freud's use of origins. However, unlike Jones and Schorske, Eliade did not impute to Freud's originology anxiety or a negative attitude toward origins. Eliade found in Freud's attribution of great power to origins echoes of archaic myths, although (unlike others) he did not suggest that psychoanalysis itself has a mythological structure and religious intent. Furthermore, Eliade referred to ontogeny rather than phylogeny—to the development of the individual rather than the species. This at least partly explains his divergence from the others, in that Eliade finds in Freudianism good and hopeful feelings about origins.

> For psychoanalysis . . . the truly primordial is the "human primordial," earliest childhood. The child lives in a mythical paradisical time. Psychoanalysis developed techniques capable of showing us the "beginnings" of our personal history, and especially of identifying the particular event that put an end to the bliss of childhood and determined the future orientation of our life. Restating this in terms of archaic thinking, one might say that there was once a "paradise" (which for psychoanalysis is the prenatal period, or the time before weaning), ending with a "break" or "catastrophe" (the infantile trauma), and whatever the adult's attitude may be toward these private circumstances, they are none the less constitutive of his being.[12]

As shall be seen, Eliade's interpretation is closer to those of Brown, Marcuse, and Erikson, in that he finds at the beginning original bliss rather than original sin. As a student of myth, Eliade was well aware of the positive feelings bound up with origins myths. However, he disregards here Freud's theory of human phylogeny, in which the origins of our most characteristically human institutions are traced to parricide.

Freud undoubtedly accorded origins great power. Philip Rieff summarized it well in the following passage.

> For Freud, a given life history, even as a given group history, must be examined in terms of the experience of crucial events occurring

necessarily at a specific historical time. What is crucial needs have happened early. There had to be a *Kairos,* that crucial time in the past that is decisive for what then must come after. Kairos may be thought of as antinomical to *Chronos,* mathematical time in which each unit is qualitatively identical. Kairotic time, on the other hand, is not qualitatively identical—rather the reverse. Thus, for Freud, memory time is always kairotic. For example, the kairotic time of childhood may overwhelm vast stretches of later chronological time.[13]

It is now possible to summarize what has been said about the genetic architectonic in psychohistory. The chapter on Freud to follow will provide illustrations. The genetic architectonic emphasizes the importance of the earliest events in a series of events. Furthermore, the early events, or moments, in a serial process continue to control later ones. Although the controlling genetic events are acted upon by a great variety of factors, they do not lose their power. Freud's Lamarckianism complicated his genetic approach, for it permitted powerful *exogenous* factors, completely independent of the physical transmission of genetic material as we know it, to acquire genetic power, which we usually consider to be of *endogenous* origin. In any case, we should not confuse modern genetics, with its emphasis upon the power of genes to reproduce themselves or replicate, with the genetic point of view of psychoanalysis, which teaches that early events control later ones. The emphasis is upon *repetition* rather than replication. Two well-known Freudian phrases—*repetition compulsion* and *the return of the repressed*—capture the spirit of the genetic architectonic in psychoanalysis and psychohistory. The conservative implications are clear. We are controlled by the vast weight and living power of the past.

THE EPIGENETIC ARCHITECTONIC

The concept of epigenesis has been elaborated and deepened by contemporary biologists, so that its current meaning bears only a slight resemblance to the original one, which William Harvey gave it when he introduced it into the lexicon of modern science in 1651. From the very beginning, it was linked to the concept of development—the gradual unfolding and elaboration of an egg or germ. To modern students of development, epigenesis is an important adjunct to the concept of genetic stability, the idea that a given set of characteristics can be transmitted through the inheritance of genes, despite the presence of exogenous factors promoting change and variation. In a seminal work, *The Strategy of the Genes,* the late Conrad Waddington elaborated the idea of epigenesis by introducing concepts of "fated path" *(chreod)* and "stable flow" *(homeorhesis)* and using them to form an image of an "epigenetic landscape." Taken together, fated path and stable flow signify the channeling of development in the presence of exogenous factors—factors external to the genetic material. The exogenous factors, which are introduced over time, affect but do not normally prevent the achievement of normal development and a final state of maturity. The epigenetic principle therefore governs a *sequence* of stages of normal development.

There is no reason to make a strong distinction between the epigenetic and genetic principles. However, for our purposes, the genetic architectonic stands for an even more conservative principle of development. The channeling of development and the most important aspects of the final state of whatever is developing appear early in the process. To put it another way, both the crucial endogenous factors of development and the exogenous ones affecting them do their effective work early in the process, even though development continues for quite a time. On the other hand, the epigenetic architectonic, although intrinsically conservative, provides a more elaborate schema for development and more occasions for the introduction of exogeneous factors affecting development. In keeping with Waddington's imagery, an epigenetic landscape has more features in it than a genetic one does, and normal development can proceed along a much more twisting path, with greater indeterminacy between onset and final state. Finally, Waddington provided not only a mapping of "epigenetic space," but also mappings of phenotypic and fitness space. Epigenetic space occupies a position between the genotype and phenotype, and in keeping with neo-Darwinian thought, the latter is subjected to a test for fitness. As shall be seen, both epigenetic space and fitness space can be used, although not in these relatively technical terms, to map psychological development and selection in an historical environment.

Erik Erikson's work illustrates the epigenetic architectonic in this study. He has used "epigenesis" explicitly and repeatedly to refer to his theory of the eight stages of human development, the centerpiece of his contribution to psychoanalysis and the foundation of his psychohistorical work.

The embryology of the human psyche takes place in a great variety of historical cultures. They are in Erikson's work what Waddington refers to as "fitness space." Culture, in a sense, *grows* each new generation, but unless something has gone awry, the new generation contributes to the larger ecology of community health and adaptation. Erikson uses the term "metabolism" of generations to describe the interaction of parents and children. In Erikson's major psychohistories, cultural communities, which are the ecological focal points of his studies rather than families, select the creative ideologies and rituals provided by gifted individuals. Thus, the children do not merely adapt themselves to an environment, they change it as well. Although their psychological embryology implacably unfolds according to an eight-stage *sequence* of development, there are a great many possibilities for variation due to the metabolism of generations and individual differences. In other words, exogenous and endogenous factors act upon but do not essentially alter the epigenetic sequence. They can affect the schedule of development and cause deviations from the norm, but not the sequence. The entire process is affected by unpredictable historical circumstances. To put it in Waddington's terms, there are plenty of features in the epigenetic landscape and abundant room for maneuvering in epigenetic and fitness space, but there is a fixed sequence of development.

To sum up, for Erikson human psychological epigenesis is an inherited and universal schema for development. Cultural communities respond to the challenges of history with both general species capacities for adaptation and the special gifts of individuals. The selection of these gifts by the community is not fated or lawlike. Thus, despite establishing a more promising structure for adaptive flexibility, Erikson's epigenetic principle and his larger ecological vision do not provide limitless possibilities. Rather, human communities must learn to maximize the possibilities of development offered within the epigenetic structure and through the gifts of individuals, or else fall before the challenge of history.

THE SYSTEMIC ARCHITECTONIC

This principle governs the maintenance of a *system* and the states of the system over time. In biology, it is ordinarily connected with a cybernetic concept. What is involved is a complex unity or whole, sustained by complex programs for integrating many levels of mutually interdepen-

36

dent subsystems. The system itself can be thought of as a superordinate whole with a program for optimal self-maintenance that governs its subordinate parts, or subsystems. At the same time, the system interacts with exogeneous factors, to which it can respond within the limits of its program. The systemic program for optimal self-maintenance might involve both development and reproduction. Systems theorists like Ludwig von Bertalanffy take an organismic approach, as opposed to a mechanistic one, and emphasize open systems, such as the one described in the above illustration, rather than the closed system of traditional mechanistic physics. They also believe that the cybernetic model of self-regulation is not adequate for an understanding of self-regulating open systems, such as organisms, and object to its use. Their aim is a *dynamic morphology*, in von Bertalanffy's words, and in this respect, they resemble geneticists like Waddington. Von Bertalanffy believed that his concept of equifinality in open systems might embrace the epigenetic landscape described by Waddington. A developing open system, such as an organism, can reach its final state despite considerable variation in the exogenous factors supporting its development. Thus, like organisms subjected to different conditions might achieve an equivalent final state.

Proponents of a systemic principle are usually concerned with the optimal states of systems, such as equilibrium or climax states. With these in mind as final states, or goals, one examines the developmental sequence and the relationships among subsystems. Without some concept of the optimal state of the whole system, it would be possible only to describe kaleidoscopic patterns among its parts. One would not express a preference for any given configuration, any particular state of the system. However, every major theoretician of psychohistory, whether aware or unaware of the systemic architectonic, uses it in the service of a concept of optimal psychological functioning, or a vision of a state of bliss, as it were, of the psychic system. In this state, all aspects of the psychic system, or self-system, contribute to optimal health or vitality. However, as shall be seen, the optimal state of the system as a whole might be achieved through the dominance of a preferred part. For Freud and Erikson, it is the ego, although in Freud's case it would probably be wrong ever to speak of a state of psychic bliss. Of the psychohistorians to be examined here, Robert J. Lifton is least inclined to employ a systemic architectonic, but he describes transcendent moments in "self-process," and the others, Brown and Marcuse, have distinctly utopian goals for the psychic system.

The hopes invested in the achievement of the optimal state of a system, and the vision of a superordinate whole governing subordinate parts, yields a great variety of ideological postures. Intelligentsia strategies accompanying the systemic architectonic take the following forms: passive theodicy (using "theodicy" in a secular sense, that this is the best of all possible worlds and it tends to get better), or the idea of the invisible hand guiding the system toward equilibrium; active theodicy, which calls for intervention in the form of "midwifery" for the purpose of achieving the optimal state of the system; and radical surgery, or engineering, in which the system has to be rearranged by main force. Systemic, or holistic thinking, might suggest the perpetual sacrifice of the subordinate parts of the constructed unity in question to the whole and its desired optimal state.

The most influential systemic visions of the modern intelligentsia have incorporated the dialectical architectonic. In these systemic-dialectical ideologies, the unfolding parts of the system (as shall be seen, dialectics either incorporates or nests within an epigenetic principle) enter into conflict with each other. Yet the conflicts serve the achievement of the optimal state of the system—indeed, the end of division and conflict, of superordinate-subordinate relationships. A vision of undifferentiated unity, the transcendence of division and hierarchy, has inspired millenarian revolutionaries, particularly anarchists. However, as noted above, the systemic architectonic can support a great many intelligentsia attitudes or postures, and it is fundamental to the construction of the great abstract unities.

THE DIALECTICAL ARCHITECTONIC

A great deal of the preceding analysis has preempted discussion of the dialectical principle. It has a special mystique, partly because of its political implications, as the "algebra of revolution" or, antithetically, as an aspect of the doctrine justifying the authority of formerly revolutionary parties which have entrenched themselves in power. It is simplest to think of dialectics as an architectonic which organizes a process of progressive change around conflicts. Development is structured according to "contradictions" or "negations," what we call conflicts or oppositions when we abandon the language of logic for more concrete images of relationship. Without contradiction or negation, conflict or opposition, development lacks a dynamic principle. The metaphor of unfolding, which is central to the epigenetic architectonic, is used by dialecticians as well. One might even think of development structured according to dialectics as a special form of epigenesis, but this is not without difficulties. The idea of epigenesis emerged from studies of developing organisms, from embryological investigations. The process of development was observed repeatedly, permitting the investigator to establish a normal sequence and schedule of development. Can the same be said for history? The only generally accepted historical vision which approaches this is Marxism. In Marxist dialectics, a given stage of history (imagined as a system) is governed by a given class inequality and class conflict. Each stage, although a constituted system with its own "laws," changes dialectically into a new stage. Although Marx had no laboratory other than books, artifacts, and his immediate historical milieu, he concluded that he knew enough to predict what the next stage of historical development would be. One might therefore conclude that dialectics is indeed a variation of the epigenetic architectonic, and perhaps a rather doubtful one.

Extrapolations from earlier to later moments in an historical dialectic are problematic, even if one can reasonably expect conflict to occur and constituted "systems" to change into something else. In the dialectical vision of the intelligentsia after the French Revolution, the idea of revolution became associated with the ultimate crisis and final conflict within a constituted system, for Marxists, the stage of feudalism. It was therefore expected that the historical stage following feudalism would generate its own crises and ultimately, its own revolution. However, in spite of the fact that each stage in the dialectic has a systemic character, the goal of the dialectic is a final end to conflict in the social world, a stage unlike the other stages. Thus, dialecticians sometimes share the millenarian outlook of systemic thinkers. It is often difficult to distinguish among them.

In the end, it is best to think of the dialectical architectonic as the focus of a complex. Dialecticians strongly adhere to the epigenetic principle of sequential development, with each stage in the sequence making an essential contribution. Theoretically, at least, no stage could arrive before the preceding one had done its work. (In practice, of course, intelligentsia activists have interpreted "midwifery" very liberally.) However, the importance of its vision of a stage beyond conflict renders the dynamic aspect of dialectics suspect. The conflict-driven dynamic seems to be mainly a means to the end usually sought in the systemic architectonic—an optimal state of the system. By combining the systemic and epigenetic principles, and adding its own dramatic emphasis upon conflict, dialectics can promise a great deal. It is no exaggeration to say that it has come to symbolize a hopeful and rich outlook on the world for the modern intelligentsia. As noted earlier, the resonance of dialectics with both an inner world of mental process and an outer world of social conflict, gives it a special élan.

Finally, dialectical thinkers often include as part of the process of development through conflict moments of qualitative change, revolutionary discontinuities. These qualitative and discontinuous changes introduce the last architectonic—the catastrophic principle. Dialecticians are not alone in their use of a catastrophic principle, for catastrophes are well-recognized aspects of morphogenesis in biology and carefully studied in the natural sciences in general. The ordinary connotation of the word "catastrophe" must be momentarily suspended and its positive contribution to structural change appreciated. Catastrophes should be thought of here as normal or expected discontinuities in morphogenesis, that do not disrupt the process of development. But they should be discussed in their own right at this point.

THE CATASTROPHIC PRINCIPLE

Despite its ordinary connotations of sudden and unexpected ruin, the word "catastrophe" in formal models often signifies an anticipated discontinuous change which contributes to the elaboration of a structure. Catastrophes are expected events in embryological development, for example. However, they are not limited to the organic world as such and, as noted above, play a major role as dramatic turning points in the dialectical architectonic of the modern intelligentsia. In the preface to *The Phenomenology of Mind,* Hegel, the master dramatist of dialectics, vividly communicates this aspect of the catastrophic principle:

> The spirit of man has broken with the old order of things hitherto
> prevailing, and with the old ways of thinking, and is in the mind

40

to let them all sink into the depths of the past and to set about its own transformation. . . . The spirit of the time, growing slowly and quietly ripe for the new form it is to assume, disintegrates one fragment after another of the structure of its previous world. That it is tottering to its fall is indicated only by symptoms here and there. . . . This gradual crumbling to pieces, which did not alter the general look and aspect of the whole, is interrupted by the sunrise, which, in a flash and at a single stroke, brings to view the form and structure of the new world.[14]

Hegel's vision of qualitative change in the dialectic of history inspired many members of the intelligentsia to intervene in the process and to hasten the appearance of the new world. When used in this fashion, the catastrophic principle becomes the very focus of radical thought, for it signifies the moment of revolution, the revolutionary upheaval ushering in the higher stage of human progress which (in Marxian imagery) had been gestating in the womb of the old order. Thus, the dialectical architectonic has a special appeal for revolutionaries, for it is a rather simple procedure to set up the dialectic to include a sequence of catastrophic but progressive conflicts. We may surmise that for many members of the revolutionary intelligentsia, the catastrophic principle as such rather than dialectics provokes their imagination.

There are also catastrophes with negative connotations in psychohistorical theory. The catastrophic principle can be used to signify a break or interruption in development. Robert J. Lifton uses catastrophes at two levels, the personal and historical, but at each level they might interrupt rather than further healthy "self-process." Although they are normally part of the dialectic of human development—what Lifton calls the *psychoformative process*—at both personal and historical levels catastrophes can assume the form of "death immersions." These precipitate "psychic numbing" and a break or interruption in both self-process and the life of communities. Lifton's disinclination for theories of historical development and his focus upon the catastrophic moments and their historical consequences distinguishes him from the psychohistorians to be studied here. He does not subsume historical catastrophes under a progressive dialectical architectonic, even though he identifies adaptive and creative responses to modern death immersions. Rather, he investigates typical responses of survivors to death immersions and both the malignant and hopeful aspects of the survivor experience. When he focuses upon the former, he is a kind of epidemiologist of catastrophe, and when he emphasizes the latter, he operates within the therapeutic mode of the psychohistorical intelligentsia. In this activist mode, he becomes a community therapist trying to facilitate the mending of the break in the life of the community.

The tendency of the revolutionary intelligentsia of the nineteenth century, following Hegel, to employ the catastrophic principle in its positive sense has not disappeared. However, the holocausts of the twentieth century have chastened the intelligentsia. The historical environment which provoked Lifton's interest in death immersions is continuous with the environment which yielded Freud's vision of a death instinct. Vast international wars, revolutions and civil wars, efforts at genocide, and the threat of nuclear devastation have been the historical environment of the psychoanalytic intelligentsia and the most important stimuli for psychohistory. This can readily be seen in the works of such prominent psychohistorians as Norman Cohn, Peter Loewenberg, Fred Weinstein, and Bruce Mazlish.[15] Anxiety about human survival—not mere survival in a numbed state of "death in life," but in a dynamic state of full vitality—strongly affects the psychoanalytic intelligentsia. Lifton's psychohistorical vision is the best illustration of the transformation of the catastrophic principle into a negative mode by an intelligentsia still assimilating the experience of the twentieth century. One should add to the impact of physical holocausts the breaks in the lives of communities and individuals caused by accelerated cultural change. Here too, the catastrophic principle has taken on a negative sense.

ARCHITECTONIC NESTING

It should be clear from the above discussion of the catastrophic principle that it cannot stand alone as an architectonic for structuring development. The catastrophic principle must work together with an least one of the other architectonics in order to function in either its positive sense, as a necessary moment in morphogenesis, or in its negative sense, as a break or interruption in a process of development. In either case, the catastrophic principle *nests* within the other principles. For example, in Marx, the catastrophic principle used in its positive revolutionary sense nests within an historical dialectic. It can be argued that any vision of history as a unitary process leads to the nesting of all other architectonics within the systemic one, just as the idea of the whole organism subsumes the idea of its epigenetic development and the catastrophes within the epigenetic process. It can also be argued that dialectics nests within the epigenetic architectonic, or else (as was suggested above) is really a variant of it. The tendency of the modern intelligentsia to make dialectics an all-purpose architectonic confuses things a bit, but a little reflection leads to the conclusion that dialectics exists for the sake of a whole or unity, rather than vice versa. The conflicts within dialectics are a means to an end, just as are the stages in an epigenetic sequence, and the qualitative or discontinuous changes brought about by the catastrophic principle (in its positive sense). All of the architectonic principles therefore tend to contribute to the final or optimal state of a system. In utopian thought about history, they most certainly do.

The genetic principle, as set forth by Freud, is the least promising architectonic for hopeful visions of human development in history. Freud's originology leads to the conclusion that organic matter is only borrowed for a time from the inorganic universe. Readers with interests in the natural sciences will be familiar with the theories of physicists and biologists about such things as entropy and negentropy. What is at issue is the future of life in the very long run. Can life prevail against disintegrative tendencies in the universe? Freud asked this question in psychohistorical form in *Civilization and Its Discontents*. To put it another way, like the catastrophic principle, the genetic architectonic can take a cruel form, the grim circularity of "ashes to ashes, dust to dust," rather than an Hegelian dialectical spiral toward self-enrichment of the Absolute Spirit. Freud's devotion to the conservation principles of physics tended to close off escape routes, despite life's temporarily widening circuit. Furthermore, he did not imagine history as an autonomous realm, with developmental principles carrying the human species toward some optimal state. This is the crux of the matter. The genetic architectonic in Freud's hands simply does not serve utopian, or even hopeful visions. It even subverted Freud's own moments of Enlightenment optimism, expressed in his hopes for the triumph of the scientific world view.

However, as Eliade and other students of religion have shown, the genetic vision can be a vision of the "perfection of the beginnings"—a beatific vision of origins, of the great creative moment. Marcuse, Brown, and Erikson all reassert this beatific version of origins by showing that good origins as well as bad ones can be recovered from the unconscious mind, and Lifton shows how origins provide an "image-base" for human vitality. In short, the genetic architectonic can be nested within the others and even operate at the *end* of history as the completion of dialectical eschatologies.

Summary

The psychohistorians to be studied below are all concerned with human development and survival. These concerns inform their structuring of both individual and historical continuity and change. Although they go about their task by investigating the workings of the unconscious mind and its strategies for giving structure and meaning to the world, their own disagreements about the human condition suggest that psychohistorians are no less prone than other intelligentsia theoreticians to inject their own wishes, hopes, anxieties, and fears into their works. Awareness about the unconscious mind and penetration of its defenses does not necessarily yield agreement about the structure of either individual psychological development or history.

History is unquestionably a *constructed unity*. The architectonics with which historians give it structure are employed imaginatively and subjectively. The systemic-dialectical visions which inspired the grand intelligentsia theories of history of Hegel and Marx had at their very centers the idea of a self-developing, self-healing, and self-solving process. History presented itself only those conflicts and problems that could be transcended and solved. Every moment in the historical process counted—everything had meaning and purpose. Alienation, conflict, crisis, and confrontations with death were dialectically transcended and made part of a continuous process yielding, in the end, wholeness and free self-development, both for the individual and the species. Freud impugned historical visions of this sort, yet Marcuse and Brown thought that they had found in Freud's own theoretical corpus the foundations for their psychohistorical utopias. Erikson and Lifton are warier of the systemic architectonic, for they associate it with dangerously *totalistic* attitudes. However, they use a dialectical architectonic in their psychohistories.

Erikson and Lifton deal with individuals, communities or groups in crisis, but offer nothing quite like the prophesies and eschatologies of the systemic-dialectical thinkers. They represent that element within the modern intelligentsia which resists visualizing History as a unified process. Nonetheless, they give structure to some portion of it, and use dialectics in a positive way, to signify dynamic psychological polarities in human development.

It would be comforting to believe that despite the splits and conflicts within ourselves and among human communities, we are all part of a developing unity or whole. It would be a great consolation to know that an all-embracing benign program structures relationships and superintends change, whatever the motives of individuals or groups; that human suffering has redemptive value; and that a better order is emerging, in which we will be able to express freely the benign qualities within us, instead of what has been forced upon us under the pressure of dialectically necessary, but temporary structures of domination. This consolatory vision, whether in its Hegelian or Marxian form, has attracted able recruits in every generation of the modern intelligentsia, and it has entered psychohistory as well.

Even as we examine the modern intelligentsia's strategies for giving structure and meaning to a threatening historical world, and provide a critique that warns about confusions of self and world, of inner and outer, we still have to confront the hopes invested in those strategies and in precisely that confusion. Norman O. Brown, for example, flouts the critique and *affirms* animism. He chooses primitive human poetry over any cultural trend that would stifle it, or create a boundary between self and world. For Brown, an attack upon the unifying vision, with its animistic (anthropomorphic) inspiration, is an attack upon life and hope, upon the poetry of being, as well as the being of poetry.

Freud himself remained a rather stern realist. He had little patience for consolatory visions and warned against the "over-valuation of psychic processes as against reality." Yet he recognized that even the scientific world view might be affected by the old animistic feeling of the omnipotence of thought. In *Totem and Taboo* he wrote:

> The scientific view of the universe no longer affords any room for human omnipotence; men have acknowledged their smallness and submitted resignedly to death and to the other necessities of nature.

45

None the less, some of the primitive belief in omnipotence still survives in men's faith in the power of the human mind, which grapples with the laws of reality.[16]

As noted earlier, Freud was guilty of structuring history according to the practice of Enlightenment theoreticians of progress, who believed that historical phases corresponded to the stages of human maturation. Thus, the animistic world view corresponded to the developmental stage of *narcissism* in the human infant. Adult moderns might regress to narcissism under certain conditions, one of them being a "libidinal hypercathexis of thinking." In simpler language, this means that when our thought becomes an object of our emotions—more precisely, a highly charged love object—we regress as individuals to an infantile stage of our own development. In so doing, we resemble our primitive ancestors, for whom animism, omnipotence of thought, and narcissism were natural, so to speak.

We might infer from this that *all* ambitious intellectual efforts aiming at vast conceptualizations of the world imply a leaning toward omnipotence of thought and narcissism, for who but individuals with supreme confidence in thought would undertake the effort? Freud was aware that narcissism did not disappear with infancy, and more recent psychoanalytic and psychohistorical thought has placed narcissism at the center of the intelligentsia's attention. Adult narcissism to many psychoanalysts today no longer connotes regression. Here, however, Freud's intention is quite clear. He wanted to unmask regressive aspects of modern thought. Freud was also alert to the resemblances between some aspects of obsessional neurosis and paranoia and all *systemic* thinking, but he sought to distinguish the external world, the "real" world as an object of scientific investigation, from the worlds created by the omnipotence of thought and narcissism, or by obsessional neurosis and paranoia. Once again, his views are well represented in *Totem and Taboo:*

It might be maintained that a case of hysteria is a caricature of a work of art, that an obsessional neurosis is a caricature of religion, and that a paranoic delusion is a caricature of a philosophical system. . . . The asocial nature of neuroses has its genetic origin in their most fundamental purpose, which is to take flight from an unsatisfying reality into a more pleasurable world of phantasy.[17]

Freud thus unmasked but did not affirm the unconscious sources of world views, even when he opened himself to the criticism that his own scientific Weltanschauung and his lifelong scientific project might be suspect. In this he differed from Brown and Marcuse, admirers of fantasy, whose utopian visions embraced animism and narcissism in particular, and the creative resources of the unconscious mind in general. Freud would have no truck with "regressive" states of mind and found no solace in mysticism. He was preeminently a proponent of conscious control and of scientific realism. A line from Schiller's poem "The Diver," quoted in *Civilization and Its Discontents,* says it well: "Let him rejoice who breathes up here in the roseate light!"

No systematic effort will be made here to psychoanalyze the psychohistorians. The speculative remarks about Hegel and Freud presented above were introduced to show how some astute critics have connected theories of history to their creators. Although similar remarks will appear below, neither psychobiography nor even standard intellectual biography will be attempted. The focus of this study is the architectonics of the major psychohistorical works of Freud, Marcuse, Brown, Erikson, and Lifton. The authors appear as representatives of quite different positions, in which different architectonics assume relative dominance. However, I hope that readers will find plenty of food for thought, and that the relatively exotic vocabulary of architectonics will not mar the presentation of works of such scope and intellectual power that they can hardly fail to stimulate and provoke.

• CHAPTER III •

Freud

THE EFFORTS to find the real Freud and to connect him with current trends in the psychoanalytic intelligentsia have, if anything, intensified in recent years. Something similar to what happened to Marx after the publication of his *Economic and Philosophical Manuscripts of 1844* for the first time, after a time lapse of more than eighty years, seems to be happening to Freud now. In the first case, the founder of an intelligentsia tradition which had been converted into a pseudoscientific political dogma was revived as a "humanist." Freud too is being revived as a humanist, although not through the discovery of any new texts. Rather, he is being reread and revised by a great many analysts and humanistic thinkers in the light of the theory of narcissism and its relationship to the organization of the ego. The "narcissistic wound" and narcissistic ambivalence rather than the Oedipus complex have become the nucleus of neurosis. The central role of women, and more particularly, mothers, in the infliction of narcissistic wounds is frequently emphasized. The terrible father has all but disappeared. But this theoretical revision is only one aspect of the contemporary intelligentsia's efforts to rehabilitate Freud in a form acceptable to them. Another aspect involves rescuing Freud from the grim biological pessimism of such works as *Beyond the Pleasure Principle*. Finally, an effort is being made to emphasize Freud's use of metaphor, symbol, and myth and to show that Freud had intended psychoanalysis to be a humanistic undertaking, rather than a mere appendage of natural science.

Freud was not oblivious to the ambiguity of his undertaking. However, the weight of the evidence is on the side of Freud scholars who believe that it is impossible to understand Freudian theory without seeing Freud as a biologist. This is truest of all of Freud's work in the 1920s and 1930s, despite the suggestion of the distinguished psychoanalyst Bruno Bettelheim that Freud recognized his departure from biology. In his recent study, *Freud and Man's Soul,* Bettelheim quoted a statement from the "Postscript" (1935) to Freud's autobiography:

> After a lifelong detour over the natural sciences, medicine, and psychotherapy, my interests returned to those cultural problems which had once captivated the youth who had barely awakened to deeper thought. These interests had centered on "the events of the history of man, the mutual influences between man's nature, the development of culture, and those residues of prehistoric events of which religion is the foremost representation . . . studies which originate in psychoanalysis but go way beyond it."[1]

What Freud means by this is not very mysterious. He is saying rather simply that he had become what we now call a *psychohistorian* at the end of his career. But the statement should not be misread to the effect that Freud had repudiated a biological conception of human development. That human mental phenomena involve culture and history as well as biological inheritance is something recognized by natural scientists as well as humanists. Freud never ceased to believe in the physical and chemical foundations of the psychological phenomena he investigated. He was well aware that his clinical method and his case studies involved the art of interpretation, and that the mental phenomena studied by psychoanalysts could not presently be reduced to physical and chemical processes. Indeed, he was well aware of the limits placed upon discourse by language. Thus, he wrote in *Beyond the Pleasure Principle:*

> We need not feel greatly disturbed in judging our speculation upon the life and death instincts by the fact that so many bewildering and obscure processes occur in it—such as one instinct being driven out by another or an instinct turning from the ego to an object, and so on. This is merely due to our being obliged to operate with the scientific terms, that is to say with the figurative language, peculiar

to psychology (or more precisely, to depth psychology). We could not otherwise describe the processes in question at all, and indeed we could not have become aware of them. The deficiencies in our description would probably vanish if we were already in a position to replace the psychological terms by physiological or chemical ones. It is true that they too are only part of a figurative language; but it is one with which we have long been familiar and which is perhaps a simpler one as well.[2]

When defending psychoanalysis, Freud often pointed to the history of other natural sciences and their struggle, over a long period of time, to clarify their concepts and definitions. He felt that critics demanded of psychoanalysis greater maturity and rigor than was fair of a young science.

Freud's *soulful* language, if it is permissible with this adjective to sum up Bettelheim's position about Freud's vocabulary in the original German, has truly suffered at the hands of translators. However, in view of the fact that the *spirit* of Freud issues as much from the natural sciences as from any area of human learning, his translator, James Strachey, did not err grievously when he rendered simple German words into Greek and Latin ones. He gave Freud the solemnity, dignity, and aura of deep inquiry connected with our intellectual forebears—perhaps he gave him what Eliade calls "the prestige of origins" associated with our Mediterranean heritage. Strachey's worst sin is the translation of *Trieb* into "instinct," for the latter connotes programmed behavior of a sort that Freud did not have in mind. However, at this point, the abandonment of the Freudian vocabulary created by Strachey and acquiesced to by Freud and his followers, would cause considerable confusion and yield only marginal gains, given the focus of this study, which is closer to Sulloway's in his book, *Sigmund Freud: Biologist of the Mind*. Freud the psychohistorian was much more clearly a biologist of mind in his reliance upon evolutionary concepts (doubtful ones, to be sure) than was Freud the artful interpreter of dreams, metaphors, symbols, and a great variety of linguistic and bodily clues to the origins of neurotic symptoms. The Freud of *The Interpretation of Dreams* and the brilliant case studies of individuals is the Freud beloved of humanists, who study language and text.

Our Freud is the young scientist who discerned the unity of all life during his work in Ernst Brücke's laboratory, when he found that the large nerve cells in the spine of *Ammocoetes petromyzon* and other "lower" species related them to animals with more developed nervous systems. He is the Freud who shared with his mentor the belief that mental phenomena might eventually be described in terms of chemical and physical attractions and repulsions, and ultimately, in quantitative measures of energy and force. It is this same Freud who stressed the *continuity* of his development in his autobiography and acknowledged his debt to Gustav Fechner, an eccentric genius whose "principle of the tendency toward stability" and psychophysical outlook in general had a strong influence on Freud's topographical theory and theory of the instincts. He even used Fechner's term, *das Lustprinzip,* the pleasure principle. Finally, the Freud of psychohistory is the Freud who was immersed in Darwinian ideas transmitted through the German academic community. Freud's debt to Darwin was immense. The evolutionary outlook informed every aspect of his psychohistorical work. It appeared in his belief that ontogeny recapitulates phylogeny, Ernst Haeckel's "biogenetic law." Darwin's theory of primal human society, set forth in *The Descent of Man,* became a fundament of Freudian pyschohistory.

At this point, some qualifications should be made. The theories to which Freud was attracted were infused with intellectual traditions, philosophical and literary, which strongly modified any mechanistic and reductionistic outlook. That is why his heritage is so ambiguous, and why he is simultaneously attractive and repellent to so many different intelligentsia traditions. But no effort will be made here to trace his intellectual genealogy. This has been done quite well in the works of several scholars, none of whom has been interested in Freud primarily as a psychohistorian.[3] Finally, most of the biological ideas, particularly the neo-Lamarckian ones, about which more will be said later, are in deep disrepute. Speculative to begin with, some of them had a brief vogue and then lost respectability during Freud's lifetime. Freud's fidelity to them, however, signified his faithfulness to his self-image as a natural scientist, as well as his preference for a rather cosmic naturalistic point of view. Thus, although he had apparently forsaken the biological approach when he abandoned neurophysiology and developed the analytic method (an artful, interpretative and humane method) of investigating and treating neuroses, he continually translated psychoanalytic material into a biological, evolutionary, and ultimately, psychohistorical theoretical framework. He remained true to his teachers, in his fashion.

The fashion was intellectual imperialism. Freud tended to assert the primacy of psychoanalytic theory, even in relation to his paternal discipline, biology. Rather than remaining filially faithful to the theories of natural science, Freud manipulated them to make them conform to his own theories and observations. He was able to exploit the heterodoxy in evolutionary theory for this purpose. When he ventured into anthropology and sociology, still young disciplines, he found precisely those theories that could be aligned with his psychoanalytic theory of the Oedipus complex. Thus, in *Totem and Taboo* he subjected the observations and theories of J. G. Frazer, Darwin, Durkheim, Spencer, and others to psychoanalytic critique and revision. Although early in his career he had emphasized the somatic sources of mental phenomena, he would be tempted to reverse the causal relationship and to experiment with the idea of a psychosomatic rather than somatopsychic pattern. In a letter to Karl Abraham written in 1917 he waxed enthusiastic about the revision of Lamarckianism by means of psychoanalysis:

> Our intention is to base Lamarck's ideas completely on our own theories and to show that his concept of "need," which creates and modifies organs, is nothing else than the power unconscious ideas have over the body of which we see the remains in hysteria—in short, the "omnipotence of thoughts." Fitness would then be really explained psychoanalytically; it would be the completion of psychoanalysis. Two great principles of change (of progress) would emerge: one through adaptation of one's own body, the later one through alteration of the outer world (autoplastic and heteroplastic).[4]

Freud's psycho-Lamarckianism, as it has been called, is primarily a theory of acquired psychological characteristics. But Freud used it in the spirit of the above quotation, in that he shifted causality in biology from genetic material to the unconscious mind. One should note parenthetically that Mendelian genetics was still new, for it had to be rediscovered in 1900 before it entered the scientific mainstream. However, Freud's obstinate refusal to give up Lamarckianism later in his life, when Mendelian inheritance was fully established, revealed fully his psychoanalytic imperialism. If current biology did not accord with psychoanalysis—then biology was wrong. For more than twenty years Freud clung to his version of human evolution.

Freud's penchant for grand, speculative theories never abated and his psycho-Lamarckianism is only one aspect of his lifelong effort to place human development in an evolutionary framework. With Sandor Ferenczi, he tried to reconstruct the great turning points, the evolutionary catastrophes that marked the evolution of living things, from the very origin of life. Ferenczi formulated a "bioanalytic scheme" with five great catastrophes, the last being the ice age when the human species emerged with a unique sexual characteristic associated with the ice age catastrophe—the latency period. Although Freud never compiled evolutionary speculation of this sort into a systematic theory, he used it extensively in his psychohistorical works. Freud's psycho-Lamarckianism and these speculative theories permitted him to sustain his own psychoanalytic point of view with respect to Haeckel's biogenetic law, that ontogeny recapitulates phylogeny. Freud found it otherwise impossible to account for his discoveries about human sexuality, the Oedipus complex, and certain phobias in contemporary human beings, and the nature of religion, ethics, and mass psychology. As shall be seen, his most startling application of psycho-Lamarckianism occurred at the very end of his career, when he wrote *Moses and Monotheism.*

Freud's psycho-Lamarckianism, first set forth in a major work in *Totem and Taboo* in 1912–13, expressed the genetic architectonic in the formula: "In the beginning was the deed." It became an axiom of his later psychohistorical work. Historical actions and experiences as well as biology contributed to the formation of the human psyche as we now know it. Perhaps to illustrate this hypothesis it is best to skip forward a bit to a later work, *The Ego and the Id* (1923), in which Freud incorporated this historical-evolutionary hypothesis into his new structural theory of the psyche:

> Through the forming of the ideal, what biology and the vicissitudes of the human species have created in the id and left behind in it is taken over by the ego and re-experienced in relation to itself as an individual. Owing to the way in which the ego ideal is formed, it has the most abundant links with the phylogenetic acquisition of

each individual—his archaic heritage. . . . The experiences of the ego seem at first to be lost for inheritance; but, when they have been repeated often enough and with sufficient strength in many individuals of successive generations, they transform themselves, so to say, into experiences of the id, the impressions of which are preserved by heredity. Thus in the id, which is capable of being inherited, are harboured residues of the existence of countless egos; and when the ego forms its super-ego out of the id, it may perhaps only be reviving the shapes of former egos and bringing them to resurrection.[5]

This quotation seems supremely cranky in the light of biology as we know it today. It states that historical experiences can sink down into the genetic code, as it were, and control human psychological characteristics, such as those underlying religious practices today. Furthermore, it gives us no way of knowing what constitutes "repeated often enough" in order for the experiences of the ego to become heritable. Freud never received support in the scholarly community for his position, although in the Soviet Union, "revolutionary" biology in the form of Lysenkoism revived the idea of acquired characteristics. What is extremely revealing about this is that Freud's use of the idea of acquired characteristics had pessimistic implications, whereas Lysenkoism signified a kind of desperate revolutionary optimism, or better still, wishful thinking. Freud used his theory of acquired psychological characteristics, of psychological phylogeny, to explain *degenerative* or at least problematic acquisitions of the human species. Even more important, psycho-Lamarckianism was a convenient way of fitting the findings of a great variety of disciplines—biology, anthropology, sociology, and history—into a psychoanalytic framework. It gave Freud's discovery, the Oedipus complex, a new mystique of origins, by making it a phylogenetic inheritance; it gave psychoanalysis, a science based upon inquiry into the minds of individuals, the power to explain human development in new terms; and it made the unconscious mind deeper by millennia and laden with historical-evolutionary power.

In *Totem and Taboo* Freud showed how psychoanalysis might illuminate the institutions and practices of primitive peoples by tying together the findings of thinkers from several disciplines, but primarily, from anthropology. If Haeckel's law (ontogeny recapitulates phylogeny) might be applied to human mental development, then the study of primitive people would shed light on the psychology of contemporary children. In *Totem and Taboo* Freud hypothesized that primitive peoples actually *did* what modern peoples only fantasize, and that these primal deeds lay at the foundation of both human neurosis and civilization. The foundation of *Totem and Taboo,* never disavowed by Freud, is the idea of hereditary transmission of historical experience. Freud's use of analogy is another central feature of the study: obsessional neurosis in modern adults resembles the normal behavior of primitives; the behavior of normal modern children resembles that of adult primitives. By making the unconscious a repository of human historical (what we would probably call "prehistorical") experience, he converted the child-primitive analogy into a psychoanalytic version of Haeckel's law. The human child, although millennia removed from the events of human prehistory, advances through stages of development similar to those experienced by the entire species. Furthermore, he inherits the tendency toward ambivalent emotions and the Oedipus complex.

In this way, Freud showed that psychoanalysis, far from being a method restricted to the investigation of individual minds, was the key to the study of collective life. He never wavered from this position. Indeed, he summed it up concisely twenty years after the publication of *Totem and Taboo* in his lecture entitled "A Weltanschauung," the thirty-fifth of his *New Introductory Lectures on Psychoanalysis:*

> If anyone were in a position to show in detail the way in which these different factors—the general inherited human dispositon, its racial variations, and its cultural transformations—inhibit and promote one another under the conditions of social rank, profession, and earning capacity—if anyone were able to do this, he would have supplemented Marxism so that it was made into a genuine social science. For sociology too, dealing as it does with the behaviour of people in society, cannot be anything but applied psychology. Strictly speaking there are only two sciences: psychology, pure and applied, and natural science.[6]

Thus, the study of the unconscious processes and inherited memories in the minds of individuals had to be connected with the investigation of human collectivities. Since no other discipline gave *systematic* access to the unconscious (Freud bowed often to the great writers with psychological insight), then it followed that psychoanalysis was a key to the study of human development. And since Freud often stated that the Oedipus complex was the great juncture in mental life, the "nucleus of neurosis," and the strait through which the experiences of infantile sexuality passed into all subsequent development, it is not surprising that in *Totem and Taboo* he concluded:

> the beginnings of religion, morals, society, and art converge in the Oedipus Complex. This is in complete agreement with the psycho-analytic finding that the same complex constitutes the nucleus of all neuroses, so far as our present knowledge goes.[7]

Freud's theory of culture rested firmly upon the universality of ambivalent emotions in human beings and the decisive role of the Oedipus complex. The postulation of love-hate emotions directed at the same object and their presence in child-parent relationships had long served as a foundation of psychoanalysis. Freud now sought the historical origins of human conscience and civilization itself in the *deed* as opposed to the *fantasy* of parricide.

Freud based his psychohistorical theory upon Darwin's hypothesis that human beings had once lived in small hordes dominated by tyrannical males. In this primal social state, older and powerful males controlled the sexual life of the horde. They forced the younger males to find mates elsewhere. In Freud's version, a tyrannical father either drives away his growing sons or castrates them out of jealousy. Eventually, the sons band together, kill the father, and devour him. The sons' act of cannibalism is the primitive *deed* upon which the psychological process of identification is modeled. Although the sons had hated and feared the father, they had also admired his strength and loved him. Their ambivalence, identification with him, and remorse for their act eventually yielded the internalization of the father's prohibitions and a sense of guilt. Thus, they established incest taboos for themselves and symbolized both their renunciation and their act of rebellion in the institutions of exogamy, totem, and totem feast. However, the solidary brother clan did not endure. A matriarchal revolution occurred, accompanied by the establishment of female deities, but matriarchy too was supplanted. Patriarchy returned and with it, paternal deities. In later works, Freud modified and elaborated his theory of the origins and evolution of religion and morality, but he defended his theory that our sense of original sin issues from the deed of rebellion and parricide, enacted repeatedly in human prehistory and inherited as a species memory.

Freud thus achieved for the human species, for phylogeny, what he had for individual psychology—ontogeny. He had used an *historical* method to overcome collective amnesia about the savage conflicts between fathers and sons and the act of cannibalism from which issued humankind's most elevated institutions. He had uncovered the source of the Oedipus complex. Real events, real deeds, real crimes had transformed the psychology of the species, and all subsequent generations of human beings inherited as an acquired characteristic the tendency to form an Oedipus complex. The theory of the transmission of acquired psychological characteristics led to the extraordinary hypothesis that our species has an inherited psychological tendency to repress its own instinctual drives. Human societies could therefore exploit an inherited tendency toward *self-repression*. Freud even surmised that we *spontaneously* repress ourselves, that is, without the influence of a social environment.

> A child who produces instinctual repressions spontaneously is thus merely repeating a part of the history of civilization. What is today an act of internal restraint was once an external one, imposed, perhaps, by the necessities of the moment; and in the same way, what is now brought to bear upon every growing individual as an external demand of civilization may some day become an internal disposition to repression.[8]

With the last sentence of the above passage, Freud seemed to abandon his originology, but we should note that in all of his subsequent psychohistorical work he emphasized the *return of the repressed* and the power of the original crime against the fathers.

Freud rarely discussed social and cultural trends toward the remission of repression in human civilization—and never the inheritance of such trends. Rather, he assumed that the inherited disposition toward self-repression had been exploited and frequently carried to extremes by successive social and cultural configurations. Freud's personal preference for instinctual renunciation, for high culture, and for strong leadership seemed, at times, to contradict his psychohistorical findings: that we suffered from an increasing sense of guilt in civilization and from too much repression. Here we emphasize Freud the therapist, who believed that the discovery of the origins of neurosis would give us control over it, and who struggled against the misery brought about by instinctual repression. He discovered two sources of repression: the first distant, the memory of primeval deeds, inherited through the id, and the second immediate, the social and cultural environment around us. Despite the considerable elaboration of psychoanalysis after *Totem and Taboo,* Freud continued to place the father-complex at the center of his psychohistorical theory of repression, although he at times referred instead to a compound parental agency. *Totem and Taboo* was not an isolated and idiosyncratic work, but the foundation for Freudian psychohistory and a necessary theoretical supplement to clinical investigation. One could not fully understand contemporary individual psychology without psychohistory—without a reconstruction of the real historical events that had caused a trend toward an increasing sense of guilt and intolerable repression in the human species. In short, psychoanalysis had to be historical in order to be theoretically complete.

Freud thus progressed in his psychohistorical perspective from analogy (neurotic and child with primitives), to a genetic explanation (ontogeny recapitulates phylogeny), and finally, to a theory of history: Historical processes reflect conflicts among components of the psyche, just as the contemporary human psyche reflects historical conflicts. This he summed up in a passage already quoted, but worth repeating:

> I perceived ever more clearly that the events of human history, the interactions between human nature, cultural development, and the precipitates of primeval experiences (the most prominent example of which is religion) are no more than a reflection of the conflicts between the ego, the id, and the superego, which psychoanalysis studies in the individual—are the very same processes repeated on a wider stage.[9]

Alert though he was to animism and the anthropomorphic psychological foundations of cosmologies, Freud seems to have been unaware of the fact that by describing history in this fashion, he, like primitive man, might be accused of transposing his internal mental processes to the larger world. But let us suspend criticism of Freud's vision of history for the moment and ask what form a history which could be nothing more than a "reflection of the dynamic conflicts between the ego, the id, and the superego" would assume? We shall follow Freud in his steps toward a systematic psychohistory.

Freud first applied the ideas of *Totem and Taboo* in a major work in 1921, when he wrote *Group Psychology and the Analysis of the Ego*. Although on the verge of completing his structural theory of the psyche, he had not arrived at the final formulation—the tripartite division presented in *The Ego and the Id*. He still used the term "ego-ideal" where he would later use "superego." When Freud descended from his speculations about human phylogeny to more immediate problems of social or group (the word "mass" might have been a better translation) psychology, especially those involving leadership in political, military, or religious institutions or movements, he also moved toward a more precise and developed psychohistorical vision. The military and political upheavals of the period 1914–1921 undoubtedly affected his point of view, but as was often the case with Freud, the stimulus of the work of others trying to explain psychological phenomena by other means challenged him to show that psychoanalysis could do it better. Thus, the extremely influential book by Gustave Le Bon, *Psychologie des foules* (1895), served as point of departure for Freud's study, and Freud surveyed other influential works as well, such as William McDougall's book *The Group Mind* (1920) and Wilfred Trotter's *Instincts of the Herd in Peace and War* (1916).

Group Psychology and the Analysis of the Ego is a striking demonstration of Freud's ability to translate with economy and elegance the observations and hypotheses framed by nonanalytic thinkers into psychoanalytic terms. For example, he showed that Trotter's theory of a herd instinct was superfluous, since *libido*, the life instinct itself, bound human beings into social groups. The nature of group ties and the behavior of human beings in the organized groups described by Le Bon and McDougall could be explained by the libidinal relations of leader and led. In view of his theory of narcissistic libido, Freud found it necessary to explain how libido attaches itself to objects rather than to the individual's own ego or, to complicate matters, how an individual fell in love with others and at the same time kept in check the instinct of aggression. Freud assumed that the initial dependent relationship of the infant and child upon its mother and father made them the first objects of love and created identifications with them. As psychic life progresses, this leads to the alteration of the child's ego and the establishment of an ego-ideal. The latter is familiarly known as conscience, which in men is normally the consequence of identification with their fathers. In love, it often happens that the love-object takes the place of the ego-ideal, so that instead of being strengthened by way of identification, the ego is put in a position of slavish subordination in its relationship to the ego-ideal. The phenomenon of hypnosis provides a striking case. The exclusion of sexual aims brings the relationship created in hypnosis closer to the leader-led tie than it does to the usual love tie, although the restriction of the group to two people in ordinary hypnosis distinguishes it from group psychology. It is not important to discuss here the distinctions between Freud's "primary groups" and the groups described by those he was criticizing or revising. What is important is how aim-inhibited libido and identification bind a group together around a love-object: the leader. In Freud's succinct summary:

A primary group of this kind is a number of individuals who have substituted one and the same object for their ego-ideal and have consequently identified themselves with one another in their ego.[10]

Freud's genetic architectonic enters the picture at this point. He could not rest content with primary groups forming spontaneously around leaders simply by virtue of libido, identification, and the ego-ideal. Rather, he returned to the idea of the primal horde presented in *Totem and Taboo*. The fathers of the primal horde retain their power over group formation in modern human beings through the leader-led relationship preserved in the memory of the species. The group therefore *spontaneously* coerces itself and expresses a human tendency to regress and to reestablish the relationships of the primal horde. It is this negative sense of membership in a group which Freud emphasizes in *Group Psychology and the Analysis of the Ego*. In a primary group of the sort described, there is a loss of individuality, conscious motivation, and individual will in favor of a heightening of the role of emotions and the unconscious mind. Individuals obey the leader's commands blindly and instantaneously in lieu of reflecting upon their actions. In individual psychology, one encounters something analogous. An individual's superego might behave toward the ego in much the same way that a tyrannical leader might toward his group. In either case, no amount of repression seems to satisfy the overseer.

Freud foreshadowed in this work his theory of the cultural superego, a psychohistorical concept which emerged after he had fully formulated his structural theory. He also revealed his own ambivalence toward the leadership function in human history. The primary task of psychoanalytic work is the strengthening of the reality principle in individuals and the establishment of conscious control over unconscious forces. The agent of the reality principle and the site of conscious control in psychoanalytic theory is the ego. Thus, any reduction of the power of the individual ego in group psychology occasions the assertion of the id's primitive heritage. It follows that the leader-led relationship as such opens the way to regression. But Freud had very great respect for leadership in its most fatherly form—this we know from his later psychohistorical writings, as well as from his biography. In his two major works on political and religious leadership, the collaborative and posthumously published biography of Thomas Woodrow Wilson and *Moses and Monotheism,* Freud presented the image of a weak son who both failed as a leader and destroyed himself and that of a gigantic father figure, who was slain because he demanded too much of his people. However, like the primal father, Moses gained a more permanent hold over them precisely because he had made such powerful renunciatory demands. In Freudian psychohistory, the strong father who demands renunciations always wins in the end.

The ego in Freud's mature structural theory occupies the position in the psyche analogous to the position of the sons of the primal horde, and the superego takes the role of the father. As a son and rebel, Freud identified and allied himself with the victims of paternal despotism, but as the leader of a movement he assumed some of the features of the father. Late in his life, Freud's sympathies as a psychohistorian rested with the heroes and leaders who had diverted the stream of history (to use his image) and created their communities' superegos in the form of laws and doctrines. In this way, he aligned himself with the superego as a psychohistorian and as a member of the intelligentsia. He himself had chosen the path of the intellect and science, a path of instinctual renunciation and sublimation as a way of life. But submission to the superego also means submission to death. Freud's therapeutic realism, the ultimate realism of psychoanalysis, consisted in strengthening the ego—in part by bringing it face to face with death—and teaching it how to endure life in the very face of death. The corollary is a psychohistory with no promise of human salvation. Freud struggled with the tensions of therapeutic ideology, in which he simultaneously recognized the immense pain inflicted by the past, and yet affirmed the value of the superego, an agent of that very past, and instinctual renunciation. This struggle is quite out on the surface in *The Future of an Illusion* (1927), which became a sort of preface to *Civilization and Its Discontents* in the development of his psychohistorical vision.

At the very outset of the essay, Freud made it clear that he had a rather low estimate of human beings in the mass. The great mass of humanity needed coercion to keep them working and exemplary leaders to induce them to control their passions and make the sacrifices necessary for culture to endure. In this respect, the replacement of the external coercion of the despotic fathers of the primal horde by an internal agency, the superego, marked an advance in human development. However, the great mass of culturally underdeveloped people presented a continuous threat to stability. Given the weakness of rational self-control in the mass, the illusions of religion, whose characteristics resembled the symptoms of obsessional neurosis, nonetheless seemed necessary for civilization. Apparently, Freud had a double standard. The educated elite, which had shown its capacity for instinctual renunciation and for rational self-control, had no need for religion. The masses, on the other hand, needed a strong external agency to control them, and this had traditionally implied the love, awe, and fear connected with religious illusions and strong authority.

The last part of the *Future of an Illusion* is written in the form of a dialogue, a device which Freud had used brilliantly in his essay "The Question of Lay Analysis," published a few months earlier. In it, Freud answers the questions posed by an imaginary interlocutor, who uses Freud's own psychoanalytic ideas against him. Freud's vision of the power of the drives in the id seemed to call for equally powerful countermeasures. One had to use the id against itself, and this meant using irrational instinctual forces, rather than the weak rational powers of the ego. Despite the cogency of this position, one suggested by the psychoanalytic corpus, Freud took his final stand as an advocate of human development, a champion of "education to reality." The social underclass, which could not be expected in its present oppressed and exploited condition to preserve civilization, needed education above all. Humanity had to subject itself to the *experiment* of enlightenment, despite the risks involved. Freud's program of enlightenment meliorism in *The Future of an Illusion* implies faith in human capacities for rational self-control—faith in *Logos,* as Freud put it. He encapsulated his faith in a well-known passage: "The voice of the intellect is a soft one, but it does not rest until it has gained a hearing."[11] Faith in the intellect in turn implies faith in the ego's ability to acquire sufficient strength to govern the underworld. Thus, in the end, Freud affirmed both the ego and its agents in the social and cultural world—the scientific elite in general and the psychoanalytic movement in particular.

It is now possible to understand Freud's ambivalent posture. His vision was genuinely psychohistorical. At an earlier stage of human history, the Oedipus complex, obsessional neurosis, and the establishment within the collective psyche of the superego, a representative of the past, had furthered human civilization. The historical agents of the superego, the powerful religious and political leaders, had played a positive role. But had humanity reached the stage where the superego and its social and cultural agents were *preventing* human development and endangering human survival?

Freud returned to these psychohistorical problems in a chastened mood in his most widely read work, *Civilization and Its Discontents* (1930). Although he resumed his attack upon the illusions of religion and pressed his case that psychoanalytic realism was the only true medicine for what ailed humanity, his very own realism tended to subvert his position. On the one hand, he extended the argument presented in *The Future of an Illusion,* that the religious world view now signified arrested development and childlike dependency. On the other hand, he showed the inadequacy of the only intelligentsia doctrine which was contesting the ground with irrational authority—"scientific" socialism. Socialism too suffered from illusions, for it did not take into account the power of the instincts. Redistributions of property would not get at the root of the problem of human misery. Freud put it simply: "Aggressiveness was not created by property."[12] It was an indestructible feature of human nature. But if the general improvement in the material position of human beings promised by socialism, and the equality promised by communism could not remove the dangers posed by aggressive drives, what could? How could psychoanalysis, a science of the individual psyche with a therapeutic procedure designed to treat individual neuroses be applied to collectivities?

If there were indeed a threat to human survival because of the inability of modern communities to deal with aggression, the manifestation of the death instinct, then psychoanalysis might be our only recourse. Psychoanalysis, in a word, *had* to take on communal ills. Its initial task was the diagnosis of cultural communities. This implied several things. First of all, it implied that one could identify the superego of a culture and its role in communal neurosis. Freud was not daunted here, for he assumed that like individual superegos, cultural superegos issued from the father-complex:

> The superego of an epoch of civilization has an origin similar to that of an individual. It is based on the impression left behind by the personalities of great leaders—men of overwhelming force of mind or men in whom one of the human impulses has found its strongest and purest, and therefore often its most one-sided expression. . . . Another point of agreement between the cultural and the individual superego is that the former, just like the latter, sets up strict ideal demands, disobedience to which is visited with "fear of conscience." Here, indeed, we come across the remarkable circumstance that the mental processes concerned are actually more familiar to us and more accessible to consciousness as they are seen in the group than they can be in the individual man. In him, when tension arises, it is only the aggressiveness of the superego which, in the form of reproaches, makes itself noisily heard; its actual demands often remain unconscious in the background. If we bring them to conscious knowledge, we find that they coincide with the precepts of the prevailing cultural superego.[13]

This suggests that the exemplary father-figure of a culture and the ethical demands made in his name by his successors and priesthood shape the cultural superego. But thus far we have only solved the initial problem. Freud sought to *diagnose* communal neuroses, and this implies a norm for communal as well as individual behavior. He encountered what appears to be an insuperable difficulty, at this point, for how would one establish the sickness or health of a cultural superego?

Freud stated the problem with great clarity in *Civilization and Its Discontents:*

> In an individual neurosis we take as our starting-point the contrast that distinguished the patient from his environment, which is assumed to be "normal." For a group all of whose members are affected by one and the same disorder no such background could exist; it would have to be found elsewhere.[14]

There is no apparent way out of this difficulty, for it is virtually impossible to imagine a definition of a normal community without cultural or subcultural bias entering into it. At best, one might look for symptoms of communal disorder. Psychoanalysis might plot the feverchart of a community by examining it in historical perspective and getting a sense of the community's development relative to its own past and to other communities. But even this would be problematic, for it is quite common in intelligentsia thought to see misery and suffering in a hopeful light—to see a process of historical development reaching a crisis (catastrophe) on the way to a new and higher stage. As shall be seen below, psychohistorians themselves cannot agree about such things. Freud showed with his last major works that he believed psychohistory to be the next assignment for psychoanalysis and his remark toward the end of *Civilization and Its Discontents* sounds very much like a self-fulfilling prophecy:

> But in spite of all of these difficulties, we may expect one day someone will venture to embark upon a pathology of cultural communities.[15]

Freud's own approach to psychohistory comes clear in *Civilization and Its Discontents*. The great phylogenetic catastrophe, the origin of the superego after the overthrow of the terrible fathers of the primal horde, was followed by periodic catastrophes which repeated in some fashion the struggle between fathers and sons. Each later catastrophe was marked by the appearance of a leader who might share the fate of the father of the primal horde in a periodic community reenactment of the "original sin." Yet the heirs to the primal father might enforce an ethic of renun-

66

ciation without demanding for themselves the privileges of the father. The founders of religious communities often bore the humble aspect of sons who rose to fatherhood only posthumously. All of Freud's ideas about cultural superegos and community health or neurosis before 1930 suggested that the subject matter of psychohistory would be great leaders and their cultural heritage; and given Freud's emphasis upon the power of religion in human development, it is not surprising that his most fully realized (although not necessarily most cogent) psychohistorical study is about a religious leader and the cultural community created by him.

Two important theoretical trends in psychohistory can be traced from *Civilization and Its Discontents.* The first leads to Herbert Marcuse and Norman O. Brown, who appreciated the challenge of the book and who employed dialectics in order to deal with Freud's dualism of the instincts, about which more will be said. The second trend moved through *Moses and Monotheism* to Erik Erikson, who created out of his own variety of psychoanalytic theory a brilliant revision of Freud's theory of great leaders in history. We will proceed directly to *Moses and Monotheism* and give short shrift to *Thomas Woodrow Wilson,* on which he collaborated with William C. Bullitt, and Freud's other efforts at psychobiography. Our concern is with the psychoanalytic theory of history, which has its own flaws, rather than with psychoanalysis practiced badly (alas, Freud too was guilty of this) on historical figures. Furthermore, the book on Wilson had no impact upon the development of psychohistory, which was well started as a discipline when it appeared in 1967. Rather, it caused mild embarrassment and some defensiveness. However there is a passage in the biography of Wilson of which Freud, who found Wilson's weakness contemptible, probably heartily approved.

> The whole stream of human life may be deflected by the character of a single individual. If Miltiades had fled from Marathon or Charles Martel had turned tail at Poitiers, Western civilization would have developed differently. And all life would have been a different thing if Christ had recanted when He stood before Pilate. When Wilson quit in Paris, the stream of Western civilization was turned into a channel not pleasant to contemplate.

> The psychological consequences of his moral collapse were perhaps as serious as the political and economic consequences. Mankind needs heroes, and just as the hero who is faithful to his trust raises the

whole level of human life, so the hero who betrays his trust lowers the level of human life.[16]

Freud wrote his own study of a genuinely powerful leader, but the study had little to do with psychobiography. Rather, it is the study of the creation of a cultural community and its collective superego. The leadership provided by Moses "deflected the whole stream of humanity." It is the kind of leadership with which Freud himself identified. Paradoxically, despite his own open preference for Jewish over Christian culture, Freud went forward with a book which was bound to offend (and did indeed deeply offend) the Jewish community. For Freud took the position that Moses was an Egyptian and that Judaism, in one sense, was a "fossil" religion compared to Christianity. Freud removed Jewish as well as Christian illusions, demanded the renunciation of the comforting wishes of religion, and offered in place of them his own brand of realism. Here he himself played the role of the rebel son, the hero struggling against the superego of his own community in order to raise its level of development. In Freud's psychoanalytic definition: "A hero is someone who has had the courage to rebel against his father and in the end victoriously overcome him." Freud might have added: and to become a father in his own right by demanding new renunciations.

Freud summarized in this single work all of his previous contributions to a psychoanalytic theory of history: the genetic point of view, the method of analogy (however apologetically), in which the structure of individual neurosis is transposed to group process, and the catastrophic principle, now clearly expressed in the concept of the traumatic events surrounding a great leader's life. Although in his last major work Freud provided for the role of innovative leaders in history, he persisted in his belief in the power of early events and remained true to originology. He was most impressed by the repetition of the pattern of the earliest rebellion against the father and the everpresent sense of guilt which renewed the power of the father in both individual and cultural superegos.

The life of Moses follows in most essentials the myth of the hero, who begins his career as a son in peril because of a father's order to kill him. Like the sons who rebelled against the fathers of the primal horde, Moses liberates the Jewish people. However, in Freud's version, the man behind the myth was a high-ranking Egyptian, probably also a priest serving the

monotheistic Pharaoh, Amenhotep IV (Ikhnaton), and his god, Aton. After
the disintegration of Amenhotep's empire and the Pharaoh's death in 1358
B.C. Moses decided to sustain the monotheistic faith by creating his own
empire. He chose as his instrument the Semitic tribes who became known
as Hebrews, and as his goal, the conquest of the land of Canaan. At a
certain point, the primitive Semites rebelled against the highly spiritual-
ized religion of Amenhotep and Moses, and subjected Moses to the fate
of the primal father: They killed him and abandoned his religion. Yet the
monotheism of Moses somehow survived the relapse of the Hebrews into
the religious primitivism of the region which they eventually conquered.
After a long period of time, monotheism once again became the religion
of the Hebrews. Freud's theory of the resurfacing of monotheism provided the occasion for an analogy with individual neurosis. He was not
content to explain the survival of monotheism by a more cautious theory—that of a stubborn tradition.

Like patients with traumatic neurosis, the early Hebrews defended
themselves against the knowledge that they had murdered their leader.
They *repressed* it. They then went through a period of latency, marked by
amnesia of the traumatic event, followed by a period of symptoms—the
neurosis proper—and a partial return of the repressed material. One should
not hurry past this formula without mentioning its suggestiveness. It became crucial for Norman O. Brown's theory of history, although in a dialectical architectonic. Freud, however, used the analogy in connection
with his genetic architectonic and the conservative principle of the compulsion to repeat the trauma. The traumatic event for the human species
was the prehistoric epoch of parricide. For Freud, the most significant
moment in the return of the repressed after a latency period of millennia,
embracing both prehistoric and historical epochs, occurred first as an
Egyptian experiment with monotheism, and then as the enduring Jewish
devotion to it, after a repetition of the phylogenetic drama. Monotheism
signified the return of the repressed, and Moses was a resurrection of the
powerful father. The Hebrews repeated the crime of parricide, repressed
the trauma associated with it, underwent latency, then an outbreak of
neurotic symptoms, and then the return of the repressed in partial form:
the religion of Moses but not the memory of having killed Moses. This
is the pattern of obsessional neurosis which, in Freud's theory of culture,
is the pattern for all religions. It involves fixation to a trauma—the spe-

69

cies trauma—the compulsion to repeat it, and the usual lack of access to material repressed in the unconscious which would reveal the nature of the human species' original sin.

Freud nonetheless believed that the repetition of original sin in this case conferred several benefits on the ancient Hebrews. Rather than being regressive and barbarizing, the monotheism of Moses carried them to a higher level of spiritual development and intellectual achievement. The idea of a single God without either a name or concrete form signified the triumph of abstract thought over sense perception. Monotheism promoted both a universalized conception of justice and a scientific world view. But it also had political value for the Hebrew community, for it strengthened their confidence that they were the chosen people. Finally, Freud believed that monotheism had therapeutic value. Even a partial return of the repressed might bring with it greater control over the repressed material and strengthen the communal ego. The reader can judge whether or not any of Freud's positions has much cogency. As an ensemble, they seem to be a statement about Freud's own values, an affirmation simultaneously of his Jewish heritage and his scientific world view. This is the central point. Freud gave the psychoanalytic intelligentsia an exemplar, a psychohistorical study in which one might affirm both progressive and therapeutic values.

However, the benefits of monotheism and the intellectual, spiritual, and psychological strength which the Jewish community derived from it were only one side of the story. The other, and more pressing issue was anti-Semitism. The Nazi entry into Vienna had interrupted the writing of *Moses and Monotheism* in 1938, and Freud was forced to seek asylum in London, where he completed the book. It was published in Amsterdam in March 1939, only a few months before Freud's death on September 23, 1939, at the age of eighty-three. These bits of historical and biographical information are interjected here to emphasize the extent of Freud's commitment to his version of scientific realism. Exiled, dying of cancer, a Jew who had suffered anti-Semitism in his career and was now faced with a new and more virulent form of it, Freud proceeded to publish a book which could neither inspire the Jewish community nor evoke the sympathies of the Christian community in which it perilously survived. *Moses and Monotheism* reveals once again Freud's "counter-political" mentality.

He explained the relationship of Judaism to Christianity and anti-Semitism in psychoanalytic terms that flattered neither Christians nor Jews.

Freud first of all hypothesized that the strengthening of the communal ego through the partial return of the repressed and the pride and confidence accompanying the spiritual and intellectual achievement of monotheism was only temporary. For reasons which remain obscure, a growing sense of guilt gripped the Jewish people and prepared the way for another stage in the return of the repressed crime of parricide. The Pauline doctrine of original sin and the idea of Christ's redemption of it signified recognition that only a son could atone for a crime committed against the father. Christianity dethroned the Mosaic father religion and substituted for it a son religion. In Jesus, God-father-son were combined, but the sacrifice of the son and its redemptive value for the community took precedence and represented a victory over the father as well. Christianity's compromise reflected the old ambivalence toward the father and resolved it in favor of the son. It was a therapeutically progressive compromise, for it signified a more advanced stage of the return of the repressed. Yet Freud remained ambivalent toward Christianity, for he believed in Judaic monotheism's spiritual and intellectual superiority. As an intellectual, he affirmed his Judaic heritage, but as a psychoanalyst he recognized the therapeutic superiority of Christianity. As a psychoanalyst, he called Judaism a fossil religion, and explained why the Jews had paid such a terrible price for refusing to accept the religion of the son and for having failed to admit that they had murdered God.

The terrible price was undoubtedly at the forefront of Freud's thought when he completed his much-interrupted study. Freud's suggestions about the psychological background of European demonology about the Jews still have great cogency, and have inspired the work of later psychohistorians, with Norman Cohn being the clearest heir to his tradition. Psychohistorians who pursue these problems today are as much inspired by the need to bear witness for the victims of history as by scientific realism. But despite Freud's sense of urgency about the "disturbances of communal life" in Europe during the 1930s, he remained to the end an analyst. He stubbornly refused to be political rather than analytical. Thus, when Arthur Koestler in 1938 discussed Nazism with him, Freud allegedly said: "Well, you know, they are *abreacting* the aggression pent up in our civilization. Something like this was inevitable, sooner or later. I am not sure from my standpoint I can blame them."[17] Freud is simply saying in so many words, "I told you so." He had indulged similarly pessimistic views in his letter to Einstein, who had asked for Freud's opinions about ways to control human aggression and prevent wars in a letter written on July 30, 1932. Freud's reply of September 1932 contained a brief account of his theory of the instincts and particularly, of the nature of the death instinct:

> The death instinct turns into the destructive instinct when, with the help of special organs, it is directed outwards, on to objects. The organism preserves its own life, so to say, by destroying an extraneous one. Some portion of the death instinct, however, remains operative *within* the organism, and we have sought to trace quite a number of normal and pathological phenomena to this internalization of the destructive instinct. We have even been guilty of the heresy of attributing the origin of conscience to this diversion inwards of aggressiveness. You will notice that it is by no means a trivial matter if this process is carried too far: it is positively unhealthy. On the other hand if these forces are turned to destruction in the external world, the organism will be relieved and the effect must be beneficial.[18]

Freud displayed here the pitiless side of a theory both naturalistic and therapeutic. This point of view permitted him to stand aside from politics during the rise of Nazism and to be perhaps too understanding about its brutality. It also permitted him to refuse to salute any political and religious colors. He would be neither brown nor red; he would only be "flesh-colour," as he had put it to Joan Riviere.[19] The same lack of partisanship informs his study of his own people. Despite his pride in Jewish cultural achievement and his sense of the "fitness" of the Jewish people, *Moses and Monotheism* became, in the end, a statement about the power of psychoanalysis to explain history. It is the most fully elaborated presentation of Freud's psychohistorical method.

Let us now summarize his position. The entire human species is fixated to repressed traumatic memories of the murder of the fathers of the primal horde. The memories could be revived under certain circumstances, despite the defense mechanisms arrayed against them. After a long latency period they returned in distorted form and the emotions and events were repeated in a new historical drama, the murder of Moses. The Hebrews reenacted the ambivalent relationship between the sons of the primal horde and the father: the love and gratitude they felt for him, as well as the awe and fear and hatred. The therapeutic benefits of the new religion gave way to feelings of guilt which the Jews expressed by increasing the strictness of their religion. In this they showed the typical compulsiveness found in obsessional neurosis. Paul's breakthrough to the idea of the redemption of the original sin through the sacrifice of a son permitted the peoples of that era—though mainly non-Jews—to throw off some of the guilt that plagued the Jewish people. But the new son religion lost many of the positive attributes of Mosaic monotheism. Hence, the Jews missed out on the therapeutic benefits of Christianity, but retained the positive spiritual and intellectual qualities of their monotheism, and their sense of being the chosen people.

Freud had thus traced the connection between the species heritage and the history of a cultural community. He had examined the formation of a particular *cultural superego* through studying the impact of a great religious and political leader upon a group. He had then discussed the strictness of the cultural superego in the same terms that he used for individuals with obsessional neuroses. Ultimately, a comparison between the balance of power between superego and ego in two cultural communities emerged from Freud's study. Whereas the cultural superego remained powerful in the Jewish community, the Christian community experienced a lightening of the burden. In short, Freud had plotted a segment of the psychohistory of Judaeo-Christian culture in terms of the changing balance of power between ego and superego. This was a new kind of history indeed. It was preeminently the history of the obsessional neurosis of the human species, examined in its communal variations.

Freud's own ambivalence made *Moses and Monotheism* a difficult and not always clear book. His therapeutic values came into conflict with his own Moses identification (about which no more will be said) and his self-affirmation as a Jew. However, the message to future psychohistorians was clear enough: Great leaders might change the balance of power in the collective psyches of their communities in favor of either the superego or the ego, but the value and meaning of the change for human development could only be determined by examining the historical context.

Freud sometimes seemed ambivalent but the message that he communicated to the next generation of psychohistorians was that too much, rather than too little guilt and repression, instigated by the superego, was the problem facing the civilized world of the twentieth century. Psychohistory, as practiced by Freud, was a therapeutic ideology in the service of the ego and its historical agencies.

The Genetic Architectonic
and the Negative Power of Origins

Despite his preference for rational control as a way of life—the ego's way—Freud could not sustain the rationalistic optimism of some of the evolutionary thinkers—Lamarck and Haeckel, for example—whose biological views he had fitted into psychoanalysis. During the later part of his life, Freud viewed both human sexuality and survival itself as problematic. He believed in sexually degenerative phylogenetic inheritances, both organic repression associated with biological evolution (erect posture, for example) and the spontaneous self-repression issuing from the inherited father-complex. The guilt transmitted through cultural superegos worked in the service of the death instinct. In psychic life, there is a kind of balance of power. The ego is the organism's defense against the unreasonable demands of the sexual and aggressive drives. In therapy, psychoanalysis intervenes on the side of the ego, whose own efforts at defense often yield a shift in the intrapsychic balance in favor of the death instinct. None of the ego's victories are without cost, for any expenditure of sublimated or aim-inhibited libidinal energy implies a *defusion* of the id's instincts and the *release* of the death instinct for the superego's aggression against the ego.

But since the ego's work of sublimation results in a defusion of the instincts and a liberation of the aggressive instincts of the superego, its struggle against the libido exposes it to the danger of maltreatment and death. In suffering under the attacks of the superego or perhaps even succumbing to them, the ego is meeting with a fate like that of the protista which are destroyed by the products of decomposition that they themselves have created. From the economic point of view the morality that functions in the superego seems to be a similar product of decomposition.[20]

The high value that Freud personally placed on sublimation seems especially paradoxical in view of the above quotation, but no more paradoxical than his admiration of strong leaders.

The theory of the instincts set forth in *Beyond the Pleasure Principle* created for the psychoanalytic inelligentsia an almost insuperable barrier to a hopeful world view, for according to the theory all stages of development were subject to a "conservative" tendency toward organic dissolution and quiescence: the Nirvana principle, a term borrowed from Barbara Low. Freud had never escaped the naturalistic reductionism of his teachers completely. Fechner's psychophysical principle of the tendency to stability dominated the theoretical outlook of *Beyond the Pleasure Principle*. Freud had accepted Fechner's theory that pleasure was an outcome of a tendency toward stability from extremes of excitation, but had found certain puzzling patterns of behavior in his patients which forced him to elaborate a theory of the instincts which would not violate Fechner's psychophysical law. Freud's patients were "fixated" to their traumas. They had a compulsion to repeat their traumas. The fixation and compulsion to repeat the trauma could not be explained by the pleasure principle and libido (sexuality) alone. Nor could they be associated with any presumed ego instincts of self-preservation. Freud speculated about the existence of a group of instincts for self-destruction—collectively, a death instinct—which worked in its own way toward stability. Thanatos worked for the dissolution of organic substances, for the quiescence of the Nirvana principle. Beyond the struggle of Eros and Thanatos there lay the inevitable return to the *original* state of all living matter—a lifeless, inorganic state.

Freud had been influenced by Ferenczi's bioanalytic vision of a sequence of catastrophes which had contributed to organic evolution in general and to the peculiarities of human sexuality in particular. The catastrophes were exogenous factors disturbing the innate conservative tendencies of the instincts "to restore an earlier state of things." The earliest form of life had existed in a state of tension between its conservative tendency to dissolve into inorganic components and its drive to persist as an organic being.

For a long time, perhaps, living substance was thus being constantly created afresh and easily dying, till decisive external influences altered in such a way as to oblige the still surviving substance to diverge ever more widely from its original course of life and to make ever more complicated *detours* before reaching its aim of death. These circuitous paths to death, faithfully kept to by the conservative instincts, would thus present us today with the picture of the phenomena of life. If we firmly maintain the exclusively conservative nature of the instincts, we cannot arrive at any other notions as to the origin and aim of life.[21]

Freud left two openings toward a more hopeful vision of development in this theory of the instincts. First, he gave the instincts at least the semblance of a history by using the catastrophic principle to explain historical modifications of the instincts, modifications which drove the organism along a circuitous route toward one of its conservative aims—death and dissolution. Second, he gave the "germ-cells" of every organism the aims of the sexual instincts (grouped under the term libido), which struggled to preserve life and make it immortal—also "conservative" aims, but in this case providing the potential for further development. Very simply, one has to survive and reproduce in order to be there when another catastrophic stimulus for development comes along. The sexual instincts working through the germ-cells oppose the aim of the death instincts. In this opposition we have the closest approach to a dialectical architectonic in Freud. The imagery Freud uses in his attempt to characterize the struggle between the sexual and destructive instincts is extremely revealing from the point of view of architectonics. With reference to the role of the sexual instincts Freud wrote:

> They operate against the purpose of the other instincts, which leads, by reason of their function, to death; and this fact indicates that there is an opposition between them and the other instincts, an opposition whose importance was long ago recognized by the theory of the neuroses. It is as though the life of the organism moved with a vacillating rhythm. One group of instincts rushes forward so as to reach the final aim of life as swiftly as possible; but when a particular stage in the advance has been reached, the other group jerks back to a certain point to make a fresh start and so prolong the journey.[22]

We often picture a dialectical process as a kind of spiral or helical form, which is driven by a principle of contradiction or negation toward unity or wholeness. But Freud's image of the conflict between Eros and Thanatos has a different form. It is an ever widening circuit, a long detour on the way to death and organic dissolution. The stubbornness of Freud's genetic vision is summed up in the following passage—a kind of reductio ad absurdum of the genetic architectonic applied to the theory of the instincts.

> It would be in contradiction to the conservative nature of the instincts if the goal of life were a state of things which had never yet been attained. On the contrary, it must be an *old* state of things, an initial state from which the living entity has at one time or another departed and to which it is striving to return by the circuitous paths along which development leads. If we are to take it as a truth that knows no exception that everything dies for *internal* reasons—becomes inorganic once again—then we shall be compelled to say that *"the aim of all life is death"* and, looking backwards, that *"inanimate things existed before living ones."*[23]

Not only did Freud refuse to structure the conflict between life and death according to a progressive dialectical architectonic, he also rejected the progressive possibilities associated with the catastrophic principle. Catastrophes might have been used to escape the conservative dead ends of repetition, restoration, and dissolution. Freud closed off this route in the following way:

> It follows that the phenomena of organic development must be attributed to external disturbing and diverting influences. The elementary living entity would from its very beginning have had no wish to change; if conditions remained the same, it would do no more than constantly repeat the same course of life. In the last resort, what has left its mark on the development of organisms must be the history of the earth we live in and its relation to the sun. Every modification which is thus imposed upon the course of the organism's life is accepted by the conservative organic instincts and stored up for further repetition. Those instincts are therefore bound to give a deceptive appearance of being forces tending towards change and progress, whilst in fact they are merely seeking to reach an ancient goal by paths alike old and new.[24]

There is no ambiguity here. Freud denied the existence of a principle of progressive development in living things and closed off every escape route for life in the struggle with death. He encouraged his readers and followers to heed Schopenhauer and accept death as the natural aim of life. But even his strongest supporters found it difficult to follow his thinking about the death instinct. Ernest Jones turned psychoanalysis upon the master himself in order to explain Freud's late theory of the instincts.

> Thus Freud always had a double attitude or phantasy about death, which one may well interpret as dread of a terrible father alternating with desire for reunion with a loved mother.[25]

One must also entertain the possibility that Freud's theory of a death instinct had been stimulated by developments in biology which reinforced his tendency to reduce everything to cosmic physical and chemical forces. In *Beyond the Pleasure Principle* he referred to experiments with infusoriae which degenerated and died because they could not successfully dispose of the products of their own metabolism. Freud related his dualistic theory of the instincts to the biological concepts of anabolism and catabolism.

In his later works, Freud put death into psychohistory with a vengeance. The slow destruction of living organisms from within could be traced in the history of the human species. The very structure of the human psyche served death. The superego, the psychic structure which succeeded the Oedipus complex both phylogenetically and ontogenetically, became the agent of the death instincts in the human organisms and in human cultures. Our egos, weak to begin with, are prone to spontaneous repression of the instincts, and serve the death instinct in this respect, for repression leads to a form of instinctual catabolism. The superego collects, as it were, the aggressive energy released by instinctual defusion, and directs it against the ego. In some cases, the products of disintegration might eventually destroy the organism. Similarly, a cultural superego might acquire sufficient strength to imperil the life of an entire community. It was only a matter of historical contexts, which would determine whether the aggression would be turned inward and lead to self-destruction, or outward, as an *abreaction,* a discharge of the pent-up aggressive

energy. Freud had attributed the latter strategy to Nazism. But in view
of the modern technologies available to nation states, the outcome might
be the self-destruction of the entire species, in either case. At the very end
of *Civilization and Its Discontents* Freud summed up his attitude toward
the swelling violence of the twentieth century.

> The fateful question for the human species seems to me to be whether
> and to what extent their cultural development will succeed in mas-
> tering the disturbance of their communal life by the human instinct
> of aggression and self-destruction. It may be that in this respect
> precisely the present time deserves a special interest. Men have gained
> control over the forces of nature to such an extent that with their
> help they would have no difficulty in exterminating one another to
> the last man. They know this, and hence comes a large part of their
> current unrest, their unhappiness and their mood of anxiety. And
> now it is to be expected that the other of the two "Heavenly Pow-
> ers," eternal Eros, will make an effort to assert himself in the strug-
> gle with his equally immortal adversary. But who can foresee with
> what success and with what result? [26]

Freud's gloomy naturalism became a challenge to his followers in the
psychoanalytic intelligentsia. All of them found ways out of his more pessimistic formulations by modifying his genetic architectonic and nesting
it in a more promising psychohistorical framework. They found sources
of future human liberation in the beginning, where Freud had found mainly
the genesis of neurosis. They completely abandoned his psycho-Lamarckianism, the idea that the entire human species had acquired heritable psychological features issuing from the conflicts between fathers and sons in
human prehistory. None of them adopted Freud's antagonistic attitude
toward religion and his skepticism toward socialism. They tended to re-
ject his scientism. Freud had adduced too much evidence showing the
power of the unconscious mind to give his own version of Enlightenment optimism much cogency. However, they all retained the psychohistorical point of view, the belief that no further human development
would be safe unless the mutual impact of the unconscious mind and cultural change were taken into account. Furthermore, they sustained Freud's

therapeutic goals, even though he had left them with a question rather than an answer in this crucial matter as well.

And as regards the therapeutic application of our knowledge, what would be the use of the most correct analysis of social neuroses, since no one possesses the authority to impose such a therapy upon the group?[27]

CHAPTER IV

Erikson

IN SPITE OF Erikson's revision of Freudian psychobiology and despite the more optimistic implications of his epigenetic architectonic, he is nonetheless Freud's most direct heir as a psychohistorian. Erikson's most fully realized and best known psychohistorical works, *Childhood and Society, Young Man Luther,* and *Gandhi's Truth* elaborate the tradition begun by Freud in *Group Psychology and the Analysis of the Ego, Civilization and Its Discontents,* and especially *Moses and Monotheism.* Indeed, Erikson affirmed his relationship to Freud's tradition despite his creative revision of Freudian psychology and psychohistory. Similarly, Freud's abandonment of Brücke's neurophysiology for psychoanalysis did not signify repudiation of the physiochemical bases of mental phenomena. Erikson remains a psychoanalyst; Freud remained a natural scientist. It follows that Erikson maintains ties to the naturalistic foundation of psychoanalysis. Of course, Erikson rejected outdated concepts and principles of the natural sciences, such as Haeckel's law of recapitulation or Fechner's law of stability and their psychoanalytic derivations: ontogeny recapitulates phylogeny, the conflict between the pleasure principle and the reality principle, and the Nirvana principle. Furthermore, Eriksonian psychobiology is far more integrated with anthropological, sociological, and historical "outer" trends than Freud's, which tended toward naturalistic reductionism.

Erikson's work belongs to a tradition which deemphasizes the role of cosmic natural forces in human psychological development and accords a much greater role to the contingencies of culture and history. Whereas Freud had seen forces similar to the universal biological processes of anabolism and catabolism at work in the human organism as drives in the human id and as tensions in civilization, Erikson visualizes a complex metabolism of individuals, generations, and larger historical trends. Erikson, although a believer in evolution, instincts, and inevitable intrapsychic conflict, does not assume that the Freudian id necessarily takes the form of the life and death instincts, Eros and Thanatos; or that the mechanistic model of the damming up of the instincts by the reality principle and civilization is the best model for the dynamics and economics of neurosis. Rather, Erikson posits species-specific problems issuing from these inherited human characteristics: the extraordinarily long period of dependency of the human child upon its caretakers; a concomitantly extended period of learning; the inequality of the relationship between the weak, dependent child and its caretakers; and the lack of fully elaborated instinctive patterns to guide the species in its basic life tasks. Whereas Freud focused upon the *force* of the instincts, Erikson emphasizes the human need for both external guidance and *mutuality* to provide a secure framework for the growth sequence and the patterns for the relatively unformed instinctual energy of the human infant. As for the instinctual energies themselves, Erikson, in this respect well within the broad psychoanalytic tradition, posits inevitable conflicts surrounding them.

The greatest contrast between Freud and Erikson occurs when one compares their perspectives on the evolution of the human species. Freud shared the anxiety about the degeneration and extinction of the species common among the intelligentsia as one trend of thought issuing from the Darwinian revolution. The "decadence" of European culture before World War I and then the war itself heightened that anxiety. The idea of the impermanency of species, indeed of life itself, had greatly impressed Freud, and in his evolutionary hypotheses about the human species and his psycho-Lamarckianism he emphasized sexually degenerative acquisitions and cultural trends which made human sexuality and survival problematic in modern civilization. The relative diminution of the power of Eros in the human species is not a problem for Erikson, nor does he concern himself with the reconstruction of the hypothetical evolutionary catastrophes that had yielded the peculiar developmental pattern of the human species. Erikson assumes the power of evolution and of the species inheritance, but is more impressed by the innate adaptive powers of integration and synthesis of the human ego than by the "vicissitudes of the instincts." He is also more impressed by the innate social characteristics which enable the dependent human infant and child to mesh its innate foundation for epigenetic development with its culture's institutionalized patterns, transmitted at first through the infant's caretakers, than with the conflict between the instinctual drives in the individual and the restrictions of society. In short, Erikson emphasizes mutuality, adaptive capacities, and learning rather than inherited weaknesses. In doing so, he revises Freud's relative pessimism about the ego's ability to achieve wholeness and develops a psychosocial theory of generational renewal—with emphasis upon the species' capacity for rejuvenation—around the concept of *identity*. Just as the Oedipus complex became the focal point for Freud's ontogenetic, phylogenetic, and psychohistorical perspectives, the concept of psychosocial identity unifies Erikson's vision of the individual life cycle, the culture pattern, the historical sequence of generations, and the unique imperatives of the historical moment. Furthermore, whereas Freudian psychohistory tended to emphasize the power of the superego, and the growing power of the death instinct, Eriksonian psychohistory tends to give heroic status to the ego's powers of synthesis and the species' powers of regeneration and rejuvenation in the face of perpetual challenges and crises.

Still another aspect of the Freudian legacy challenged Erikson. Freud had emphasized repetition in history—the replaying in different historical contexts of a fixed repertoire of father-son conflicts. Leaders played the central role, first by liberating a community and then by creating anew the community's superego. The return of the primal father and the rebel sons and the repetition of their modes of leadership, with appurtenant psychic benefits and losses, became Freud's characteristic scenario for psychohistory on the grand scale. As noted above, Erikson continues Freud's tradition in many respects: He places great leaders at the center of his own psychohistorical dramas and he also asserts that they play familiar roles before a communal audience; but the familiarity does not issue from historically acquired phylogenetic memory traces. Furthemore, Erikson locates the significance of the drama in the actuality of the reenactment of an earlier scenario. "Actuality" is a concept resembling Marx's notion of praxis, as one can see from the following definition:

83

actuality, the world verified in immediate immersion and interaction. . . . *Reality* . . . is the world of phenomenal experience, perceived with a minimum of distortion and with a maximum of customary validation agreed upon in a given state of technology and culture; while *actuality* is the world of participation, shared with other participants with a minimum of defensive maneuvering and a maximum of mutual activation.[1]

Quite clearly, Erikson emphasizes here the truth-in-action forged by the individual ego, in conjunction with a community, but he connects the moment of actuality and creative reenactment with the individual and communal past—indeed, the shared unconscious past. There is resonance here with Freud, whose ultimate therapeutic purpose was to strengthen the weak human ego. Erikson, in effect, gave the communal ego power to strengthen itself through the mutuality of great leaders with their communities. Thus, while recognizing the role of the great leaders, Erikson revised the one-sidedness of the relationship between the great leader and his community, and emphasized their mutual activation.

Mutual activation is the crux of the matter; for human ego strength, while employing all means of testing reality, depends from stage to stage upon a network of mutual influences within which the person actuates others even as he is actuated, and within which the person is "inspired with active properties," even as he so inspires others. This is *ego actuality;* largely preconscious and unconscious, it must be studied in the individual by psychoanalytic means. Yet actualities are shared, as are realities. Members of the same age group share analogous combinations of capacities and opportunities, and members of different age groups depend on each other for the mutual activation of their complementary ego strengths. Here, then, studies of "outer" conditions and of "inner" states meet in one focus. One can speak of actualities as co-determined by an individual's *stage of development,* by his *personal circumstances,* and by *historical and political processes.*[2]

The above quotations present in summary form Erikson's epigenetic principle at a psychohistorical level: the idea of a sequence of development, the meshing of individual and communal processes of development. The desired outcomes are *growth,* through the achievement of a firm psychosocial identity, for the individual, and adaptation, in the form of both *regeneration* and *rejuvenation,* for the community. At both a conscious and unconscious level, the achievement of a positive psychosocial identity signifies an inner sense of continuity, self-integrity, and self-affirmation, which encourages whole-hearted action in a given historical setting. In addition, the epigenetic architectonic is future-oriented, for Erikson visualizes *historical actuality* as "the attempt to create a future order out of the disorder of the past."³ The most desirable type of leadership adapts an entire community for the future by working at the inner frontier of unconscious obstacles and maladaptations, as well as at the outer frontier of political, social, and economic disorders and maladaptations. To put it simply, the great leader acts as therapist for the community's collective ego. He restores impaired ego functions and mobilizes those whom he leads according to the ego's rational powers *and* its capacity for faith, for an attack on the obstacles to a more desirable future. In contemporary history "actuality" signifies the truth-in-action of innovative leaders, whose expansive psychosocial identities will eventually mesh with the readiness of their historical communities to abandon the narrower identities of "pseudospecies" for a more inclusive and adaptive human identity. Eriksonian psychohistory thus orients itself to the better identities of the *future,* even when diagnosing the ills inherited from the past. Here Erikson carries on Freud's task of enlightenment and universalism in a different, less scientistic and more religious voice, which proposes a psychoanalytic Golden Rule in the concept of mutuality.

As shall be seen, Erikson's epigenetic architectonic resembles a systemic-dialectical one, in its teleological character, its future-orientedness, its formulation of stages of development organized around polarities, and its values of synthesis and wholeness. However, unlike traditional dialectical systems, Erikson's epigenetic one is not driven by an implacable logic of development. Rather, each moment of conflict in the sequence of development presents an opportunity for growth for the individual, progress for the community and movement toward an all-species identity. Only leaders imbued with psychohistorical actuality can make the breakthroughs on the inner frontier that simultaneously consolidate and advance the gains made on the outer frontier by human communities possessing advanced technologies. The progress of the entire system depends upon a special kind of leadership. Erikson ultimately places the burden of development upon the extraordinary gifts of individuals whose egos can synthesize, at a critical moment, the available inner and outer possibilities. Above all, they must have the giftedness to overcome their own inner conflicts inherited from their pasts, the splits in their egos, their fear, anxiety, and dread of the future. The special gifts of Erikson's great leaders yield new ideologies and rituals for communities suffering in Erikson's terms from "identity vacua," and the most gifted leaders share enough similarities to warrant a common label, that of *homo religiosus*. All of them suffer from what Erikson calls an "existential curse" and all of them have a genius for introspection. Kierkegaard is one of Erikson's heroes of the inner frontier and not surprisingly, Erikson's psychoanalytic vision and psychohistorical dramas have an existential character. A decisive and active choice must be made at a critical moment in order for the mutuality of leader and led to mesh in psychohistorical actuality.

With considerable ingenuity, Erikson subverts Freud's position on the value and role of religion. As was suggested above, Freud's position on religion was affected by a combination of attitudes: his intellectual elitism, his "realism," his enlightenment goal of universalism, which presumably could only be achieved through the scientific world view, and his therapeutic outlook, which permitted him to see some value in religion. Despite the last attitude, the vast weight of Freud's arguments militates against the illusions of religion, whereas Erikson, in effect, offers religion as a vehicle for actuality, and the emphasis upon actuality, as opposed to realism, may be crucial for understanding the difference in attitude between Erikson and Freud.

Furthermore, Erikson finds universal implications in religious ideologies and ritualizations which, to all appearances, are too timebound and groupbound to sustain the larger burden of liberating the human species from its destructive rages. His positive attitudes towards early Christianity, Protestantism, and Hinduism, for example, issue from Erikson's evaluation of their significance for human ego strength and identity formation, just as his appreciation of *homines religiosi* issues from his perception of their kinship with Freud—their genius for introspection. Erikson apparently sees religion in psychoanalytic terms and in the corpus of his work gives psychoanalysis the power to explain the phenomenon of religion, although at times he gives the impression that he is a believing

Christian. What is most important, he gives religious leaders a crucial role in human development, not just in the past, but in the present as well.

Erikson's peculiar blending of psychoanalysis, existentialism, and religion, and his awareness of the contributions of psychoanalysis (unintended, to be sure) to contemporary malaise, supports his own style of activism—which he himself would probably prefer to call "actuality." Several of his psychohistorical works have the qualities of a psychoanalytic-existential *Bildungsroman* and *In Search of Common Ground: Conversations with Huey Newton* (1973), the published transcript of a dialogue with the leader of the Black Panthers which took place in New Haven in 1970, reflects both Erikson's concept of actuality and his care for the future of his adopted nation. His studies of American, Russian, and German identity in *Childhood and Society* (1950, 1963) and *Dimensions of a New Identity* (1974) reveal a sustained commitment to responsible insight into modern transformations of historical communities. *Young Man Luther* (1958) and *Gandhi's Truth* (1969) show how great ideologists and ritualists renew their communities by providing access to inactivated sources of human strength and adaptiveness. Placing himself on the side of the *homines religiosi*, Erikson speaks for an emerging style of leadership in a world of human pseudospecies armed to the teeth. Whereas Freud presented Moses as a leader in a longterm trend toward spirituality and intellect, Erikson offers Gandhi's truth-in-action as the last major breakthrough on the inner frontier—a breakthrough of evolutionary significance.

The foregoing introduction sketches out significant similarities and differences between Freud and Erikson without specifying the features of Erikson's ego psychology, his psychosocial theory of epigenesis, and his major psychohistorical works. The discussion below will begin with the biological assumptions behind Erikson's theory of human ontogeny, proceed to his epigenetic schema, and then to their psychohistorical applications. *Childhood and Society*, Erikson's first book, summarizes all of these aspects of his work and prefigures the later studies. Published in 1950 and reissued in an enlarged edition in 1963, it is a book of great and continuing influence.

In *Childhood and Society* Erikson affirms his affiliation to the Freudian tradition, in his profession of fidelity to the biological basis of psychology and the theory of infantile sexuality. Although he does not try to establish physiochemical bases for psychological processes, he does launch himself from the soma—the human body, its organs, and their innate characteristics. Erikson recognizes instinctual sexual energy—Freud's libido—as an essential human endowment, but he changes its position within the psychic system as a whole. Freud, of course, had made the id instincts the first cause and moving force of his psychic system. Erikson finds this approach too reductionistic and sees the developing human ego as something other than a mere superstructure satisfying and simultaneously defending itself against the id instincts. Furthermore, he rejects the idea of a death instinct and substitutes for it the force of *rage,* which is aroused and then repressed when the sense of *mastery* in developing human beings is frustrated. The inevitability of such frustration and repressed rage in a species characterized by extremely long infantile and childhood weakness and dependency and the problem of how to dispose of repressed rage remain central for Erikson. In the developing infant and child both sexuality and the sense of mastery focus themselves in zones of the body: oral-sensory, anal, and genital. The organs located at these zones operate according to different stages of development: incorporative, retentive, eliminative, and intrusive. The organ modes are the basis for socialization. For example, the interaction of mother and child at the breast determines the child's experience of *getting,* the social modality related to the organ mode of incorporation. With the development of teeth the incorporative mode enters a second stage in which *taking* and the social modality of holding onto objects dominate the interaction of mother and child.

Psychological development usually initially depends upon the way in which the developing organism is greeted by its social environment in the form of its mother, and although cultural patterns differ greatly, every culture must provide a framework for nurturing a child and developing its sense of mastery. However adequate the framework, the growing human being inevitably encounters some frustration at each step in the sequence of development. The process of teething brings with it an unavoidable trauma and the first major catastrophe in human development: weaning and separation from the mother. To this infantile catastrophe Erikson attributes the human sense of having been disconnected from a beneficent unity and expelled from paradise. It also marks the onset of powerful sadistic and masochistic trends associated with the dilemma of teething and controlling the mother's breast at the same time. Thus, although Erikson avoids the theory of a death instinct, he does not submit in its place a utopian vision in which the emergence of human destructiveness and aggression can be completely avoided. Rage at the pain of teething and the frustration of weaning dramatically illustrate the inevitability of the emergence of these trends. Erikson shows that a growing child faces failures at every stage of development which add to the sense of evil issuing from the first major catastrophe, just as its sense of the goodness of the world issues from the initial blissful experience of being cared for. In Erikson's system each stage of development in the eight-stage process can be resolved in favor of adaptation or maladaptation, depending upon the ratio of positive to negative senses, for example, in the oral stage, the ratio of a sense of basic trust to one of basic mistrust. The adaptive strengths and weaknesses contribute to a psychosocial identity, the latter the joint creation of a natural sequence of growth, immediate caretakers, and a cultural pattern. Finally, the institutions of every society have a definite relationship to the senses associated with each stage of development. Thus, religious faith reflects the *basic virtue* of *hope* derived from a sense of *basic trust,* whereas the ideas of evil, inner dividedness, and doom in religious doctrines carry over some of the negativity associated with the trauma of the oral phase. In evolutionary terms, the basic virtues are the foundation for ongoing cultural and social vitality.

The issue of sphincter control during the anal phase provides the basis for a new turning point in development, a new conflict, now between a positive sense of autonomy and a negative sense of shame and doubt. These positive and negative psychological senses are associated with the organ modes of elimination and retention and the social modalities of letting go and holding on. The social principle of law and order, judicial institutions, and ultimately, a sense of justice, can be traced to the resolution of the conflict over autonomy and shame or doubt. The basic virtue of *willpower* is associated with a positive resolution of the conflict.

The above brief summaries of the two phases in Erikson's epigenetic chart are presented here to show how inner and outer, nature and nurture, "drive fragments" and culture, work conjointly in an epigenetic process, usually through the mediation of the family. Clearly, by formulating conflicts at each phase as polarities with positive and negative significance for growth and adaptation, Erikson has added a dialectical dimension to his epigenetic system, and like many dialectical visions, his contains catastrophes. They are the crises, or turning points in each phase: "moments of decision between progress and regression, integration and retardation."[4] It is probably easiest to conceptualize this process as a kind of psychological embryology. For Erikson, human development, unlike instinctive animal development, unfolds psychosocially and depends upon culture to supply the patterns and emphases of the social modalities to assemble "drive fragments." Long after biological growth has ceased, psychobiological growth must continue in order for a human being to realize the potentialities of the human life cycle and to sustain the metabolism of generations. The chart of psychosocial epigenesis presented here[5] is a convenient schema which belies the richness of Erikson's vision, the "actuality" of his psychoanalytic experience, and the breadth of his explorations of different cultural patterns. In the ensuing treatment of Erikson's psychohistorical work, more positions on the chart will be discussed.

It remains to examine Erikson's best-known contribution to ego psychology—his concept of identity—and his method for relating psychosocial identity and community history. It might be useful, once again, to think of the concept of identity as the focal point of Erikson's epigenetic scheme in contrast to the Oedipus complex in Freud's genetic system. In orthodox Freudianism, the Oedipus complex and its resolution determines the character of the child's identifications with its father or mother, and its psychological masculinity or femininity, in Freudian terms, the ratio of an active to a passive orientation. According to Freud, identifications are modeled on introjection. The human ego evolved from the phylogenetic experience of actually devouring one's father—the "myth" of *Totem and Taboo*—and retains contact with the primitive infantile experience of introjection. One internalizes one's father by way of identification with him and in human ontogeny identification is the source of the superego. In Erikson's epigenetic scheme, fragmentary childhood identifications are superceded in adolescence by a sense of identity.

In keeping with his approach to Freud's theory of the instincts, Erikson treats identifications, identity elements, and other early psychological mechanisms as fragments to be integrated sequentially by the developing human ego into a mature whole. In *Childhood and Society,* he described the achievement of ego identity during the fifth stage of development in these terms:

		1	2	3	4	5	6	7	8
VIII	MATURITY								EGO INTEGRITY VS. DESPAIR
VII	ADULTHOOD							GENERA-TIVITY VS. STAGNATION	
VI	YOUNG ADULTHOOD						INTIMACY VS. ISOLATION		
V	PUBERTY AND ADOLESCENCE					IDENTITY VS. ROLE CONFUSION			
IV	LATENCY				INDUSTRY VS. INFERIORITY				
III	LOCOMOTOR-GENITAL			INITIATIVE VS. GUILT					
II	MUSCULAR-ANAL		AUTONOMY VS. SHAME, DOUBT						
I	ORAL SENSORY	BASIC TRUST VS. MISTRUST							

The integration now taking place in the form of ego identity is, as pointed out, more than the sum of the childhood identifications. It is the accrued experience of the ego's ability to integrate all identifications with the vicissitudes of the libido, with the aptitudes developed out of endowment, and with the opportunities offered in social roles. The sense of ego identity, then, is the accrued confidence that the inner sameness and continuity prepared in the past are matched by the sameness and continuity of one's meaning for others, as evidenced in the tangible promise of a "career."[6]

There are numerous clarifications and elaborations of the concept of identity in Erikson's work and the adjectives which he places before it ("ego," "personal," "psychosocial") alter the meaning somewhat, but Erikson's intentions cannot be doubted. The concept of mature psychosocial identity subsumes a systemic principle. Continuous *wholeness* is the ego's systemic achievement, the outcome of its ability to sustain the integrity of an open system, as can be seen in the following quotation:

In discussing identity, I have used the terms "wholeness" and "totality." Both mean entireness; yet let me underscore their differences. Wholeness seems to connote an assembly of parts, even quite diversified parts, that enter into fruitful association and organization. This concept is most strikingly expressed in such terms as wholeheartedness, wholemindedness, wholesomeness, and the like. As a *Gestalt,* then, wholeness emphasizes a sound, organic, progressive mutuality between diversified functions and parts within an entirety, the boundaries of which are open and fluent. Totality, on the contrary, evokes a *Gestalt* in which an absolute boundary is emphasized: given a certain arbitrary delineation, nothing that must be outside can be tolerated inside. . . . It is an alternate, if more primitive, way of dealing with experience, and thus has, at least in transitory states, a certain adjustment and survival value. It belongs to normal psychology.[7]

Thus, with mature psychosocial identity a principle of continuity is introduced into Erikson's epigenetic system, but not the continuity of a closed and static system, in which parts are subordinated to a whole, as in a totalistic system. However, Erikson recognizes that even totalistic orientations have adaptive value at some moments. Severe failures of the interaction of the individual and the culture in psychosocial process often lead to pathological states, in which the ego's integrative function is impaired. The catastrophe associated with adolescence, the identity crisis, may yield identity diffusion and role confusion at pathological extremes of maladaptation. On the other hand, a creative young individual may resolve an extreme identity crisis in a profoundly original way, with important historical consequences for a community sharing similar problems of identity.

Erikson follows a rather straightforward formula in his two most important psychohistories, *Young Man Luther* and *Gandhi's Truth.* Each of them is a case study of a *homo religiosus* and each is focused upon a moment of crisis, an epigenetic turning point in a great man's life, the creative resolution of which serves a large community in a state of crisis. One sees foreshadowings of the later works in *Childhood and Society,* particularly in the chapter entitled "The Legend of Maxim Gorky's Youth." A brilliant effort to base an analysis of traditional Russian national character and the psychology of revolutionaries upon a film adaptation of

Maxim Gorky's memoirs, it has the salient characteristics of Erikson's later works: It is a sensitive and skilled interpretation based upon scant historical knowledge. Above all, it has the *Bildungsroman* quality of *Young Man Luther,* an emphasis upon positive over negative, upon the young hero's strength, his capacity to pass through a variety of psychosocial trials on the way to a new Russian identity.

> Each scene and each significant person thus represents a temptation to regress to the traditional morality and to the ancient folkways of his people, to remain bound by the traditional superego within and by serfdom without. On the positive side, Alyosha is seen to become sure of himself, as if he had taken a secret vow; and he seems to devote himself with deepening fidelity to an unformulated goal.[8]

The term "fidelity," of course, has technical status in Erikson's epigenetic system. It is the "cornerstone of identity" and signifies a positive resolution of the identity crisis—a favorable ratio of identity to role confusion, and the achievement of an essential psychosocial virtue. Without the ego-quality of fidelity, youth cannot commit itself wholeheartedly to its culture's tasks. With it, the individual is saved—the community rejuvenated.

Alert readers can find throughout Erikson's work abundant evidence that he is aware of the possibility of negative or tragic outcomes, that he knows the perils of historical challenges to traditional societies, and the enormous difficulties confronting reformers and revolutionaries who must work on the inner as well as the outer frontier. Erikson's all too brief accounts of historical denouements of the struggle for the new individual and corporate identities through new ideologies and rituals provide stark contrasts with the dramatic unfolding of the future leader's struggle, and the moment of creative breakthrough at both an individual and historical level. The creators of new ideologies and rituals, a vanguard of historical leaders, like Freud's Moses, may pay with their lives in the end. After assuming power, such leaders often demand more than their followers are willing to give, or fall victim to the vagaries of political and social movements which they did not seek and which they cannot control, or even succumb to their own epigenetic weaknesses. Freud had shown how murdered leaders exercise power by shaping the cultural superegos of their communities. Erikson, on the other hand, shows that gifted leaders provide what is needed for adaptation at an historically critical moment in community development; but that they cannot control the future. Communities therefore need innovative leadership at every critical moment in their history. Here too we see the difference between Freud's genetic and Erikson's epigenetic architectonics.

Erikson's leader-centered psychohistory can be distinguished from Freud's in still another crucial aspect: In Freud's vision the leader stands above and apart from the group; in Erikson's, he is a member of a generational community of sufferers. This points up the central importance of mutuality in Erikson's psychosocial theory of development. Erikson's psychohistorical method involves a search for connections between the suffering of the great leader and the suffering of the group. The hypothesis of shared suffering also permits Erikson to use psychoanalytic language designed to describe endopsychic structures and processes in the study of communities. In an illuminating article in which he describes his method of research for his biography of Gandhi, Erikson establishes a psychohistorical principle of complementarity:

> From the psychohistorical viewpoint, then, the question is not, or not only, whether a man like Gandhi inadvertently proves some of Freud's points (such as the power of the emotions subsumed under the term Oedipus complex), but why such items which we now recognize as universal were reenacted in different media of representation (*including* Freud's dream analyses) by particular types of men in given periods of history—and why, indeed, their time was ready for them and their medium.[9]

Nonetheless, as a psychohistorian Erikson remains surprisingly close to the founding father. In an effort to steer between the "originological fallacy" (Freud's own genetic outlook) and the other extreme, the "teleological fallacy," (a systemic-dialectical eschatology in the Hegelian tradition) Erikson shows his own fidelity to the spirit of psychoanalysis.

"Reenactment" is his creative compromise—a concept which permits him to disavow mere repetition of the ontogenetic and phylogenetic "curse" of the father complex and yet give Freud his due. The *existential* curse in the lives of Erikson's *homines religiosi* issues from the father-son relationship of each new generation, and their creative reenactment of the curse

94

in the "garb of the historical day" at the right moment is what awes and liberates an historical community. Phylogenetic inevitability is replaced by a universal and inevitable generational conflict, in which the father-son struggle remains central for certain types of creative breakthrough. By emphasizing the existential moment and by eschewing deterministic theories of progress, Erikson avoids the teleological fallacy. Thus, reenactment permits Erikson to connect an historically unique situation and moment with analogous situations in which a certain type of leader at least temporarily resolved a generational conflict for an entire community, thereby reactivating paralyzed psychological resources and strengthening the community ego.

As shall be seen, Erikson's leaders do not necessarily conform to the image of the father or the rebel son. "Actuality" demands situation-specific responses. For example, at a given moment in its history, a community might need a maternal style of leadership. This last idea was apparently alien to Freud, despite his passing reference to an historical phase of matriarchy. Nonetheless, Erikson does show kinship with Freud when he speaks of community needs and the ministration of a leader—in effect, a great therapist—to those needs. Here he could find precedent in Freud's analysis of Paul's adaptation of Christianity to the Mediterranean community—the gift of a religious outlook with therapeutic value. However, the gifted leader and the community need not inevitably connect. Gifted lives may be squandered; and even those leaders who command the stage for a moment and satisfy community needs are only saviours pro tem. Here, the existential spirit of Kierkegaard prevails over Hegelian teleology. But in order to understand Erikson's position fully, it is best to examine his major psychohistorical works, *Young Man Luther* and *Gandhi's Truth*.

Among religious ideologies, Protestantism had special significance for Erikson. Although he did not characterize Catholicism as a fossil religion, as Freud had done with Judaism when comparing it to Christianity from a psychoanalytic point of view, Erikson implied something similar in *Young Man Luther*. In order to develop, all modern peoples had to protest against traditions which could no longer serve their spiritual needs or sustain their activity in the world. Luther, the first successful protestant in modern history, is Erikson's exemplar, but the future Bolshevik, Alyosha in "The Legend of Maxim Gorky's Youth" is also a kind of protestant. Erikson uses the word generically, to denote a stage in the development of human conscience in which "conscience is not based upon the paroxysms of the sin-and-expiation cycle, but on a discipline of mind."[10] Liberation from a negative conscience and the recovery of ego-strength does not occur in the same way among all historical communities, but it is the essential movement on the inner frontier for human development in the modern world. Therefore *Young Man Luther* might be seen as Erikson's response to the questions put by Freud in *Civilization and Its Discontents:* Would the human species through cultural development learn to control their unruly drives? Would they be able to avert the catastrophe looming ahead as a consequence of human technological mastery? In *Young Man Luther* Erikson offered Luther's ideology as a partial answer to Freud's question, and in the epilogue to his study poses another question, a rhetorical question which signifies, once again, his fidelity to Freud's psychoanalytic point of view:

> But will revolutions against exploiters settle the issue of exploitation, or must man also learn to raise truly less exploitable men— men who are first of all masters of the human life cycle and of the cycle of generations in man's own lifespace?[11]

Protestantism is an ideology which nourishes less exploitable identities and hence less exploitable men. Redistributions of property, the destruction of entire classes and the emergence of new political elites and bureaucracies might signify liberation at a given historical moment, but so long as communities as a whole fail to internalize the new identities imbedded in protestant ideologies, they tend to resubmit themselves to new masters, both inner and outer. Thus *Young Man Luther* presents as heroes those who have the inner strength to create ideologies of liberation, the source of which is the ego. In simplest terms, the communal ego liberates itself from negative conscience through the efforts of heroes of the inner frontier. In cultures struggling to free themselves from traditional folkways and orthodoxies the ego's ideological representative is protestantism in the generic sense. Luther is Erikson's vehicle for presenting his psychoanalytic interpretation of liberal ideology.

> Luther's emphasis on individual conscience prepared the way for the
> series of concepts of equality, representation, and self-determina-

tion which became in successive secular revolutions and wars the foundations not of the dignity of some, but of the liberty of all.[12]

Erikson's truly impressive achievement in *Young Man Luther* is his sometimes brilliantly inventive—though not always cogent—integration of Luther's life history with larger historical trends. Luther's relationship to his own north-German spiritual, social, and economic milieu is developed with the virtuosity already displayed by Erikson in *Childhood and Society*. Erikson insists—despite Nietzsche's indictment of Luther—that Luther was a man of the Renaissance. In addition, Erikson tries to integrate the achievements of his great *homo religiosus* with technological advances, and other changes on the outer frontier which could not fail to affect human identities and roles in the modernizing European world of the sixteenth century. Finally, with equally impressive virtuosity Erikson looks backward to the waning Middle Ages and forward to the industrial age and the era of the great political and social revolutions. There is something almost Hegelian in the scope of Erikson's psychohistorical integration. Despite his preference for open systems and existential indeterminacy, at times his psychohistorical positions seem programmatic, if not teleological. The *fit* between the great man and so many trends suits Erikson's vision of a greater scheme of things. *Young Man Luther* becomes a starting point for inquiry into matters of wider scope than the particular identity problems of Western or Northern Christendom.

However, it is best to begin a discussion of the book as such with Luther as Erikson's psychiatric case, for the young Luther is Erikson's entry point into all of the inquiries mentioned above. Erikson organizes his psychohistorical inquiry around moments of great meaning in Martin Luther's career—moments which historians of other persuasion interpret far differently. These are moments revelatory of Luther's identity crisis and his breakthrough to a new identity. Erikson's psychoanalytic "third ear" tells him that Martin's alleged raving in the choir of the monastery at Erfurt (the date is uncertain, but Luther was in his early or mid-twenties), in which he shouted "I am not!" can be connected with earlier and later evidence and fit into a pattern of identity crisis. Luther's identity crisis assumed a classical Oedipal form in that it revolved around a father-son conflict, but several ontogenetic peculiarities made it the identity crisis of a *homo religiosus:* First, Luther had a "precocious and relentless" conscience; second, he experienced an "existential curse," Kierkegaard's language for what the psychoanalysts call a "cover memory" or a "screen memory"; third, he experienced the integrity crisis early in his life and simultaneously with his identity crisis. Thus, he seemed old and full of melancholy while very young, for the negative sense of the integrity crisis is despair about the meaning and order of one's life and one's culture's style of life.

The generational conflict in *Young Man Luther* is connected with a father's drive for upward mobility and the family's transition from rural and peasant folkways to those of a mining community and an urban way of life. Erikson's reconstruction of the family romance is based upon such fragmentary evidence that it has little cogency, but it is nonetheless of great value, in that it shows how psychosocial history might be done well were evidence available. Luther's conflicted relationship with his father, Hans, and the unconscious hatred issuing from it is at the center of the story of his creative breakthrough:

> The theological problems which he tackled as a young adult of course reflected the peculiarly tenacious problem of the domestic relationship to his own father; but this was true to a large extent because both problems, the domestic and the universal, were part of one ideological crisis: a crisis about the theory and practice, the power and responsibility, of the moral authority invested in fathers: on earth and in heaven; at home, and in the market-place, and in politics; in the castles, the capitals, and in Rome.[13]

The second theme of the family romance, Luther's relationship to his mother, plays a crucial role in Erikson's explanation of Luther's recovery of faith, but one has to have great faith in Erikson's powers of reconstruction, for the evidence for the mother-son relationship is even scantier than that for the father-son conflict. However, Erikson's speculations are plausible: that a combination of upward mobility, transition to urban values and roles, passionate ambition, the use of cruel and authoritarian methods of child rearing by both parents alongside the father's techniques for binding his son to him, might create unconscious conflicts in a certain type of young man; and that the resolution of these conflicts might inspire (by unconscious analogy) an attack upon more exalted forms of authority. A gifted youth from a mining town in the northern part of

Germany did eventually (and unwittingly) initiate a rebellion whose ideology served a broad array of political, social, economic, and cultural ambitions, as well as the condition of European psyches and souls. The crucial assumption behind Erikson's psychohistorical approach is that without Luther's new ideology, the growing trend toward technical, cultural, and political innovation would have been stifled for lack of an ideology to promote inner ego strength. Only a gifted *homo religiosus* who had been beaten into anxious obedience could raise the question of obedience for a communal audience and invest it with historical meaning.

One should note parenthetically that Erikson's *homines religiosi* offer to their communities precisely what Freud had refused to give: consolation. They are "living bridges to an eventual clarity of existence, or at least to a sense of consolation which makes it possible to produce, create and serve without debilitating despair."[14] In order to appreciate Erikson's profound departure from Freud in this respect one need only place the above position side by side with this passage from *Civilization and Its Discontents:*

> Thus I have not the courage to rise up before my fellowmen as a prophet, and I bow to their reproach that I can offer them no consolation: for that is what they are all demanding—the wildest revolutionaries no less passionately than the most virtuous believers.[15]

The method of analogy is no less prominent in Erikson's work than in that of lesser psychohistorians. The holy family reflects the earthly family. If earthly fathers are wrathful, then the heavenly father may take on a grim demeanor. In order to support the hypothesis that Luther's existential dread was not idiosyncratic, Erikson turns to Jan Huizinga's *The Waning of the Middle Ages* and extends Huizinga's conclusion to North Germany during Luther's youth. Erikson concludes:

> Thus it is probable that in Martin's childhood and youth there lurked in the ideological perspective of his world, perhaps just because the great theologians were so engrossed in scholasticism, a world image of man as inescapably sinful, with a soul incapable of finding any true identity in its perishable body. This world-image implied only one hope: at an uncertain (and maybe immediately impending)

moment, an end would come which might guarantee an individual the chance (to be denied to millions of others) of finding pity before the only true Identity, the only true Reality, which was Divine Wrath.[16]

Few contemporary social scientists would accept either Huizinga's or Erikson's conclusions, since we have no direct access to such psychohistorical phenomena as late medieval and early Renaissance identity vacua, any more than we have direct knowledge of the feelings of guilt which pervaded the Mediterranean world in Paul's era, according to Freud. However, without such hypotheses, psychohistory would lose much of its interest. Erikson urges us to see the European community of the late fifteenth and early sixteenth centuries in the light of the first half of the twentieth century, with its own awareness of new death-dealing technologies and anxieties about changes in politics and culture. The European world after 1914—Freud's world when he wrote *Civilization and Its Discontents*—thus provides Erikson with the basis for a plausible *historical analogy*. In his valuable essay, "On the Nature of Psychohistorical Evidence," Erikson quite explicitly shows how the method of analogy serves him at several levels:

> For recorders and reviewers alike, however, events assume a momentous character when they seem both unprecedented and yet mysteriously familiar—that is, if *analogous events* come to mind that combine to suggest a direction to historical recurrences, be it divine intention someday to be revealed or an inexorable fate to which man may at least learn to adapt, or regularities which it may be man's task to regulate more engineeringly, or a repetitive delusion from which thoughtful man must "wake up."[17]

Luther's resolution of his identity crisis, his transformation from an obsessively obedient son and priest to a creative rebel and ideologue is the central theme of Erikson's study. Luther's first act of rebellion, his repudiation of Hans Luder's choice of a career in the law for him and his entry into the Augustinian monastery in Erfurt in 1505 could not itself resolve the problems issuing from a negative conscience with its attendant existential anxiety and dread. All of this could only provide young Luther with a *moratorium*. The concept of moratorium provides the occasion for still another Eriksonian analogy—between Luther's period of gestation and that of other creative but conflicted young men. Luther unwittingly used monasticism as a method for working through his identity crisis. He unconsciously postponed his decision about a future identity by choosing what was a negative identity from his father's point of view, and virtual nothingness from his own. Darwin, Freud, George Bernard Shaw, creative geniuses all—and a destructive genius, Hitler—had analogous moratoria, what we would recognize today as neurotic or even borderline psychotic breakdowns, before they broke through to a new identity and the genius of their creativity. But for Erikson, the crucial analogy is between Freud's and Luther's *insight* after long and lonely struggles in the inner depths.

It is now possible to make some general remarks about Erikson's use of the case study. His cogency derives from his provocative analogies. However unconvincing his evidence for any one of his hypotheses about Luther, his evocation of the *pattern* of development of a certain type of human creativity is compelling. Erikson uses a variety of analogies to serve his larger purposes, for which the story of Luther's development appears to be only a vehicle. The story of Luther's childhood occasions a critique of child rearing; and the story of his moratorium prefaces a discussion of the plight of neurotic adolescents and the conditions under which the fortunate among them might realize their talents. Luther's near psychic self-annihilation and his recovery are only the dramatic center of a psychoanalytic *Bildungsroman* in which the nominal hero's perilous journey serves mainly as a dramatic vehicle for Erikson's psychoanalytic prescriptions. But if much of the case study of Luther's identity crisis seems brilliantly contrived, Erikson's remarks about ideology are inspired and forceful.

Erikson's discussion of ideology in *Young Man Luther* in the chapter entitled "The Meaning of Meaning It" pulls together all of the threads—psychoanalytic, biographical, and historical—running through the book. It is a psychohistorical tour de force. Equally impressive is Erikson's deceptively simple connection of the concept of ideology with his notion of psychosocial identity:

> In this book *ideology* will mean an unconscious tendency underlying religious and scientific as well as political thought: the tendency at a given time to make facts amenable to ideas, and ideas to facts, in order to create a world image convincing enough to support the collective and the individual sense of identity.[18]

Erikson presents Luther's doctrine as a Renaissance ideology, despite the fact that by Erikson's own admission, his hero "seems blind" to the Renaissance. In order for the Renaissance to extend itself and to become a genuinely revolutionary movement, it needed an ideology—and a leading ideologue who could liberate Christian Europeans from the chilled and constricted ego space of the late medieval world. Erikson's psychohistorical thesis about the Renaissance is quite straightforward:

> It cannot escape those familiar with psychoanalytic theory that the Renaissance is the ego revolution *par excellence*. It was a large-scale restoration of the ego's executive functions, particularly insofar as the enjoyment of the senses, the exercise of power, and the cultivation of a good conscience to the point of anthropocentric vanity were concerned, all of which was regained from the Church's systematic and terroristic exploitation of man's proclivity for a negative conscience. . . . The Renaissance gave man a vacation from his negative conscience, thus freeing the ego to gather strength for manifold activity.[19]

It was Luther who extended the Renaissance to the "conscience of ordinary man," a lingering late medieval conscience described by Erikson as "negative," "tragic," and "hypertrophied," by recovering his own capacity for creative activity through a restoration of his own ego-initiative. Luther's struggle for justification against an obsessive conscience and his breakthrough against it, which occurred during his lectures on the Psalms, was dramatized by the notorious revelation in the tower privy. The latter provided Erikson with an opportunity for discussing the epigenetic truth of the relationship of organ modes (in this case, retention and elimination) to the emotional phenomena of revelation and repudiation: the revelation of justification by faith in Christ and the repudiation of the Devil, symbolized by excrement.

Luther's breakthrough for Erikson signified both personal progress from youth to adulthood and communal progress, in that Luther's ideology of faith provided the inner resources for a Renaissance identity. The protestant identity, with its individuality, acceptance of inner conflict, and reliance upon the ego's capacity to synthesize opposites, prefigured Freud's psychoanalytic version of human psychological maturity and health. No attempt will be made here to present in its entirety Erikson's description of the spiritual exercise of passivity—a species of psychological internalization of Christ's passion—as the ego's method for gaining mastery over negative conscience (superego) and the id's drives. It should be clear, however, what Erikson means when he writes, "Christ now becomes the core of the Christian identity." The last quotation implies a profound existential transformation from passive reception of judgments handed from an external authority on high, to active participation in suffering and recognition that the inner pain of self-judgment must be endured. The inner authority functions without external props and yields up the "individual's truly meant self-judgment." This is what Erikson means by "meaning it."

Epigenesis and the Ego

The ego's ability to transform a passive posture into active mastery (a type of reversal often encountered in dialectics) represents ontogenetically "the internalization of the father-son relationship; the concomitant crystallization of conscience; the safe establishment of an identity as a worker and a man; and the concomitant reaffirmation of basic trust."[20] It is important to note too that Luther's realistic recognition of the power of *libido* signifies for Erikson the conditions under which the ego dominates the superego rather than vice versa. To put it in structural terms, the ego's ability to gain control of the psychic *system* and to steer it toward an *optimal state* depends upon its ability to assume a correct relationship to both of the other substructures of the psyche—the superego and the id—and that ability in turn depends upon realistic *insight,* whatever the ideological idiom of that realism. The best ideologies therefore contain both faith and realism.

The importance of ideologies, whether religious or political or both, for the mobilization of groups has long been recognized. However, not before Freud's *Moses and Monotheism* did anyone venture to show how the inner life of an entire historical community might be transformed. It remained for Erikson to revise Freud's ideas—indeed to invert Freud's position—by making men of faith the bearers of Freud's insights and promoters of realism, work, love, and mature, autonomous ways of life. The human ego *itself* and its historical agents, such as Luther, who know how to marshal its strength through their capacity for systematic intro-spection are the heroes of the inner frontier. Eriksonian psychohistory shows how their epigenetic development contains the strengths and weaknesses of the culture's patterns and reigning ideology; how this will be reflected in the identities that ordinary members of all social strata can achieve; and how the gifted few can redeem the many and create new identities, if the historical moment and their communities are ready for them and their ideologies of human liberation and rejuvenation.

Luther became a saviour pro tem, in this case, because of his capacity to recover basic trust—the epigenetic foundation of faith—from a state of existential despair. The dialectical architectonic is also central to the ego's functioning in Erikson's system. It nests within his epigenetic schema. The ego synthesizes opposites and can transform a state of passivity into active mastery by recovering a sense of mutuality from its accumulated epigenetic strength. Luther's ideological achievement therefore did not merely signify liberation from the doctrinal authority of the Catholic Church, but liberation *for* self-development through ego-strength. Lu-ther provided Europeans with the appropriate ideology for forging a ma-ture identity—an identity based upon both faith and realism. Erikson seems to say that the internalization of Christ gives the ego a sense of self-creat-ing autonomy—it both wills its life and lives (or gives) it freely. One could hardly wish for a more dramatic psychoanalytic argument that Luther gave Renaissance anthropocentrism an inner core of "meaning it," which in-spired modern individuality and a sense of freely chosen, wholehearted, confident action. By grasping the meaning of Christ's passion, Luther overcame the paralyzing effects of the crippled and fragmented identity transmitted by the late medieval religious ideology. His ideology of faith signified a restoration of his own inner wholeness and actuality, and it promised in turn to mitigate the inevitable curse of human generational conflict by altering the metabolism of generations in favor of greater mu-tuality. A new ideology of faith replacing the "terrorism" of the Catholic Church would support new identities in both divine and earthly families, and make living and working more wholehearted, in the Eriksonian sense. Introspective genius which thus realizes itself in ideological creativity and community leadership can eventually affect the entire human species. Thus, the suffering of the gifted few can redeem the many, but they—the *hom-ines religiosi*—can only achieve actuality as saviours pro tem. Every historical community must choose its own innovative leaders, its own heroes of the inner frontier.

The central role of ideologies and ideological leaders in Erikson's own childhood, adolescence, and young manhood no doubt affected his psychohistorical vision. Freud too had lived in a world in which ideological heroes had tried to universalize their new doctrines, but he had assiduously distinguished prevailing religious and secular ideologies from the psychoanalytic point of view and repudiated efforts to combine psychoanalysis with them, even when he found in them (as he had found in Marx's theory) valuable insights into some historical phenomena. As noted earlier, he had shown no inclination to apply dialectics to a material and historical world. Erikson, on the other hand, infuses his epigenetic theory and psychohistories with a dialectical spirit. Unlike Hegelians, however, Erikson implies that dialectics is nothing more than the ego's method for reconciling the conflicts and inner division issuing from the developing human being's experience of its body and its contact with a nurturing but also frustrating environment. Furthermore, the ego can only achieve its reconciliation under the correct circumstances—when the intrapsychic balance of power is in its favor—what Erikson calls a state of "ego-dominance." And the fundamental epigenetic strength supporting ego-dominance issues from the human experience of *mutuality of recognition* in the very first stage of human development when the mother (in ordinary circumstances) establishes basic trust in her child. The inner achievement of ego-dominance brings with it the ego's special time-space quality, which Erikson describes in the following terms:

> To the ego, eternity is always now. . . . To the ego the past is not an inexorable process, experienced only as a preparation for an impending doom; rather, the past is part of a present mastery which employs a convenient mixture of forgetting, falsifying, and idealizing to fit the past to the present, but usually to an extent which is neither unknowingly delusional nor knowingly dishonest. The ego can resign itself to past losses and forfeitings and learn not to demand the impossible of the future. It enjoys the illusion of a present, and defends this most precarious of all assumptions against doubts and apprehensions by remembering most easily chains of experiences which were alike in their unblemished presentness. To the healthy ego, the flux of time sponsors the process of identity. It

is thus not afraid of death (as Freud has pointed out vigorously); it has no concept of death. But it *is* afraid of losing mastery over the negative conscience, over the drives, and over reality. To lose any of these battles is, for the ego, living death; to win them again and again means to the ego something akin to an assumption that it is causing its own life.[21]

The victory of the ego signifies mastery over the past, a healthy attitude toward the future, and a sense of self-initiated activity in the present—a spirit of *causa sui* and free will. With this achievement, death has no sting. One can readily translate Erikson's vision of the state of ego-dominance into Hegelian and Marxian visions of freedom.

Ego-dominance and the time-space quality associated with it are a necessary inner achievement in a world whose time-space characteristics have been changed by new technologies of communication and which has generally achieved impressive mastery over nature. The continuation of such technological mastery in the modern world and the strengthening of the Renaissance anthropocentric vision—now the modern vision of man as prosthetic God, in Freud's terms—depends upon this inner rearrangement in favor of the ego and the concomitant faith, realism, initiative, individuality, present-mindedness, and freedom sponsored by ego-strength. The new protestant identity (in its generic sense) fits the new technologically oriented environment and has the right qualities for modern industrial civilization. In a word, in *Young Man Luther* Erikson made ego-dominance the foundation of modernization and Luther a heroic fighter in the service of the ego and of human adaptation to and extension of a modernizing outer frontier, despite his personal blindness and even aversion to the changes occurring there. That is why it is possible to refer to Luther as the *nominal* hero of Erikson's *Bildungsroman*. The real hero, of course, is the ego.

Erikson's great sympathy for Luther and his appreciation for the value of a rejuvenated Christianity might lead one to suspect that he had chosen some combination of Christianity and psychoanalysis as the correct modern ideology. But his book on Gandhi suggests an even larger program. *Gandhi's Truth* does for adulthood, the crisis of generativity, and Hinduism, what *Young Man Luther* did for youth, the identity crisis, and Christianity. Furthermore, *Gandhi's Truth* reflects the progress of Erikson's own career as a therapist—a movement through problems of child-hood, to those of adolescence and youth, and finally, to those of adult-hood. Erikson's psychohistories adroitly mesh his immediate therapeutic concerns with his larger concern about the human condition. Whereas his earlier psychohistorical work had been focused on ideology, during the period when he wrote *Gandhi's Truth* he took ritual as his central theme. This signified a further step in the progress of his study of human conflict and mutuality, always undertaken with a sense of the value of psychoanalytic insight for conflict resolution at an historical level, where human "pseudospecies" often confront one another with mutual annihi-lation in mind. If *Young Man Luther* is Erikson's vehicle for showing how an ideology of ego-dominance can rejuvenate a community suffering from an identity vacuum and serve modernization, then *Gandhi's Truth* is his vehicle for offering a creative ritualization of conflict in an era when the struggle among pseudospecies, whether religious, racial, national, or so-cial, might lead to the extinction of the entire species.

During the course of his researches on Gandhi, Erikson extended his vision of the epigenesis of psychosocial identity to include the ontogeny of ritualization, which he elaborated upon in *Toys and Reason, Stages in the Ritualization of Experience* (1977). Erikson's psychoanalytic theory of ritualization is based upon the hypothesis that there is an innate human need for regular "mutual affirmation and certification."[22] Human cultural institutions, which reflect the senses associated with Erikson's epigenetic stages, also reflect the human need for rituals and ceremonies, which sus-tain and re-integrate at higher levels earlier human experience, especially play experience, but most important of all, the initial human experience of mutuality. This is illustrated in the chart shown below.[23]

Erikson's chart of ritualization, like his epigenetic chart of human on-togeny, is based upon the idea that the mutuality of mother and child is the original social experience, the foundation of hope and faith, the source of a religious sense of the numinous, and of "charisma hunger" in hu-manity. Here, Erikson subverts Freud's theory of the centrality of the father in religious and group phenomena. Whereas the the theme of the mater-nal contribution to ideological rejuvenation had been overshadowed by the father-son relationship in *Young Man Luther,* in *Gandhi's Truth* and preliminary articles, Erikson completed the process of standing Freud on his head by suggesting that a style of leadership issuing from the mu-

Ontogeny of Ritualization

infancy	mutuality of recognition					
early childhood		discrimination of good and bad				
play age			dramatic elaboration			
school age				rules of performance		
adolescence					solidarity of conviction	
elements in adult rituals	NUMINOUS	JUDICIOUS	DRAMATIC	FORMAL	IDEOLOGICAL	GENERATIONAL SANCTION

tuality of mother and child is the closest human approach to an adaptive instinctive pattern for the ritualization of conflict. Erikson's interest in ethology and in Konrad Lorenz's description of ritualized threatening behavior in social species close to *homo sapiens* reflected his new aspiration: the promotion of a ritualization "through which men, equipped with both realism and spiritual strength, can face each other with a mutual confidence analogous to the instinctive safety built into the animals' pacific rituals."[24]

Erikson accentuates the importance of the earliest stages of mother-child interaction in his theory of ritualization to the point where it becomes his own optimistic originology. He emphasizes sources of strength in infantile experiences, the repetition of which in creative ritualization has great adaptive value for the human species. The internalization of mutual recognition, affirmation, and certification of the mother-infant relationship sustains our inner hope of paradisical union and wholeness, when it is reintegrated at higher levels in both the ontogenetic and historical process. Ultimately, creative ritualization offers the hope that we may transcend the exclusive identities of our pseudospecies and achieve a universal ethics. Erikson defines pseudospeciation as the evolution of human groups:

> which behave as if they were separate species created at the beginning of time by supernatural will, and each superimposing on the geographic and economic facts of its existence a cosmogeny, as well

as a theocracy and an image of man, all its own. Thus each develops a *distinct sense of identity,* held to be *the* human identity and fortified against other pseudo-species by prejudices which mark them as exta-specific and, in fact, inimical to the only "genuine human endeavor."[25]

What Erikson hopes for is a breakthrough to a universal ethics which will provide a new, inclusive human identity. The ideological achievements of creative young *homines religiosi* had supported new identities adapted to an emerging technological civilization, but something beyond that is needed now. The new trend in Erikson's thinking about human leadership can be seen clearly in the following passage from *Identity: Youth and Crisis* (1968):

> The overriding issue is the creation not of a new ideology but of a universal ethics growing out of a universal technological civilization. This can be advanced only by men and women who are neither ideological youths nor moralistic old men, but who know that from generation to generation the test of what you produce is the *care* it inspires.[26]

The role of the feminine, or more precisely, maternal characteristics of the species in determining the issue is central to Erikson's thesis about Gandhi's style of leadership and to his appreciation of other *homines religiosi* with maternal qualities. St. Francis, about whom Joan Erikson, his wife, wrote a short study, became another of his maternal heroes and Erikson suggests that psychoanalysis itself operates in a maternal mode.[27] Once again, he discovered that the psychoanalytic method of insight and therapy shared features with the insights and methods of *homines religiosi* who might save the species from self-destruction. His concern with racial struggle in the United States and his commitment to leaders who might creatively renovate Gandhi's ritualization of conflict is reflected in his dedication of his *magnum opus* to Martin Luther King. Thus, *Gandhi's Truth* carried the burden of Erikson's concerns of the late 1960s, as well as his ultimate hope for a universal ethics.

Gandhi's Truth, Erikson's most eloquent statement about religious actuality and its relationship to psychoanalysis, is even more complex as psychohistory than *Young Man Luther*. It is one of the first major works of psychohistory to deal systematically and openly with the problem of counter-transference experienced by the historical investigator during his encounters with the records of the past. Because he was studying events for which there were living witnesses, Erikson used interviews in his research. Erikson's essay describing his research methods, "On the Nature of Psychohistorical Evidence: In Search of Gandhi," has been cited already.[28] It summarizes with considerable clarity Erikson's method for dealing with the transferences, counter-transferences, and complementarity that he encountered at each level of research in his examinations of recorder, reviewer, and follower. Erikson outlines here the procedure by which psychohistorians might critically examine the available data and mesh the epigenetic process of an historical life career with that of a community. The essay also presents Erikson's major psychohistorical theses about the role of introspective genius in the development of historically momentous styles of leadership. Finally, it is still another chapter in Erikson's long effort to rescue Freud from his grimness and his repudiation of all of the prophets and saints, religious and political, of his era. *Gandhi's Truth*, like *Young Man Luther*, joins Freud, the introspective hero whose method provides systematic insight into the reality of problems of human psychological development created by biological evolution, to Gandhi, the religious leader who struggled for a universal ethics grounded in a form of Hindu religious actuality—Satyagraha. For Erikson, psychoanalysis and Satyagraha together offer "clear insight into our central motivations and pervasive faith in the brotherhood of man."[29]

That *Gandhi's Truth* is Erikson's vehicle for promoting his therapeutic version of the Golden Rule can hardly be doubted. So it was with *Childhood and Society* and *Young Man Luther*. Erikson summarizes his position on the Golden Rule in *Insight and Responsibility*, where he offers a preview of his work on Gandhi and Satyagraha.

> My base line is the Golden Rule, which advocates that one should do (or not do) to another what one wishes to be (or not to be) done by [another]. . . . For the only alternative to armed competition seems to be the effort to *activate in the historical partner what will strengthen him in his historical development even as it strengthens the actor in his own development—toward a common future identity.* . . .

At our historical moment it becomes clear in a most practical way that the doer of the Golden Rule, and he who is done by, is the same man, *is* man. . . . While the Golden Rule in its classical versions prods man to strive *consciously* for a highest good and to avoid mutual harm with a sharpened awareness, our insights assume an *unconscious* substratum of ethical strength and, at the same time, unconscious arsenals of destructive rage. . . . It will be the task of the next generation everywhere to begin to integrate new and old methods of self-awareness with the minute particulars of universal technical proficiency.[30]

Indian culture had some of the old methods of self-awareness and Gandhi was able to use them innovatively. Erikson's brilliant evocation of Indian culture and Hinduism cannot be recounted here, any more than his discussion of Christian cosmology and medieval religious philosophy in *Young Man Luther*. Suffice it to say, Erikson is a master at sketching culture patterns and connecting them with his epigenetic vision. The Hindu concept of *dharma* proves to be analogous to Erickson's own concept of identity, for like psychosocial identity, dharma is "that which integrates the individual experience and yet is always communal in nature." It is "a consolidation of the world through the self-realization of each individual within a joint order."[31] However, Gandhi's gift to India and to humanity as a whole—assuming that innovative leaders who are able to adapt it in different historical settings come forth—is the *ritualization* called *Satyagraha*. Erikson chose to organize his book around the first use of Satyagraha in India, at Ahmedabad in 1918, the intersection of Gandhi's crisis of generativity with a set of historical conflicts, both local and global, which continue in altered forms to threaten to annihilate the human species. Satyagraha is Gandhi's instrument of religious actualism, a product of his middle age and the epigenetic moment when men and women "must have defined for themselves what and whom they have come to care for, what they care to do well, and how they plan to take care of what they have started and created."[32] In the Hindu life cycle, the crisis of generativity coincided with the state of householdership *(Grhastha)* during which procreation, productivity, family life, and communal life are a person's dominant concerns. In a great *homo religiosus,* however, the gift of religious actualism prevents ordinary householdership, just as it prevents the attainment of the monastic or saintly ideal on a smaller stage.

III

For the true saints are those who transfer the state of household-ership to the house of God, becoming father and mother, brother and sister, son and daughter, to all creation, rather than to their own issue. But they do this in established "orders," and they create or partake in rituals which will envelope and give peace to those who must live in transitory reality.[33]

Like the chapter entitled 'The Meaning of Meaning It" in *Young Man Luther,* the section of *Gandhi's Truth* entitled "The Leverage of Truth" contains the heart of the book and the burden of Erikson's higher purpose. Erikson draws together many of the themes that pervade his work: the unequal relationship between parent and child, therapist and patient, and the need for actuality in their relationships. The great *homo religiosus* can provide, even though only temporarily in a given historical context, that confrontation with death and nothingness out of which comes impressive ego-strength and the power to actualize others. The immediacy of ego-strength, the nowness of truth-in-action, signifies for Erikson the capacity for rebirth, renewal, and regeneration. When human groups are actualized by leaders like Gandhi they are revitalized, for "to be ready to die for what is true now means to grasp the only chance to have lived fully."[34] The power of actuality embodied in Satyagraha and the Indian struggle against English imperialism ultimately has universal significance and implications for a universal ethics in the future. Actuality in Erikson's terms is also "the potential for unifying action at a given moment."[35] As Satyagraha, actuality performs in history what ego-strength achieves in the individual—it faces death and nothingness and uses truth-in-action to create ever more inclusive unities out of conflicting elements. Gandhi's ritualization of conflict, his militant nonviolence, serves all of Erikson's purposes, and is accorded evolutionary significance as a new method, akin to psychoanalysis, for dealing with the vicissitudes of the instincts and reinstating in the human species "what in the animal is so innocently and yet so fatefully given."[36]

Gandhi's Truth achieves in masterful fashion Erikson's assimilation of psychoanalysis to religion and politics, and to existential and dialectical thought. His epigenetic principle depends upon agencies (the ego, the psychoanalyst, the *homo religiosus)* of unification and wholeness which, in the best of conditions, have the power to reconcile the inevitably conflicting forces in both the individual and society. The insight of *homo religiosus* is all the more important at a moment in history when only a nonviolent resolution of conflict can assure a future for the human species. Satyagraha is the historical-evolutionary analogue of psychoanalysis in that:

> in both encounters only the militant probing of a vital issue by a nonviolent confrontation can bring to light what insight is ready on both sides. Such probing must be decided on only after careful study, but then the developing encounter must be permitted to show, step by step, what the power of truth may reveal and enact. At the end only a development which transforms both partners in such an encounter is truth in action; and such transformation is possible only where man learns to be nonviolent toward himself as well as toward others.[37]

The replacement of the superego's and the id's power by the ego's strength is the central concern in his psychology, and the construction of a heroic image of the forces which can confront the enemy (whether inner or outer) with disciplined courage, with scientific realism and religious faith, and in such a way that the reconciliation of the past with the present makes a better future possible—are the foundation of Erikson's effort to be true to Freud and yet to offer hope.

Erikson believes that the insight-through-suffering of great *homines religiosi* and the truth-in-action of their styles of leadership may be the last recourse of a technological civilization whose intelligentsia have created several revolutionary, and violent, doctrines of human liberation. But he offers no assurance that the intersection of great lives with community needs—indeed, with evolutionary needs—will save humanity from self-destruction. In the individual, the ratio of positive to negative senses and the accrual of ego-strength at each crisis of development depends upon a great variety of factors at each level of epigenetic reintegration. In the species as a whole, historical moments are subject to forces working for unity and disunity, for more inclusive human identities or for pseudospeciation. Erikson's psychohistorical vision, despite strong similarities with those of systemic-dialectical thinkers like Hegel, sustains its epigenetic indeterminacy and existential tension. Ego-strength is the meeting place of the epigenetic, dialectical, and systemic principles in Erikson's work. The ego unifies and carries forward the accrued strength of the psychic system; it integrates polarities; it reconciles the present with the past; and it creates the foundation for ever greater wholeness and unity. Indeed, it is the executive agency of our hope for the future.

• CHAPTER V •

Marcuse and Brown

E VERY GREAT new vision of the human condition has challenged the interpretative power of the intelligentsia. Erikson's revision of Freud vividly demonstrates how psychoanalysis can be assimilated to religious and existential points of view and rendered more dynamic and optimistic through the use of epigenetic and dialectical architectonics. An Hegelian spirit of reconciliation pervades Erikson's work, but he avoids deterministic theories of progress or dialectical formulas describing Good and Evil in History, except insofar as he shows how psychosocial polarities, especially that of positive and negative identity, carry a sense of Good and Evil. The two dialectical psychohistorians who will be examined in this chapter present far more developed theories of history than did either Erikson or Freud and, as one might suspect, do tend to see Good and Evil in History. Marcuse and Brown both show the impact of left-Hegelian approaches to history, but Brown carries on a Romantic and mystical tradition and Marcuse a Marxian one. Freud's theory of repression is the most important link between them. Both place Freud's idea of repression at the center of their theories of history; and both set themselves the task of answering the question posed by Freud in *Civilization and Its Discontents:* Is it possible under the present conditions of technological civilization, human repression and the unleashing of Thanatos, to visualize a strengthening of Eros and a positive outcome for the human species? Marcuse and Brown were far more adept at developing a theory of history around Freud's theory of the instincts and his idea of repression than they were at presenting unambiguous programs for human survival. However, during the decade of the 1960s and early 1970s, their radical visions attracted wide followings. Through them psychohistory entered the counterculture (or contraculture) of that era and the New Left.

Herbert Marcuse's devotion to the idea of history and to dialectics would presumably place him at a far remove from Freud's naturalism. Nonetheless, he found a useful naturalistic basis for his utopian vision in Freud's theory of the instincts. This in itself might at first seem odd, given the profoundly conservative implications of Freud's version of the genetic theory of the instincts. But Marcuse and other serious thinkers of the left by the late 1930s (if not earlier) could no longer ignore the lessons of the Russian Revolution. They began to ponder, with the help of psychoanalysis, the reasons for the appearance of new forms of domination— even atavistic forms. They no longer believed that only a stubbornly persisting capitalism stood in the way of human liberation. The search for critical terra firma—to be more precise—for a foundation for a radical and optimistic theory of history, led Marcuse and several of his colleagues, many of whom like Marcuse emigrated to the United States from Nazi Germany and reestablished the Institute of Social Research in New York City in 1934, to Freud. Oddly enough, Freud's genetic outlook contained elements which an inventive dialectician might integrate into a radical critique of contemporary civilization and even a hopeful outlook—although the latter was a far more difficult task than the former. Freud's theory of the instincts and repression and his formulation of the origins and meaning of the Oedipus complex were subjected to the left-Hegelian style of thought of the Frankfurt school of critical theory.[1]

The primacy of social and political over mainly therapeutic purposes distinguishes the approach of the critical theorists from Freud or Erikson. They and others in the Marxian tradition used Freud's psychosexual approach and his theory of the unconscious to add another dimension to their critique of "bourgeois" civilization. The first Freudo-Marxist, Wilhelm Reich, showed not only how *deep* socioeconomic domination went but how far liberation would have to go. Social and economic liberation alone would fail unless sexual repression were also abolished.[2] Stalinism had spurred Reich, who refused to abandon hope for a materialistic solution to human misery, to argue that full human liberation involved the abolition of sexual repression. In a word, social and political revolution could not succeed unless accompanied by a revolution in sexual behavior. Reich eventually abandoned his Marxism for a cranky sexual reduction-ism which owed only its inspiration to Freud. However, Reich's theoret-ical role as synthesizer has been appreciated by students of the left for what it was: an original effort to combine two distinctive (and apparently incompatible) explanations of human misery and two theories, only one of which aspired to a program of human liberation through social and political movements. Freud's occasional, although on balance hostile, re-marks about Marxism or about events in the Soviet Union hardly consti-tute a developed position. On the other hand, his behavior as leader of the psychoanalytic movement left little doubt about his attitude that sci-ence and politics do not mix well, any more than religion and science do.

The mystique of Marxian socialism was and is powerful enough to at-tract thinkers from a great variety of intellectual traditions. Marcuse was a species of Marxist before he followed Reich's lead, but his general the-oretical approach is better called left-Hegelian, in that Marcuse aban-doned, when necessary, any ideological position which threatened to be-come part of a structure of domination in history. Left-Hegelianism is, in principle, a doctrine of permanent revolution. In practice, it is a per-manently critical posture, a constant theoretical vigilance for the dialec-tically negative moment, a perpetual search for the theoretical and prac-tical basis for an assault against the existing order. Left-Hegelianism launched itself in the second quarter of the nineteenth century largely as a critique of German idealism, and some of its peculiarities can only be understood by studying the intelligentsia of that period. However, in spite of its dynamic—indeed revolutionary—posture, it had absorbed from metaphysical idealism not only dialectics but an idea of reconciliation at some moment in the future. All Hegelians pursue an idea of wholeness as the end of the dialectical process. However, unlike Hegel, who tended to reconcile the present with the past, the left Hegelians sought to preempt the future. Like all Hegelians, they recognized the necessity of each mo-ment of the dialectic, but they turned their faces toward the future, which by definition was the historical path to rational progress, unity, and hu-man self-fulfillment.

Marcuse's long career reflects, more than anything else, his fidelity to left-Hegelianism. Freud became a useful appendix. He permitted Marcuse to develop a more elaborate and thorough critique of domination in human history. Marcuse's psychohistorical work is part of a major project—by no means his only—to explain the seeming failures of Marxism without abandoning revolutionary socialism's unrealized social and political programs. One might therefore see Marcuse's work as an interesting chapter in an elaborate effort to update the left-Hegelian critique of bourgeois civilization. He presses into service those aspects of Freud and Marx which can be fitted to a critique of the present historical moment and applied to a program for the future.

Finally, one should note that Marcuse was not alone in his effort to follow Reich's lead. Several of the thinkers associated with the Institute of Social Research sustained their commitment to dialectics and socialism but, like Marcuse, transcended dogmatic, party-oriented theorizing and showed great receptivity to psychoanalytic theory. Erich Fromm also became an early Freudo-Marxist and produced a popular critique of modern culture in his influential book, *Escape from Freedom,* in 1941. The rise of Fascism, the degeneration of the Russian Revolution into Stalinism, and a great variety of disturbing political, social, and cultural phenomena (prominent among them, anti-Semitism) in the mass democracies inspired ever more elaborate theories, diagnoses, and prescriptions among the intelligentsia. Fromm, however, in developing his critique renounced the very aspects of Freudian theory which Marcuse believed provided the basis for a *radical* critique. In *Eros and Civilization* (1955), Marcuse's major work of psychohistorical theory—and indeed the only one which will be discussed here—Marcuse set out to rescue Freud from "revisionists" like Fromm, who had abandoned Freud's theory of the instincts. In doing so, Marcuse showed great dialectical virtuosity.

Unlike the revisionists or neo-Freudians, Marcuse embraced Freud's theory of the instincts, but he did so as a radically historical thinker and not as a proponent of biologism or naturalism. Rather, he did it in a spirit akin to that of Marx, when Marx chose an infrastructure of forces of production for his theory of history. The instincts for Marcuse were not immutable, even though they retained their original aim: pleasure. Moreover, Marcuse accepted Freud's theory of a death instinct and the idea of the Nirvana principle. Marcuse's historical approach to the instincts is based upon the rather straightforward idea that changing historical environments alter the program of the pleasure principle by confronting the id instincts with a new reality principle and altered forms of domination of the ego and superego. The latter agencies enforce the various historical versions of the reality principle by way of repression. For Marcuse, repression is mainly historical and he swiftly passes by Freud's most pessimistic reflections on organic repression and the inheritance of degenerative acquired characteristics. Thus, the ego and superego always act as a bilevel superstructure of domination, which have to be acquired anew by every human generation in new historical forms. All the while, individuals in all generations retain unconscious memories of a time of infantile bliss when they did not have to compromise the program of the pleasure principle—when they strove for "integral gratification."[3] In short, the aim of the instincts is preserved as unconscious memories which can be restored with the help of psychoanalysis or spontaneously by means of fantasy (imagination). It may seem odd that Marcuse should place so much emphasis upon the recovery of the past, given the future-oriented character of left-Hegelianism. But Hegelians, whether of the right or the left, believe in the *sublation (Aufhebung)* of the past rather than its disappearance. In this particular use of the unconscious ontogenetic past, Marcuse found the basis for a critique of repression. It is an irreducibly genetic aspect of his theory—despite his dialectical orientation and his position on the mutability of the instincts.

It is worthwhile to note once again that the Hegelian philosophy posits an *original* wholeness. After self-alienation and dialectical development Hegel's Absolute Spirit, enriched by that very development, becomes whole again. At the end of the process, a dialectical union of freedom and necessity is achieved. Marcuse describes the unconscious mind not only as the source of the drive for integral gratification, but as the locus of the "immediate identity of necessity and freedom,"[4] for integral gratification is the absence of want and repression. The unconscious thus preserves our drive for wholeness and *that,* evidently, is immutable.

If the unconscious id instincts represent the radical past which can be pressed into the service of human liberation in the present for the sake of the future, the superego functions as the reactionary representative of past reality principles and serves to adapt the individual to a "punitive" present. Thus, the unconscious is a mixed blessing. It contains modifications of the instincts which have been imposed by the reality principle alongside the unmodified memory of gratification. This ingenious interpretation of Freud's theory of the conservative nature of the instincts, repression, and the unconscious mind permits Marcuse to identify the enemy within as well as the inner source of human liberation. In the process, of course, he inverts Freud's position, for Freud believed in strengthening the reality principle.

Unlike the original structure of the instincts, the infrastructure, as it were, of the human psyche, the ego and the superego are historical acquisitions and the repressive reality principles which they serve are impermanent. This historical approach to the reality principle and repression is paralleled by Marcuse's historical interpretation of the character of human sexuality. Once again, he posits an original erotic wholeness, described as "polymorphous perverse" by Freud. However, unlike Freud, who believed that the stages of psychosexual development in the infant, child, and adolescent were biologically fixed stages of maturation, Marcuse believed that adult genital sexuality represented not *maturity* but *desexualization* through cultural imperatives imposed upon human beings throughout their life cycle. Different historical civilizations mutilated human erotic wholeness in different ways, but the problem of *scarcity,* whether absolute scarcity or organized scarcity imposed by mechanisms of domination in a given society, always underlay the necessity for work. The work imperative in turn demanded the transformation of the human body into an instrument of labor rather than one of love. Marcuse distinguished his historical approach from Freud's mistaken (in this instance) biologism by using the term "surplus repression" to signify "the restrictions necessitated by social domination" and the term "performance principle" to denote "the prevailing historical form of the reality principle."[5] Thus, the amount of repression imposed upon human beings above the minimum amount necessary for survival in civilization ("basic repression") is a function of sociohistorical forms of domination.

Freud had observed human sexuality under conditions of surplus repression and the prevailing performance principle of European bourgeois society of the late nineteenth and early twentieth centuries and had mistakenly assumed that he was observing biologically given stages of development. He erroneously concluded that sexuality in the human species was inherently problematic. Marcuse assumed that phylogenetic peculiarities gave the human species a special grace:

The power to restrain and guide instinctual drives, to make biolog-ical necessities into individual needs and desires, increases rather than reduces gratification: the "mediatization" of nature, the breaking of its compulsion, is the human form of the pleasure principle. Such restrictions of the instincts may first have been enforced by scarcity and by the protracted dependence of the human animal, but they have become the privilege and distinction of man which enabled him to transform the blind necessity of the fulfillment of want into de-sired gratification.[6]

One should note that the agent for this "mediatization" in orthodox psy-choanalysis can be nothing other than the human ego, and Marcuse takes the position that we have a history distinct from natural necessity pre-cisely because we have an ego and repression. In the end, Marcuse must somehow infer from human history the characteristics of human beings in a society which could reduce repression to some "basic" level. As can be seen in the above quotation, he accepts the existence of the instinctual drives but implies that human beings are not so much *driven* as *driving*. He thus effectively transforms the meaning of *Trieb* and removes it from the realm of natural necessity. In doing so, he himself becomes a kind of revisionist, for his assumption that human beings live in history rather than nature is quite contrary to the spirit of Freud, who did not make radical distinctions between the realms of nature and history. In the end, Marcuse has to define a new kind of ego, which can operate more freely, yet still control and shape the drives. Here he demonstrates his radicalism relative to the other revisionists, the ego-psychologists. But first of all, he must describe the historical conditions under which a new kind of ego might emerge.

Despite the complexity of his ideas, Marcuse offers a rather old-fash-ioned theory of progress in the left-Hegelian tradition. There is a move-ment from natural necessity, to historical necessity based upon political, social, economic, and cultural forms of domination, to liberation from these structures of domination and the achievement of a new kind of freedom issuing mainly from the conditions of abundance yielded by the last phase of domination. The Marxian inspiration is apparent. Marcuse set himself the task of enriching Marx and assimilating Freudian concepts to the idea of alienated labor. In doing so, he rejected the pessimistic and stoic strains in Freud and pressed Freud's Eros into service as the agency of liberation. The Freudian theory of the primal horde and the origin of the superego became for Marcuse a useful myth about the "dialectic of domination" rather than a grim, and insurmountable, phylogenetic curse. To be sure, Marcuse was forced to confront the internal (according to Freud, inherited) Oedipal sources of Thermidorian reactions to rebellion, liberation, and sensual gratification. The failure of modern revolutions suggested inner or psychic compulsion to reinstitute repression, by way of identification with the overthrown father-institutions and father-symbols. Marcuse's preliminary task as a psychohistorian was to define the conditions under which a revolution might succeed at *all* levels. Here, he had nothing to fall back upon but a combination of left-Hegelian dialectical teleology and optimism about the transformation of modern technology into a condition of gratification rather than alienated labor.

Marcuse could only assume that the historically most developed forms of domination would create the conditions for their own dialectical transformation, a typical left-Hegelian approach to historical progress.

> The theory of alienation demonstrated the fact that man does not realize himself in his labor, that his life has become an instrument of labor, that his work and its products have assumed a form and power independent of him as an individual. But the liberation from this state seems to require, not the arrest of alienation, but its consummation, not the reactivation of the repressed and productive personality but its abolition. The elimination of human potentialities from the world of (alienated) labor creates the preconditions for the elimination of labor from the world of human potentialities.[7]

In other words, Marcuse saw the end of the performance principle in sight and the possibility of a nonrepressive civilization. But Freud presented a formidable set of problems, for he had not only taken the position that libido had to be repressed in order for human beings to survive in civilization, he had posited the existence of a death instinct.

Marcuse accurately charted Freud's theory of the evolution of the relationship of the life and death instincts, and appropriately assumed that the relationship between the instincts, the extent of their fusion *(Mi-*

schung) or defusion *(Entmischung)* depended upon exogenous (environmental or historical) forces. Here indeed Freud had taken an historical approach. *Civilization and Its Discontents* had posed the problem of the defusion of the death instinct in historical terms and related it to the increasing power of the superego in civilization. But there seemed to be no easy way out of Freud's circular problem: The superego was an inherited structural feature of the human psyche; it could be modified but not eradicated. Freud placed his hopes—as have all psychoanalysts in his tradition—upon the ego's ability to cope with the superego's unreasonable and sometimes destructive demands. Marcuse, not satisfied with Freud's meliorism (in the service of a bourgeois social order), disposed of the problem of the death instinct and superego by revising Freud's theory of the normal relationship of the ego to the id. Ultimately, Marcuse inverted the relationship by developing the truly radical theory of a revolution in intrapsychic relations corresponding to the revolution in the relations of production in the social world and to the new institutional arrangements in the nonrepressive world of the future. The ego would no longer serve a repressive reality principle (performance principle) and would be free to ally itself with Eros. Consequently, the ego would be eroticized and the superego would disappear. In essence, Marcuse argues that Eros would manifest itself in forms other than those observed in conditions of the prevailing historical reality principle—and would become strong enough to rule intrapsychic relations.

Marcuse performed on Freud a surgical procedure similar to the one Marx had performed on Feuerbach. He separated the "revolutionary" elements, those that might be used as part of a critique of contemporary civilization, from the ahistorical and "idealistic" trends in his thought. But like Marx, Marcuse had absorbed into his own thinking a teleological dialectical principle, which could not be combined with a nonteleological, nondialectical naturalism. Indeed, like Marx, he had separated the elements of Hegel's philosophy which might serve revolutionary activism from those which served passive acceptance of the status quo. In Freud, Marcuse found only one potentially revolutionary element—the concept of repressed Eros. The liberation of Eros would signal the end of repressive civilization, of the traditional Western ego in the service of Freud's god, *Logos,* and the beginning of a new eroticism in all areas of life, including work.

Marcuse's historicity, like Marx's, serves his utopian conclusions, but unlike Marx he no longer places so much faith in productivity. Marcuse rather emphasizes the power of the human *imagination* to reinstate the original unity, harmony, and wholeness of the psyche. "Imagination envisions the reconciliation of the individual with the whole, of desire with realization, of happiness with reason."[8] The reconciliation of the pleasure and reality principles is Marcuse's utopia, and it implies the disappearance of the Freudian ego and the conflict between the individual and society which Freud had assumed was inevitable. Marcuse rejects both Marx's Prometheanism and Freud's Stoicism for the subversive myths of Orpheus and Narcissus.

> The images of Orpheus and Narcissus reconcile Eros and Thanatos. They recall the experience of a world that is not to be mastered and controlled but to be liberated—a freedom that will release the powers of Eros now bound in the repressed and petrified forms of man and nature. These powers are conceived not as destruction but as peace, not as terror but as beauty. It is sufficient to enumerate the assembled images in order to circumscribe the dimension to which they are committed: the redemption of pleasure, the halt of time, the absorption of death; silence, sleep, night, paradise—the Nirvana principle not as death but as life.[9]

Here Marcuse reveals the systemic aim of his dialectics—a state of homeostatic unity, which can only be achieved when all opposites are reconciled, when all relationships can be integrated into a harmonious whole. Unlike Erikson, who achieves his optimal state through the agency of the strong adaptive ego and the original experience of mutuality, Marcuse chooses narcissism as the *fons et origo* of his utopia.

More clearly than most radicals in the Hegelian tradition, Marcuse reveals the aims of the dialectical architectonic: the *restoration* of unity and wholeness, the end of time and history as we now experience them, and an end to conflict and anxious striving. The quest for origins does not uncover original sin, as with Freud, but original bliss, as with Erikson. Like Erikson—but in a more systematically dialectical mode—Marcuse uses the past as an agency of liberation in the construction of his future order. However, Marcuse's dialectic does not make use of exceptional individuals. It issues from the Marxian sociological tradition. Yet it goes beyond Marx, for Marcuse, like other members of the Frankfurt school, was appalled by the immense power of the economic, social, political, and cultural totalisms of modern technological civilization, and the seeming constriction of individual ego-space. Anxiety about a loss of individualism in a totalitarian environment—here too there are similarities with Erikson— is joined to the fundamental Marxian concern with alienated labor. In Marcuse's utopia the individual is regrown and reintegrated into society at a dialectically higher level of freedom. But given the totalism of the social environment, Marcuse had to show an almost desperate inventiveness in order to find in the Freudian theory of narcissism the narrow bit of ground from which to launch a radical critique. He spent much of his later career trying to identify the concrete historical vehicles of liberation and the second edition of *Eros and Civilization* (1966) contains a "Political Preface" to that end. However, only Marcuse's theoretical conclusion and his psychohistorical optimism will be discussed in summary here, in order to show the characteristics of the dialectical architectonic in psychohistory.

Marcuse's optimism rested finally upon his *récherche du temps perdu* within the context of Freud's theory of the instincts and left-Hegelianism. Once freed of the pressure of surplus repression, libido would assume benign forms. The eroticizing of the body would not express itself as an explosive release of polymorphous perverse activities, in forms which are hideous or regressive in a strict sense, but in diffuse forms and expressions issuing from nonrepressive self-sublimation in cultural activity. Under the correct conditions, narcissistic libido would be reactivated and then overflow onto others in love, cultural activity, and work. Under the governance of Eros a new sensuous rationality would emerge, a rationality of gratification. The historical dialectic in Marcuse's vision is Marxian, in that the development of a technology of production and alienated labor provide the basis for a new phase in human development, but the genetic key to his utopia is the psychoanalytic recovery of an original erotic wholeness. The original erotic wholeness is finally described by Marcuse as a relationship between infant and mother—a Narcissistic-maternal unity—the reestablishment of which had always been too threatening psychosexually to the weak human ego. But the "return" of the Narcissistic-maternal orientation is made possible "under the power of the mature ego and in a mature civilization."[10] Marcuse thus reaches into the past beyond Freud's patriarchal reality principle to a maternal one, whose time to reassert itself in human history has arrived.

One should pause here to note the similarity with Erikson, whose primordial mutuality is that of mother and child. The mother-child relationship for Marcuse too proves to be crucial for any advances in human morality. But rather than the source of the numinous, it is the basis for a new reality principle. Its recovery through memory (aided by psychoanalytic consciousness) is therefore liberating and future-oriented rather than primitively regressive. The end of the era of the father is possible in a civilization in which the agencies of socialization and acculturation reduce the role of families and fathers to a minimum. Oddly enough, life without father can be more problematic than life with him under certain conditions in modern culture. The price paid for the reduction of the role of the father is, according to Marcuse in his pessimistic voice, the subjection of the individual psyche to the process described in Freud's *Group Psychology and the Analysis of the Ego*. However, Marcuse ignores the evolutionary theoretical foundation of *Group Psychology*, in which attraction to the leader is a function of the human psyche's phylogenetic memory of the primal father. For Marcuse, mass psychology is exemplified by Nazi Germany and by forms of mass culture and "repressive desublimation" described in his other popular work of psychohistory, *One-Dimensional Man* (1964). *Eros and Civilization* presents the utopian alternative to the democratic authoritarian trends of modern times by showing that life without father might be superceded, under the right conditions, not by the totalitarian state or the subtler controls of bourgeois culture, but by a new era under a maternal reality principle.

The eroticization of life therefore depends upon the remembrance of things past translated into historical action. The historical liberation from surplus repression would affect the goal of the death instinct:

> The instinctual value of death would have changed: if the instincts pursued and attained their fulfillment in a nonrepressive order, the regressive compulsion would lose much of its biological rationale. As suffering and want recede, the Nirvana principle may become reconciled with the reality principle. The unconscious attraction that draws the instincts back to an "earlier state" would be effectively

counteracted by the desirability of the attained state of life. The "conservative nature" of the instincts would come to rest in a fulfilled present. Death would cease to be an instinctual goal. It remains a fact, perhaps even an ultimate necessity—but a necessity against which the unrepressed energy of mankind will protest, against which it will wage its greatest struggle. . . . Men can die without anxiety if they know that what they love is protected from misery and oblivion.[11]

Thus, the strengthening of Eros changes the aim of Thanatos, without hiding from human beings the inevitability of death. But in a civilization of sensuous reason, in which human beings choose their sublimations freely and with a new kind of rationality, a civilization in which they are *for themselves* instinctually in a Hegelian sense, they can struggle with death rationally and perhaps remove its sting.

Readers who wish to examine the gloomier side of Marcuse will find much material, but aside from a gloomy and not altogether clear ending, in which Marcuse suggests that the "accumulated guilt of mankind against its victims" weighs heavily in the balance against the return of original bliss, *Eros and Civilization* remains within a hopeful dialectical tradition.

In his utopia, Marcuse visualizes a time when the traditional antitheses of reason and feeling, spontaneity and consciousness, work and play, and the Freudian instincts, Eros and Thanatos, are dialectically united (or in the last case, joined in a different relationship) under a nonrepressive (maternal) reality principle. The second part of *Eros and Civilization* is very appropriately entitled "Beyond the Reality Principle," for Marcuse reverses the pessimism of Freud's *Beyond the Pleasure Principle,* a truly gloomy work. Marcuse's method is in keeping with ancient trends in Western thought—trends revivified by Hegel and Marx. He prophesies both a return to origins and a reversal: The earliest stage in an historical sequence will reappear in the end in altered form as the most advanced stage; the masters (the rich and powerful and the technologies they control) will be overthrown by the slaves (the proletariat performing alienated labor). The return of the repressed and the revolt of the oppressed are Marcuse's vehicles for establishing utopia. One can understand the great appeal of *Eros and Civilization* to an intelligentsia generation seeking a way out of the dangers of history through an integral radical vision uniting two great, although apparently antagonistic currents in Western thought; and one can appreciate Marcuse's creation of a set of terms to denote the historicity of the intrapsychic balance of power. The prognostications of Marcuse and others about the disappearance of the traditional Oedipus complex and the superego still have great appeal for those who work within the theoretical framework created by Freud.

An even more provocative thinker than Marcuse, Norman O. Brown employed the dialectical architectonic in the service of psychohistorical radicalism as well. Although Brown and Marcuse intersect at many points, Brown's dialectic is less dependent upon exogenous factors, such as historical development of the technology of production. The centrality of the idea of repression in Brown and his vision of history as the return of the repressed—a "forward-looking *récherche du temps perdu*"—are perhaps the major psychohistorical features which he shares with Marcuse. However, even more faithful to Hegel in this respect than Marcuse is, Brown sees history as the phenomenology of mind itself, with the mind's self-repressed aspects returning (like the self-alienated Spirit) to restore a primordial wholeness at a new level. Brown's theory of the historical unfolding of human self-repression also has strong (and conscious) resemblances with Hegel's phenomenology of mind. Human beings create history and new structures which, like exoskeletons, must be cracked and shuffled off, but these structures have a different meaning from Marcuse's structures of domination. They are explained by Brown's theory of sublimation and the workings of the death instinct and do not represent simply a series of new versions of a repressive reality principle. However, like Marcuse, Brown remains in the dialectical mode in this sense: At the moment of highest development of sublimation (in Marcuse, alienated labor), the process of the return of the repressed offers a way out. Brown radically devalues the role of fathers as agents of repression and sublimation. In doing so, he offers a far more original theory than Marcuse, who simply made fathers the familial representative (until recent history) of repressive reality principles. Finally, whereas Marcuse had identified the repression of Eros as the source of the problem, Brown, explicitly following the later Hegel, made death the starting point of his dialectic. History moves not by the repression of Eros but of Thanatos. This is the central thesis of Brown's brilliant contribution to the theory of psychohistory, *Life Against Death* (1959).

Brown's decision to make a naturalistic outlook the foundation for his psychohistorical theory immediately separates him from Marcuse. As noted above, history for Marcuse represented a stage of development beyond natural necessity. Marcuse has no explanation for historical change other than Marxian historical sociology based upon a theory of the development of forces and relations of production. Brown, on the other hand, does not believe that economic forces drive human beings through history, or that each stage of economic and social change represents, above all, another step in the conquest of scarcity. History and historical economic and social forms are driven by unconscious desires rather than by economic necessity and rational (taken in a dialectical sense) responses to it. Scarcity is not a central problem for Brown. Whereas thinkers in the Marxian tradition assume that each new economic and social configuration (in Marcuse, each new reality principle) has its own "laws," they always assume that the vast majority of human beings in all such configurations have been exploited and subjected to scarcity. Thus, to the casual student of history in the Marxian mode, the classes that controlled the means of production in history tended to be the beneficiaries of economic and social systems with vast numbers of victims. Despite the fact that Marxists do not moralize as theoreticians of history, it is difficult not to judge exploiters as wicked and exploited as noble victims. Brown, a thoroughly democratic thinker in his aims, tends to see all economic and social arrangements of domination as symptoms of the human species' neurosis and makes it difficult to distinguish among the victims. Brown rather visualizes the entire human species as a victim of its own weakness, its own species flaw. The species flaw is a *natural* flaw and history has no structure other than the one given to it by a naturally flawed human psychology. In short, we have a history because of our nature, and since Brown's interpretation of psychoanalysis holds that we are by nature neurotic, it follows that our history too has a neurotic character.

Brown undertook the solution of a problem that Freud had posed but never solved: that of describing a *normal* culture. It is not difficult to see that a normal culture would have to be inferred from theoretical postulates, since Freud gave his followers no reason to believe that a nonneurotic culture had ever existed. The evolution of the species and its prehistoric experiences had given the species unique psychosexual weaknesses, the bases for psychic conflict and neuroses, and these had become so dangerous that human survival might be doubted. Brown astutely avoided Freud's psycho-Lamarckianism and launched his speculative theory from assumptions about the peculiarities of the human species compared to other animal species. His point of departure is the assumption (which might give a logician pause) that other animal species are normal precisely because they do not have histories. Only man, the neurotic animal, has a history and he has a history because he represses himself. Repression creates the "dialectic of neurosis,"[12] which in turn is the dialectic of history. Historical cultures are all symptom-formations.

Freud's own mixture of pride in human cultural achievement and dismay about the weakness and murderous qualities of the species are not repeated in Brown. Sublimation, so highly prized by Freud, is central to the problem of human neurosis for Brown. Brown's theory of sublimation is a major departure from Freudian orthodoxy and will be discussed below. Suffice it to say here, Brown correctly identifies a rationalistic current in Freud and a commitment to cultural progress and rejects them, just as he rejects them in Marx. For Brown, history is part of the solution to the human dilemma only insofar as it provides the key to its own abolition. In Brown's eschatology—and he is quite explicit in his commitment to an eschatology—salvation comes not through Freud's rationality and realism, but through the subversive discovery of the unmutilated pleasure-seeking of infancy. Like Marcuse, Brown seeks in human infancy the wholeness which existed before repression and sublimation— paradise before the expulsion.

There are some obvious but misleading similarities between Brown and Marcuse. The principle of restoration or recovery of the wholeness of infancy, when narcissistic libido could not distinguish self from other and overflowed from infant to mother uniting the two in erotic bliss, provides the image of instinctual paradise. This is the paradise lost of their psychohistorical dialectics. In Marcuse, progress at first occurs only at the *material* level of domination of nature and society, but the individual ego suffers until the dialectic of history leads to human erotic liberation. Brown similarly sees a process of increasing mastery of nature, but most human forms of cultural mastery and striving reflect a progressive loss of the human body's erotic wholeness. Rather than a social and political revolution based upon material progress, it is psychoanalytic *consciousness* which emerges from the dialectic of neurosis in history and which, by discovering the origins of neurosis, also discovers a way out of the dialectic. Unlike Marcuse, whose dialectic is ultimately rational and who quests for an orderly sensuality and a new rationality of gratification through self-sublimation of Eros, Brown is antirationalistic and seeks an end to sublimation. Thus, the superficial similarities between them should not obscure Brown's radical anti-materialism and his allegiance to a mystical utopian tradition.

Brown's first task was to transform Freud's dualistic theory of the instincts into a theory of the undifferentiated dialectical unity of the instincts. He explains the vicissitudes of the instincts by a radically one-sided and endogenous interpretation of the development of the human infantile ego. More than any of the thinkers mentioned, Brown emphasizes the weakness and dependency of the human infant. Neoteny, or fetalization, distinguishes the human animal. During its period of prolonged dependency the human child's pre-Oedipal relationship to its mother engenders first a polymorphously erotic pure pleasure-ego, which recognizes no distinction between self and other, between ego-and object-libido. The libidinal aim of union is achieved in the act of feeding at the breast; the human infant's exuberant narcissism abolishes the distinction between itself and the outside world. How then do the instinctual wholeness of infantile sexuality and the infant's union with the world disintegrate? What is the source of human ambivalence? Freud had postulated both a reality principle and a death instinct, the former the source of repression and the latter a destructive or disintegrative drive. Whereas Freud had assumed that the death instinct worked in all living things in the same way, Brown assumed that only in the human species did Eros and Thanatos exist in a state of conflict. In orthodox Freudianism, the chaotic id makes demands that split the ego and tax its powers of synthesis. In Brown's radical revision, the id becomes a *systemic* agency of natural harmony and unity, and the ego becomes the agent of disintegration. The problem for Brown becomes one of explaining the origins of psychological conflict and instinctual duality in the human child and the progressive loss of the erotic paradise of infancy.

The problem is exceedingly complex, for Brown's explanation of the defusion of the life and death instincts (if we accept the hypothesis of an original undifferentiated unity of the instincts in infants) must emerge from his naturalistic position, and self-consistent naturalism does not readily support a hopeful world view of the sort which Brown consciously seeks to derive from psychoanalysis. But Brown brilliantly achieves his aim by making all of history a series of projections of unconscious fantasies which, when properly understood by psychoanalysis, provide a way out of history. For most psychohistorians, exogenous factors—things external to the mind and impinging upon the mind—are in some sense autonomous. They are not creations of the mind. For example, the historical structures of domination in Marcuse's theory of history, like the cultural configurations or patterns in Erikson's, affect the intrapsychic balance of power within a larger historical dialectic or metabolism of generations. Such structures and patterns can be thought of as material conditions or symbolic environments, but they are unavoidably there and comprise the "outer" to the psychic "inner." The interaction between inner and outer has taxed many of the most profound thinkers of every era, but Brown's idea that the outer is a projection of unconscious fantasies gives his theory an unusually endogenous character. For Brown, history is a symptom of the defusion of the life and death instincts, a product of the innate weakness of the human ego. In order to find a way out of history one first has to display the weakness and its symptoms and then "restore to man his animal nature."[13] To be human, to have a history, is to be *unnatural* and diseased. Thus, Brown's hopeful dialectic entails a recovery of nature through a recovery of the early and brief period in human ontogeny when a natural unity of the instincts existed. The problem is evidently more one of terminology than anything else, for if it is natural for human beings (who, after all, did not choose to be fetalized) to experience psychic conflict, then it seems pointless to try to reserve for the adjective "natural" only benign connotations. What Brown means by "natural" is clear enough—it is the unconflicted, homeostatic, and ahistorical condition of animals in a state of nature. Dualism signifies conflict, neurosis, restless striving, and history.

It would appear that the foremost thinkers in the dialectical tradition in psychohistory, if not in general, use dialectics in the service of a *systemic* aim and that history, the medium of dialectics, has value only insofar as it can be transcended. To call Brown's eschatology "systemic" may seem odd, but his alliance with mystical religious traditions should not obscure his commitment to monistic naturalism. He is well aware of the theological tradition to which his theory of psychohistory can be comfortably joined, but like Freud, Erikson, and Marcuse, he remains committed to saving psyches whose basis is the human soma. Salvation in Brown too means strengthening the human capacity to live and enjoy the present moment fully. Thus, to transcend history means to find an eternal equilibrium, to live forever in the present, to become a prelapsarian child again.

Brown's interpretation of Freud's theory of the instincts is a first step toward his goal of overcoming Freud's dualism and the metaphysical pessimism associated with it. By making the Nirvana principle the natural principle working behind both life and death instincts, Brown reaffirms Fechner's conservative principle of stability. Using reasoning similar to Marcuse's with respect to repression, Brown hypothesizes that the pleasure principle's restless and dynamic manifestations are *historical* rather than *natural* expressions of libido. That is, Marcuse assumed we had never observed Eros in a situation other than an historical one of surplus repression and imagined how Eros would manifest itself after liberation. Brown went so far as to assume that the pre-Oedipal child lived according to unrepressed Eros and therefore according to the Nirvana principle. The unrepressed human child, which lives outside of historical time in an eternity of self-gratification and play, is clearly the model for the God of the mystics. Finally, then, the task Brown set himself was that of describing the loss of the child's polymorphously erotic body and psychic wholeness, but to do it in naturalistic terms and presumably in keeping with Freud's theory of the instincts. He did so by shifting the catastrophe of repression from the Oedipal to the pre-Oedipal phase of human development.

Like Marcuse, Brown avoided the implications of Freud's most pessimistic conjectures about human phylogeny and organic repression. However, Brown did make self-repression central to his theory of ontogeny. His is an extraordinarily inventive reading of the early stages of human development. The crux of his position lies in his interpretation of the human infant's response to separation anxiety. The experience of separation from the mother is equivalent to the experience of dying to the child. In its anxious flight from death, the weak human ego begins to use the death instinct to construct fantastic projects in relation to the love object with which it had experienced joyous narcissistic union in the early oral phase. Emphasis should be placed on the word "fantastic." The weak and dependent human infant's early projects are doomed, but both the projects and their failure issue from the natural state of affairs in the human family. Brown assumed that the powerful instinctual ambivalence which then emerges in the human child—a simultaneous intensification and defusion of the life and death instincts—continues throughout its life. The most momentous consequences of the flight from death are, however, the ego's constriction of the body's eroticism in the oral, anal, and phallic phases, each of which is an aspect of the ego's fantastic projects. Instead of seeking "loving union with the world" the child first employs the death instinct to deny the painful aspects of the world and in denial creates the prototype of all repression. This serves the child's fantasy of becoming independent of want. But each stage of development brings its own frustrations and new projects. The fantastic project of the anal phase involves a transformation of the death instinct, which initially was converted into the mental process of denial (or negation) into active aggression. Thus the death instinct is pressed into the service of the weak human ego first as an introverted principle of denial or negation and then—with fateful consequences—as an extroverted principle of aggression.

One might pause for a moment to examine Brown's interpretration of the instincts. Quite clearly, he sees life as affirmation and death as negation when they are translated into psychic attitudes. Defusion of the instincts is a consequence of the ego's anxiety. Anxiety, the ego's response to separation, in effect triggers negation, fantasy, and the dynamic development of the death instinct, which it shapes into unnatural forms. But in view of the relationship of the death instinct to libido, the libidinal organizations too undergo a dynamic development. For each negation there is an affirmation, but the dialectic is one of flight from reality. It yields a transformation and desexualization of the originally polymorphously erotic body given by nature. The weak human ego therefore is the problem, not the blind and chaotic instincts described by Freud. The ego *converts* the death instinct into a principle of denial or negation and then constructs the hypercathexes of the erogenous zones which we know as the "natural" oral, anal, and phallic phases of psychosexual development. Brown has proposed that the ego's flight from death is the supreme force in human ontogeny and history. According to his dialectical interpretation, the ego's flight from death creates the neurotic, active manifestations of the death instinct and simultaneously, the neurotic libidinal activity which we mistakenly attribute to natural drives. The only reasonable conclusion is that the anxiety of the ego is a most powerful psychological force, if it can so fundamentally alter the disposition of the instincts and, finally, deny the very body to which it is attached. It would also follow that Eros and Thanatos are *weak* relative to the ego's anxiety, since they are forced by the ego to follow unique paths unintended by nature, and that the ego itself is in some sense *strong,* in order for it to sustain its fantastic and frequently self-destructive projects through millennia.

By means of dialectical formulae Brown creates the impression that he has abandoned id psychology, for his emphasis upon the ego's reorganization through anxiety and fantasty of what was given by nature makes the ego an impressive force in his system and gives it much more power than Freud gave it. Brown does so provisionally only in order to make his case that the id instincts are not what they appear to be in orthodox Freudianism. He gives the instincts their traditional power to fight back and his entire eschatology depends upon the return of the repressed. Nonetheless, he has profoundly altered Freudian theory. For Freud and most of his followers, including ego psychologists, the weak ego is assailed by impulses so powerful that they paralyze or modify it. For Brown, the ego's anxiety and flight from death enables it to split apart the natural undifferentiated unity of the instincts. For Freud, one of the ego's central functions is to face reality, whereas for Brown the ego's de facto function is to construct fantasies. The common ground shared between Freud and Brown is the idea that the ego represses the instincts. Brown's manipulation of Freud's theory of the instincts only points up the weaknessess and undeveloped aspects of Freud's picture of the ego.

Brown's interpretation of the phenomenon of self-repression extends through the Oedipal phase of development, when the castration complex forces the abandonment of the last distorted project of narcissism in infant and child—the fantasy that it can be its own father. Brown's version of the Oedipal phase will not be presented in detail, but it is a crucial break in development. The project of becoming one's father brings with it a final catastrophe: the creation of a false individuality based upon a denial of separation and death, the internalization of the parents as superego, and the resolution of the infant's psychological bisexuality into psychosexual maleness and femaleness. Here we encounter the theme of androgyny and an important aspect of Brown's association of psychoanalysis with mysticism, both Western and Eastern. It is also one of the extraordinarily influential ideas in Brown's theory of psychohistory. There can be no doubting its influence on the counterculture of the 1960s.

The child which emerges from the failures of its distorted and fantastic narcissistic projects to become both Self and Other is split into erogenous zones of its own construction, into a false individual, part parent (superego) and part child (ego), and into maleness and femaleness, depending upon which psychological gender has been repressed. The huge remainder of the child's primal wholeness exists in a repressed state. But the history of human culture is, in essence, the history of sublimations of *adults*, whose continuing flight from death instigates new projects—projects as fantastic as those of infancy and childhood—which succeed the Oedipal fantasy of becoming one's own father. The Oedipal project is transformed into the religious quest for immortality.

Brown's ontogenetic theory of self-repression explains the disintegration of an original, natural, dialectical unity of the instincts, and of union and separateness in the human family. But his theory of human ontogeny is merely a prologue to his theory of culture. The key to Brown's psychohistorical theory of culture is the concept of sublimation. Freud's own ambiguous position on sublimation has troubled Freud scholars for decades and Brown noted the difficulties and biases in Freud's position. Freud's well-known personal preference for sublimation as a way of life is not shared by Brown, who neither believes in nonrepressive sublimation nor accepts sublimation issuing from repression as a satisfactory way of life. Brown decisively repudiates Freud's Enlightenment preference for the intellect and his reliance upon the ability of reason (a function of the ego) to rise above and control the wild instincts. Brown's theory of culture is closely allied with his own therapeutic project. He rejects sublimation as self-therapy and Freud's talking cure (rather, treatment) as a method for dealing with either individual or cultural neurosis, in view of the fact that neither of them could yield a satisfactory way out of the human dilemma. We either suffer from guilt and self-sacrifice or make others suffer because we direct our aggression outward; or else we adapt ourselves by way of traditional psychotherapy to a world of repression—hardly a way out. Therapy must therefore assume a new *social* form as a method for changing repressive culture. The task becomes that of creating a psychoanalytic theory of culture which might serve to bring about a nonrepressive culture.

Brown eloquently professes the dialectical eschatology: One further intellectual effort, one last bite of the apple of the tree of knowledge is needed in order to throw off the sublimated and neurotic existence which prepared us for the effort. The more advanced we are in sublimation, the closer we are to the final return of the repressed. Brown's dynamic, dialectical theory of adult sublimations and their relationship to the early phases of ontogeny issues from one of Freud's psychohistorical postulates: that some historical phenomena can be understood—as in *Moses and Monotheism*—by way of analogy with neurosis. Brown makes the increasing return of the repressed both the basis for his diagnosis of communal ills and his eschatology. Once we can understand the development of culture by way of psychoanalysis, we are on our way to mastering it. In other words, once we have a psychoanalytic theory of history, we can abolish history.

However, Brown's revision of Freud alters both the phylogenetic grounds for repression and the nature of repression. The radically different theory of repression and sublimation in Brown yields, in the end, a rejection of the reality principle as Freud knew it—and a rejection of Freud's preferred treatments of neurosis. Like Marcuse, Brown sees Freud's affirmation of the ego and of sublimation as the expression of an historical trend in Western civilization. Brown's critique of the traditional Western repressive ego (*Logos*) and his notion—also similar to Marcuse's—that a new kind of nonrepressive ego is possible, can easily be read as a critique of Freud. Brown's choice of Dionysus as his subversive culture hero reflects his rejection of the Apollonian ego and traditional Freudian therapy in favor of Dionysian cultural therapy.

The Apollonian ego constructs culture by means of fantasy and sublimation. Brown's idea that sublimations are based upon fantasy rather than the repression of real instincts follows from his theory of ontogeny. The ego organizes the body sexually by constricting sexual space into the erogenous zones. The constricted sexual space has the fantastic character imparted to it by the negation of the remainder of the body, denial of separation and loss, and the grandiose and unrealizable projects of distorted narcissism. Sublimations in turn launch themselves from this fantasy world and are therefore two removes from the reality of the human body and its instinctual endowment:

> Sublimation is the continuation not of infantile sexuality but of infantile dreaming; it comes to the same thing to say that what is sublimated is infantile sexuality not as polymorphously perverse but as organized by fantasies into the sexual organizations. . . . Sublimations are formed out of infantile sexuality by the mechanism of fetishism; sublimations are denials or negations of the fantasies of infantile sexuality, and affirm them in the mode of affirmation by negation. The original fantasies are negations; sublimations are negations of negations. The original activity of the infantile sexual organizations was symbolic; sublimations are symbols of symbols. Thus sublimation is a second and higher level of desexualization; the life in culture is the shadow of a dream.[14]

The world of culture created by the ego—and indeed all of human history—is an insubstantial world. Yet by its very externality it serves the crucial function of revealing what has been negated and denied. The psychological mechanism of projection of intrapsychic (or endopsychic) processes makes culture a viewing screen or map of what has been repressed for those with the special hermeneutic skills associated with psychoanalysis. Freudian psychoanalysis itself can then be understood as an historical product, the penultimate step in the return of the repressed, and Brown's psychohistorical revision of Freud—a revised psychoanalysis plus dialectics—the ultimate critique of culture.

Dialectics and Unification

It would appear then that psychoanalysis and dialectics provide a map of the inner and outer world, the psychological and cultural world created by autoplastic and alloplastic methods—by repression, fantasy, sublimation, and projection. Psychoanalytic consciousness and dialectics can provide not only a psychohistory, but a way out of history. As a systemic dialectician, Brown seeks restoration of a lost unity and history, as we know it, becomes a long but necessary journey into the empyrean, into a world of symbols and abstractions which, when properly interpreted, open the way to reconciliation with our lost, desexualized bodies. More important, psychohistory's critique of the Apollonian culture and the Apollonian ego is, in dialectical terms, the ultimate negation of negation—the last abstract system, whose aim is self-abolition in favor of affirmation and the Dionysian ego. This is where Brown's eschatology leads. Yet we are left with a project: the *construction* of a life-affirming Dionysian ego to replace the Apollonian ego and the *resurrection* of the body. But the project evidently must begin as a critique of culture and then proceed as cultural revolution guided by psychohistorical consciousness which embraces dialectical thinking. Brown noticed in passing[15] that the purpose of dialectics—the overcoming of division and conflict—had been identified with the ego's synthetic function by Freud and his followers. We are left with the impression that Brown, no less than Erikson, believes that the human mind has the power to heal itself, to make itself whole again. It follows that dialectical consciousness issues from the mind's self-restorative activity, but in Brown's case, the ego's self-healing is aided by the id, serves Eros, and (it would appear) leads to the restoration of the polymorphously erotic body and psychological androgyny. Ultimately, the strengthened ego transforms itself into a Dionysian ego—a body ego—completing the process of the return of the repressed.

In *Love's Body* (1966), his next major work after the publication of *Life Against Death*, Brown introduces a variety of political themes and identifies the cultural trends which might serve his dialectical purposes. Like Erikson and Marcuse, he sees in religion an ally, and like Marcuse searches for a way to abolish all structures of domination—intrapsychic or cultural. The composition of *Love's Body* itself reflects Brown's repudiation of formal systems and his belief that symbolic consciousness and poetry are the appropriate vehicles of liberation. At the political and social level, Brown calls for the abolition of all false boundaries.

> Dionysus, the mad god, breaks down the boundaries; releases the prisoners; abolishes repression; and abolishes the *principium individuationis,* substituting for it the unity of man and the unity of man with nature. In this age of schizophrenia, with the atom, the individual self, the boundaries disintegrating, there is, for those who would save our souls, the ego-psychologists, "the problem of Identity." But the breakdown is to be made into a breakthrough; as

Conrad said, in the destructive element immerse. The soul that we can call our own is not a real one. The solution to the problem of identity is, get lost. Or as it says in the New Testament: "He that findeth his own psyche shall lose it, and he that loseth his psyche for my sake shall find it.".[16]

The repudiation of Eriksonian identity is quite explicit here, and it is connected with a more radical psychohistorical vision than Erikson's. But despite this radical program of inner and outer unification, Brown's main concern seems to be to find the correct vehicle for his message. *Love's Body* is mainly about symbols and language and their relationship to the resurrection of the body. Brown casts himself in the role of poet and prophet of an apocalypse. His is a total apocalypse and as its prophet, he signals an end to our reality principle. As in schizophrenia, "all things lose their definite boundaries, become iridescent with many-colored significances."[17] The abolition of the human ego as we know it and its transformation into a Dionysian ego would not only mean an end to our present form of consciousness, to history and all of its neurotic patterns, but even to language as it is now constructed. Thus, having taken the last bite of the apple, constructed the last theory of history, and interpreted the symbolic map which yields a way out, Brown has said everything worth saying. What is left is the symbolism and poetry of silence—but not quite. Brown's last book, *Closing Time* (1973) continues the themes of *Love's Body*: language, symbols, poetry, and unity.

Brown makes transparent what most dialecticians try to hide: that the human imagination contends with insoluble problems and often solves them by means of word magic. The final result is a subversion of Freudian scientism, elitism, and pessimism in favor of animism, mystical unity, and eschatology. The resurrected body proves to be a body which recognizes no distinction between inner and outer. It is a mystical body.

Fusion, mystical participation. Primitive animism is suffused with unconscious identification of subject and object: *participation mystique*. Civilized objectivity is non-participating consciousness, consciousness as separation, as dualism, distance, definition; as property and prison: consciousness ruled by negation, which is from the death instinct. Symbolical consciousness, the erotic sense of reality, is a return to the principle of ancient animistic science, mystical participation, but now for the first time freely; instead of religion, poetry. . . . Apocalypse is the dissolution of the group as numerical series, as in representative democracy, and its replacement by the group as fusion, as communion.[18]

As an animist, Brown affirms the omnipotence of thought and narcissism of the mind's poetic faculty discussed in the second chapter. More precisely, he glorifies our poetic capacity for creating symbols of unity and community. Realists in the Freudian tradition would find here only confusion and regression. Brown's subversion has all of the marks of the revolt of a poet and religious prophet against analytic science—an outcome made all the easier by Freud's own complex heritage. To call it simply revolt is to suggest a narrower and perhaps meaner purpose than Brown professes. By admitting openly that he is engaged in subversive poetry and affirming poetry and prophesy as a way of life, Brown has made a brilliant effort to change the character of Freud's connection to the Romantic tradition and to join psychoanalysis to mystical religious traditions. But there is a final irony. Despite his communitarian and presumably democratic aims, Brown's complexity, erudition, and eccentricity make him accessible only to an elite audience, and one suspects that his long-term appeal will be to the intelligentsia (young, middle-aged, or old) who have discovered that analytic reason not only has limits, but is limiting. For them, a reading of Brown may be the last bite of the apple, but like those who have discovered the path to mysticism in the past, they will very likely find themselves to be an isolated spiritual elite.

The above discussion of Marcuse and Brown reveals that Freud's rich heritage can be joined to traditions which Freud himself had approached in different ways for different purposes. With the aid of dialectics, they surmount Freud's system and claim that it is part of the problem, as well as part of the solution to human misery. The separation of the human species from nature, the dissolution of the natural unity of the instincts, the structure of the human psyche, the clash between individual and society, the division of the human species, and the structure of history were all related to the central issue of repression. As systemic-dialecticians, Brown and Marcuse tend to see all division as temporary and all superordinate-subordinate relationships as problematic; and they see the solution to the problem of human misery and self-destruction emerging from within the system itself. There can be no accidental forces—no deus ex machina. The dialectical architectonic defines historical conflict in such a way that it is transcended in an ultimate unity or wholeness, in which inner and outer are in perfect harmony, or in which the distinction between the two becomes meaningless. The task of the dialectical imagination is to find appropriate terms and vehicles of liberation and unification, and Marcuse and Brown are exemplars of dialectical skill. Like Erikson, they placed themselves in the service of healing communal ills.

• CHAPTER VI •

Lifton

R OBERT J. LIFTON'S WORK, like the catastrophic principle within it, can be thought of as a discontinuous or qualitative change in the development of the theory and practice of psychohistory. As a theoretician, he identifies himself as the proponent of a new paradigm in psychology—the "formative" paradigm. Although formative theory is quite a departure from orthodox psychoanalysis and varieties of neo-Freudianism, Lifton includes Freud and Erikson in his intellectual genealogy, and the influence of Erikson in particular can be seen in his earlier work, such as *Thought Reform and the Psychology of Totalism* (1961). One finds in Lifton's autobiographical statements about his intellectual roots an illustration of his theory of "grounding," which will be discussed below. Affirmation of continuity with a theoretical and clinical tradition in psychoanalysis coexists with commitment to a major change in the theory and practice of psychoanalysis. These changes had long been prepared by heretics and innovators in more than one generation of analysts, but Lifton's change is a conscious and systematic effort to create a new paradigm for psychology from within psychoanalysis. In this respect, he shows the influence of Thomas Kuhn's seminal work, *The Structure of Scientific Revolutions* (1962). Thus, Lifton builds upon the ideas of early heretics like Otto Rank and Jung without repudiating the contributions of the orthodox. He views the emergence of the formative paradigm in psychology the way an intellectual historian or historian of science would.

Lifton is also vividly aware of the contribution of his own life experience to the creation of the new paradigm. Rapid shifts in cultural ambience, the experience of the Great Depression, World War II, the Holocaust of European Jewry, the invention and use of nuclear weapons, and more than two decades of warfare conducted by the United States in Asia had both direct and indirect impact upon him. His major works of psychohistory have been about upheavals in East Asia, an area of the world affected by civil war, invasion, nuclear bombing, revolutionary movements of the most extreme and destructive sort, and rapid cultural change. Furthermore, Lifton conducted his work in the field, in the form of psychiatric interviews in his early work, and later, in "rap groups" for *Home from the War* (1973) his study of U.S. veterans of the Vietnam War. Of the psychohistorians examined here, of course, only Erikson in his work on Gandhi used the method of psychiatric interviewing. In a sense, then, Lifton is to psychohistory what the first anthropologists who went into the field were to their armchair colleagues, and this is a function of his interest in twentieth-century problems. However, it would be wrong to emphasize investigative technique as opposed to theory when comparing Lifton to other psychologists and psychohistorians. Rather, it is his theoretical departure from the others which is most significant.

Quite a theoretical distance separates Lifton from Freud, Erikson, Brown, and Marcuse, all of whom were grounded in the thought-world of the nineteenth century in important ways. Both Freud and Erikson perpetuated the fascination with men of power and genius that had dominated much of the European intelligentsia since the Napoleonic era. One could find in Freud's naturalism some characteristics associated with the intellectual trends of *Naturphilosophie* and Romanticism. Marcuse and Brown, both encyclopedic minds, and both fully aware of their intellectual ancestry, had special affinities with Hegel, Marx, and other nineteenth-century (and much earlier) utopians and heretics. Lifton shares with Erikson, Brown, and Marcuse an aversion for positivistic, mechanistic, and dualistic visions, and a repugnance for twentieth-century totalism, but he is distinctly a member of a different intellectual trend, a group of thinkers in several fields who have committed themselves unreservedly to the neo-Kantian view that the human species is best known as *homo symbolicus*.

Lifton's emphasis upon image, form, and symbol in human psychology is a far more radical departure than it would at first seem, given the importance of symbolism in psychoanalysis. However, Lifton has given images, forms, and symbols a new position at the very foundation of human development and vitality. The idea of instincts or drives and Freud's quantitative concept of energy go by the wayside, and with them, related concepts of defense and psychic structure. Lifton replaces them with a more compact theory in which a paucity of biological attributes, particularly an innate tendency to form mental imagery about death and the continuity of life, account for the most prominent psychological features of the human species. Lifton did not attach the power of imagination to any specific subsystems or substructures within the human soma or psyche, although he has speculated about the relationship of brain lateralization to human psychology. The traditional Freudian psyche becomes a fluid self, and the self can no longer be identified with a substructure of the psyche charged with assessing reality—the rational ego—or with something quite as stable as Erikson's ego identity. By clearing the psyche (self) of these structures and divisions, Lifton removed some of the most important features sustaining endopsychic anthropomorphism in its psychoanalytic forms.

As noted earlier, thinkers in a variety of traditions have tended to find external analogues or homologues for endopsychic phenomena. They have identified aspects of the larger world analagous to Reason, Feeling, or Will, Activity or Passivity, Consciousness or Spontaneity. In turn, they have promoted within the larger world the agencies corresponding to the psychic attributes they affirmed in themselves and warned against those that they feared or were anxious about. Thinkers within the psychoanalytic tradition usually promote the ego and its agencies. Lifton avoids this type of anthropomorphism. Even more important, by replacing the force of the life and death instincts with the power of the imagination, Lifton removed the source of psychoanalytic interpretations of history based upon the conflict of Eros and Thanatos.

However, despite his abandonment of the traditional Freudian notion of conflict, Lifton sustains the idea of struggle in a dialectical architectonic. The human imagination works dialectically. Unlike many dialecticians, he establishes dialectics in his theory as a purely *mental* principle associated with imagination and creativity rather than with any metaphysical or "material" structures or forces. Here he comes closer to the dialectic connected with Erikson's epigenetic polarities and existential indeterminacy than to the dialectical eschatologies of Marcuse and Brown.

Lifton does not pretend that he knows the end of the dialectical process or treat the process as if its stages were predetermined. His focus upon the breaks within the dialectic of individual self-process and community symbolization strongly distinguishes him from dialecticians within the Hegelian tradition, for whom catastrophes are always nested within an epigenetic process, and the latter in turn subordinated to a systemic aim. For utopian dialecticians, nothing is for nought, whereas for Lifton, in some individuals, and in some historical communities, the psychoformative process is destroyed or deeply impaired by catastrophic traumas.

Lifton's major theoretical summing up, *The Broken Connection* (1979), is a systematic effort to summarize his views and to display the formative paradigm's ability to explain the most important aspects of human psychology in a superior fashion. Lifton traces the formative dialectic through the human life cycle in *The Broken Connection*. The most radical change in the paradigm is the replacement of the old Freudian idea of life and death instincts (the latter never congenial to most psychoanalysts) with the idea of a psychoformative process, whose success depends upon an uninterrupted dialectic of imagery about death and the continuity of life. Lifton's shift of emphasis in his paradigm to the unique human capacity for imagination implies a deemphasis of endogenous as opposed to exogenous factors in human development. In this respect he is closer to Erikson, Marcuse, and Brown than it would at first appear. Although all of the psychohistorians discussed thus far accepted an idea of innate drives, they either gave exogenous factors in human development significant power to shape instinct, as Erikson and Marcuse did in their theories, or subtly inverted the relationship between nature and culture, as Brown did in his work after *Life Against Death*. Brown had begun by affirming Freud's naturalistic vision but ended in *Love's Body* and *Closing Time* by emphasizing poetry, symbolism, imagination, and representation as the major forces governing the human condition. Although Brown never renounced the instinctual and somatic bases of fantasy and its cultural forms (sublimations), the data with which he worked were cultural, and his "way out" appears to begin, at least, with cultural revolution.

Lifton does not abandon a psychobiological framework. Rather, he incorporates into formative theory recent trends in biology, especially in ethology, which revise instinct theory in favor of less programmed behavior and a more open system. Prominent among the biological and ethological findings which he finds serviceable for his formative theory are widely accepted views about the fetalization of the human infant (neoteny) and mammalian attachment behavior. In Lifton's theory, there is a progression in human development from the physiological to the symbolic. It occurs as an epigenetic-dialectical process, in which the higher stages include the lower ones. The distinctive human capacity for imagination attunes human beings in a unique fashion for life in cultures and the latter govern human activity by means of symbol systems, complexes of developed images. To put it in simplest terms, our biological inheritance attunes us to be controlled by images, which both direct us to our sources of nourishment in infancy and energize us in our more complex cultural activities in our maturity.

With respect to human ontogeny, formative theory hypothesizes that the human infant possesses only a plan in the form of an image, and it describes the image as an "interpretive anticipation of interaction with the environment,"[1] a "structured anticipation of interaction with the environment," or finally, "a schema for enactment."[2] In short, the human neonate is not *tabula rasa,* but inherits a psychobiological plan for action, which, however inchoate it is, both affects its caretakers and then actively responds to their behavior. The innate plan is, in simplest terms, a genetic plan for survival, for the maintenance of the life of the organism. In time, it develops into the image of the self—the organism's "self-symbol" in Lifton's terms—and this becomes the driving force of the formative process. Lifton constructs his psychology around complex symbolizations issuing from uniquely human forms of struggle for vitality and self-development. He believes it is possible to do so without placing sexuality (libido) and aggression at the center of the picture. By not doing so, he radically alters the traditional psychoanalytic infrastructure of human development.

In the genetic and epigenetic visions of human development, both individuals and groups are superstructures for hereditary drives and patterns of development. Freud had emphasized the power of the past in his depth psychology; Erikson emphasizes the power of human cultures to assemble full psychosocial patterns of development from fragmentary instincts and an epigenetic sequence; and Lifton emphasizes the continual reshaping and renewal of the human quest for vitality and self-development in response to the spur of death. It is the human capacity for *imag-*

147

ination, for creating a rich variety of symbolic forms addressing the issues of life and death, which distinguishes the human species from other species with a lesser endowment and a more limited capacity to respond to the challenges of changing environments. Quite clearly, Lifton's vision too embraces evolutionary theory, and takes into account distinctive human evolutionary acquisitions.

The cogency of Lifton's approach depends upon his ability to deal with the richness of human psychological and psychohistorical phenomena more adequately within the terms of his theory than either orthodox Freudian psychoanalysis or its many revisions can within theirs. Lifton consciously shifts the center of attention away from sexuality as well as from instinct, so that traumas, anxiety, and guilt issue from conflict around the polarities of life and death imagery. For example, whereas Freud subordinated anxiety about death to castration anxiety in his theory, Lifton reverses the relationship, and whereas Freud saw life and death *instincts* locked in enternal conflict, Lifton proposes a dialectical, unitary vision of the relationship between life and death imagery. In short, the vicissitudes of the repressed instincts are replaced by the vicissitudes of the distinctively human power of imagination.

In the very beginning, there are only "image-feelings," which are experienced as equivalents of life and death. The death equivalents are: *separation, disintegration, and stasis.* Lifton calls them "precursors and models for later feelings about actual death."[3] They are epigenetically assimilated into the individual's life experience and continue to be associated with death long after the birth trauma. Of the three death equivalents, separation is the crucial experience. Lifton therefore joins those psychoanalysts who place separation anxiety at the origin of a lifelong dialectic. The antitheses of the death equivalents are, respectively: *connection, integrity, and movement.* The life equivalents require the stimulus of the negativity of the death equivalents in order to develop the full vitality of the human neonate. It is clearer in Lifton's dialectic than in most that the dialectical principle *itself* is the symbolic juncture of the life equivalents of connection, integrity, and movement. The first experience of death and life equivalents, the birth experience of extrusion and emergence, imprints itself and initiates the dialectic. In this fashion the groundwork is laid for the infant's *image-base* derived through its initial attachment to its caretaker, ordinarily its mother, and for a *dialectical integration* of imagery of connection and separation.[4] This early "felt" imagery begins the dialecti-cal process of more structured image-formation and symbolization. The process is propelled forward by means of the negative stimulus of the ex-perience of death equivalents. The crucial position of death equivalents in Lifton's theory and the dialectical method suggest an affinity with Brown, but the resemblance ends here, for Brown remained loyal to the theory of the instincts. Lifton also clearly distinguishes the development of the inchoate image, through the experience of birth and the nurturing caretaker, from Erikson's first epigenetic crisis of basic trust versus mis-trust, with its somatopsychic and cultural foundations.[5] In Lifton's the-ory of development, the succeeding steps in human ontogeny are punc-tuated by advances in the imaginative process: from felt imagery to structured imagery—the use of pictures and words—and finally, to highly developed symbolizations of life and death equivalents.

Lifton remains within the genetic architectonic to this extent: The lengthy and complex dialectic of death and life imagery has a genetic ba-sis in the inchoate image and the imprint of the birth experience. As is the case with most epigenetic-dialectical processes, the early moments are preserved in some way throughout the process of development. Lifton also emphasizes the uniquely long period of dependency and weakness of the human neonate, and these too are genetic inheritances. However, there is no nostalgia for beginnings in Lifton and the power of origins is pre-sented rather as a psychobiological fact. The unique vulnerability of the young of the human species recurs as a theme in all psychoanalytic thought, as well as in all contemporary psychobiological visions of human devel-opment. Neither the return of original bliss in a dialectical eschatology nor the burden of original sin need be associated with origins, and Lifton avoids either the hope or pessimism bound up with such uses of the ge-netic architectonic.

Lifton based his formative paradigm, at first tentatively and then more surely, upon the assumption that the human experience of a multitude of small threats in both proximate and ultimate dimensions of human ex-perience is necessary for human vitality and development. Like negativity in the Hegelian dialectical tradition, in the formative paradigm the ex-perience of death equivalents and their transcendence in a creative psy-chological process drives the dialectic of human development. At the level of ultimate experience, elaborate systems of symbols, such as religions and

ideological systems, take the place of the immediate (proximate) physio-
logically stimulated experiences of threats to the organism. As a psychohistorian, Lifton emphasizes threats so traumatic that they cause a break
in the psychoformative process, a temporary—or in the worst case, permanent—cessation of the psychological dialectic of imagery about death
and the continuity of life. The break occurs in human communities when
exogenous catastrophes, death immersions brought about by unexpected
natural disasters or slaughter brought about by warfare, or endogenous
processes of change vitiate communal forms of symbolic immortality. The
most dramatic cases—those involving mass death—yield groups of survivors with a deeply impaired sense of the continuity of life. The survivor
may lose the power to create new forms of life imagery which might as-
similate and transcend the death immersion. *Psychic numbing* is the psychological response to the anxiety generated by the threat of death, whether
in immediate or ultimate forms. To put it another way, both individuals
and communities can become so traumatized in the face of death that
they lose the ability to feel, to express their full vitality. The flight from
death brings with it a flight from life as well. Lifton therefore affirms the
Freudian tradition in this respect: He upholds the view that human beings
must face death in order to live well. However, Lifton's emphasis is quite
different. Freud wanted human beings to give up their *illusions* about immortality, whereas Lifton wants human beings to live with death *anxiety*
so that they can transcend it and sustain their *symbols* of immortality. A
quotation from Heinrich Böll appears repeatedly in Lifton's work: "The
artist carries death within him, like a good priest his breviary."

Lifton's paradigm seen in one light is a response to what he calls "the
cosmology of death" of the twentieth century. He has studied more systematically than any major psychohistorian the traumatic moments which
cause a break in the dialectic and fix the numbed psyche into a posture
of mere survival, a kind of death in life. His sense of the vulnerability of
the formative process to death anxiety and psychic numbing inspires his
central concern as a psychohistorian—the communal correlatives of a break
in the formative process. These are breakdowns of the community's symbols of immortality and an impairment of its ability to create new ones.
Both the individual and the community are therefore vulnerable to breaks
in the dialectic. Such breaks are catastrophes in the ordinary sense of the
word rather than examples of the benign negativity ordinarily associated

with the dialectical architectonic—the negativity needed to drive along a healthy process of life and death imagery. Lifton's catastrophic principle expresses his own anxiety about a widespread loss of vitality in the modern world, among the symptoms of which are a loss of passion and vigor in activity and subjective experience. In simplest terms, the break in the dialectic implies a loss of feeling and a cessation of creativity.

The concept of psychic numbing, which issues from Lifton's studies of the traumatic syndrome and survivor experience, is central to his explanation of the break in the formative process. We will therefore examine it in greater detail. First, it should be noted that there is an idea of *dosage* implicit in Lifton's theory in that threats, anxiety, and even a degree of psychic numbing in some contexts, can contribute to the psychoformative process. The traumatic syndrome connotes a powerful dose of death imagery, but even then does not inevitably imply an irreversible or permanent state of impairment. One can easily think of circumstances in which a diminished capacity to feel, even when an involuntary and unconscious response to an acute trauma, might have temporary adaptive value. But this is true only up to a point. An overdose might produce instead what is in effect the mind's death, a "break in the lifeline," in D. W. Winnicott's formulation. In Lifton's succinct statement of his own position, it consists of *"the mind being severed from its own psychic forms."*[6] There is an accompanying paralysis and dissociation of knowledge from feeling—in short, separation, disintegration, and stasis. The unitary dialectical self-process, which is the essential life of the mind, is suspended despite the continuation of the life of the organism—hence, death in life.

In order to grasp more fully Lifton's concept of psychic numbing, the source of every every major type of mental disorder in formative theory, we must examine his systemic ideal, so to speak. The systemic architectonic occupies an unusually recessive place in formative theory, but it is nonetheless important. Lifton's optimal state of the psychic process can be described as a state of perfect harmony and equilibrium in an open system. It is the state of the self-system at a farthest remove from the disintegrated state issuing from severe psychic numbing. In orthodox psychoanalysis, there are a variety of optimal states: those associated with direct gratification of the drives, those issuing from a close approach to the superego's ideals, and from a state of "ego dominance" as described by Erikson. Each suggests equilibrium and harmony. In Lifton's formative theory, there is no psychic structure called "ego" which experiences anxiety and deploys defense mechanisms for dealing with it or achieves control over the other psychic structures. Nor is there a superego for the ego to please, or an id to be satisfied. Rather, the unitary Self has strategies for integrating all dimensions of experience.

The crucial terms are *grounding, centering, and decentering*. The lack of elaboration of these concepts in Lifton's theory may be related to his repudiation of static and mechanical models of the psyche. However, they play the role in formative theory that the integrative and synthetic powers of the ego do in traditional psychoanalysis. It is no accident that Lifton often uses gerunds rather than nouns for terms in formative theory, for his psychology is more attuned to a notion of mental activity, to mental process rather than to the idea of mental structures. "Grounding" implies an epigenetic principle or, in dialectical terms, a principle of sublation, in which earlier moments in a process are transcended, yet retained. It signifies "the relationship of the self to its own history, individual and collective, as well as to its biology."[7] Without this historical foundation, a healthy process of centering and decentering would be impossible. Lifton specifies three dimensions of experience which the self normally orders by means of centering: temporal, spatial, and emotional. Of these three dimensions, the emotional one plays the most significant role. Lifton describes it as the "core of the self." The centering of emotions involves "making discriminations in emotional valence between our most impassioned images and forms (what we call the 'core of the self') and those that are less impassioned and therefore more peripheral." The following quotation gives a clearer sense of Lifton's idea of the core of the self:

> Emotion is the means by which the human mind articulates, gives form to and energizes the organism on behalf of that which is perceived as most important. In our paradigm this is likely to concern the following core areas: love, sexuality, and personal bonds; learning, working, and making; death, play, and transcendence; home and place; relationship to society and environment; and nurturance and growth. These are so designated because we sense them to be at the core of our existence, of our struggles and images around life and death.[8]

The idea of emotional valence replaces the old Freudian quantitative notion of libidinal cathexes, charges of sexual energy connected with mental

representatives of desired objects; and the idea of the core of the self subsumes Erikson's concept of psychosocial identity.

The centered self has qualities similar to those associated with a secure
sense of identity in Eriksonian psychology. However, while Erikson's
epigenetic principle involves maximization of the positive senses at each
stage of the development of psychosocial identity on the way to that sense
of identity, Lifton's more fluid dialectic has less specific aims. Moments
of perfect centering yield transcendent or peak experiences, which are
nothing less than ecstatic, mystical experiences. Time and death are momentarily obliterated. The individual experiences:

> the harmonious merging of immediate and ultimate experience (self
> and world), past and prospective imagery, and of the varying emo-
> tional shadings that ordinarily complicate life. . . . With inner forms
> in harmony, psychic action is intense and focused, and there is a
> free flow of psychic and bodily energy—all in the "continous pre-
> sent." Whether the initiating events seems primarily psychic (as in
> contemplation or meditation) or physical (as in the sex act), or is
> some combination of these, the resulting awareness and energy flow
> are in the truest sense, psychosomatic.[9]

Moments of transcendence are needed for the human sense of immortality, an essential ingredient of psychological health. However, in Lifton's
notion of self-process, optimal states are followed by decentering, a loos-
ening of the integration of the three dimensions of psychic experience.
What is clearly involved is a dynamic equilibrium in an open system, into
which new experience can be integrated and the self-system centered once
again at a dialectically higher level, so to speak. Thus, Lifton sustains a
genuinely dynamic and open dialectical vision and eschews any final equilibrium or harmony, any Nirvana of the self-system.

It is now possible to discuss Lifton's concept of mental disorder in terms
of grounding and centering. Disruptions of this dynamic equilibrium of
grounding, centering, and decentering affect the formative process and
diminish the experience of vitality. Mental disorders occur when the continuity of the self implied by grounding is disrupted. The *continuity* of
the dialectical process of image and symbol formation—a kind of perpetual preservation and recreation of the self—is central to the integrity of
the self-system. Without both continuity and dynamic development, the

self cannot integrate experience. Despite some connections with the left-Hegelian tradition, Lifton's emphasis upon the dialectical process rather than upon the achievement of a final state of the system, and the absence of subsystems or hierarchies (aside from the core of the self and the idea of emotional valence) distinguish him from the systemic-dialectical thinkers. His vision of the fragility of the dialectic of individual development, his focus upon traumatic moments in the microcosm of life history and the macrocosm of community history gives Lifton a unique position in psychohistorical theory. Mental disorders in individuals and psychological epidemics (shared symptoms) in communities issue from breaks, negative catastrophes which do not contribute to development or promise an ultimate systemic integrity, as they do in the visions of the Hegelian left. To return to the idea of dosage implicit in Lifton's catastrophic principle—a little negativity is a good thing, too much can bring the dialectic to a halt. In Lifton's theory psychological traumas no longer issue from an innate pattern of conflict between instincts and repressive agencies; they occur when an inner plan for action encounters an unpredictable historical enviroment.

We must now examine Lifton's historical vision and the concepts associated with his theory of historical change. Lifton's vision of history is less anthropomorphic than that of the psychohistorians already studied, in that he does not transpose to history the structure of neurosis like Freud and Brown did or, like Erikson and Marcuse, find agencies representing the ego or id in history. It is not surprising, though, that symbols and symbolization take the place of those inner structures, for the idea of *homo symbolicus* organizes Lifton's theory of history as well as his psychological theory. Thus, he establishes psychohistorical polarities around death and life corresponding to those in individual psychology. At one end, one finds in historical communities breakdowns of collective symbolization or formulation and a "negative psychohistorical triad of desymbolization, death anxiety, and denial."[10] The positive triad of viable symbolization, minimal death anxiety, and maximum acceptance of death occurs in communities that are able to sustain and create imagery of immortality. The concept of "dislocation" in Lifton's psychohistorical theory embraces all historical situations in which communities are "out of joint" with the cosmologies that contain their symbols of immortality. Lifton is well aware of the chronic human discomfort in culture, but believes that it is possible to distinguish historical dislocations and aberrant moments in community history from the usual problems of human existence. But in order to discuss such dislocations and aberrations, it is first necessary to examine briefly Lifton's theory of symbolic immortality.

He posits five modes of symbolic immortality. A *sense* of immortality is usually achieved through combinations of the five modes. The first mode, the purely biological perpetuation of self through procreation and kin, can become "biosocial" when one's sense of connection extends beyond family to tribe, ethnic group, polity, race, or species. The second mode involves the conquest of death through religious belief in salvation of some sort. The third mode sustains a sense of immortality by means of the belief that it is possible to live forever through good works or achievements, which will have enduring influence. The fourth mode operates through the idea that one merges into nature, lives forever in it materially, and shares its eternal qualities. The fifth mode of immortality issues from transcendent experiences of the sort that occur when centering is virtually perfect, when the individual has a mystical sense of oneness with the world, or feels the Dionysian ecstacy of overflowing the usual constricting boundaries within the self and between the self and the world. During such experiences time and death are momentarily abolished. The fifth mode, in Lifton's view, is essential to a human sense of connection and continuity.

Opposed to the five modes of symbolic immortality are complexes of death imagery or death symbols, the most lethal of which yield the twentieth century's cosmology of death—a vision of the end of the world through total nuclear destruction. Lifton has devoted his career as a psychohistorian to the study of the historical dislocations in human communities issuing from the death immersions of the twentieth century, but particulary those occurring during and after World War II. The phenomenon of thought reform in the Chinese revolution (popularly called "brainwashing") provided him with his first psychohistorical laboratory for investigating by means of psychiatric interviews the human response to dislocations. In the book based upon the study, *Thought Reform and the Psychology of Totalism,* Lifton still discussed continuity and change in human psychology in Erikson's idiom of identity. However, in the final chapter, entitled "Open Personal Change," he presented in inchoate form a unitary, dialectical perspective and the idea of renewal through the innate power of human imagination. Lifton offered "open change" as an ideal model, antithetical to totalistic impositions of change and the coercive reshaping of human identities. He was at first inclined to see open change as a feature of the lives of great men. Here too Erikson's influence is suggested. But Lifton had already moved toward the position that, far from being an ideal and rare condition, open change might be an aspect of all human development. Partly under the inspiration of Joseph Campbell's study of myths, and partly through his reading of modern literature, particularly the work of Camus, in which he found numerous images of creative transgression and rebellion, Lifton abandoned the concept of identity in favor of the idea of continuous renewal and the formative paradigm. One might see this as his creative response to the phenomenon of totalism.

The theme of totalism does not disappear in Lifton's work, but it does not remain a central preoccupation, as it did for at least two generations of thinkers, who saw old authoritarian systems replaced by new totalitarian ones. Totalism became for Lifton one typical and highly destructive response to historical dislocation, and therefore it is his theory of dislocation which must be our initial concern.

There is no simple formula for historical dislocation. The term "dislocation" does not imply any specific event, cause, or process, but rather a relationship between human communities and their symbolic universes, particularly between them and the symbols which sustain their sense of immortality. Lifton does not himself have an inclusive image of historical structure or development, and the metaphorical language which he uses ("dislocation," "out of joint") does not imply a general model of historical development. Indeed, Lifton is fully aware of the tendency to sustain the anthropomorphic Freudian image of history as "the intrapsychic struggle of the individual writ large." He criticizes Marcuse, for example, for confusing mental with social phenomena. The formative paradigm alerts Lifton to the creative principles employed by historians when they impose structure upon history, and their metaphors often strike him as mechanistic. Lifton translates his own preference for open systems and fluid process into a dialectical principle in psychology, but he does not do the same for history; he does not attempt to give history itself a dialectical structure. However, throughout his psychohistorical work he makes direct connections between historical dislocation and mental disorders shared by large communities.

Dislocation is unpredictable and is most easily discussed in terms of its consequences, which do follow a pattern: dislocation, totalism, victimization, and violence. Historical dislocation occurs when the complexes of symbols which ordinarily give meaning to life by symbolically connecting human beings and supporting their sense of immortality, no longer fit the communities which created them. A quotation from Joseph Campbell sums up the last situation: "A God outgrown becomes immediately a life-destroying demon. The form has to be broken and the energies released."[11] The failure can occur suddenly, as a result of historical upheavals, or gradually, as a consequence of long-term cultural change. In either case, the old symbols fail. *Desymbolization* occurs in upheavals which force abandonment of old symbols and unqualified acceptance of new ones— the coercive pattern of totalism; or else the old forms and symbols remain and seem deadening to a younger generation, stimulating generational rebellion in labile cultures such as our own. Lifton's own sympathies lie with the rebels who, in the spirit of Camus, experiment creatively with transgression and rebellion but also observe limits. They avoid the total, systemic solutions described in the following quotation:

> Totalistic programs seek a once-and-for-all resolution of dilemmas around death imagery and human continuity. Their impulse is not merely to "stop time" . . . but to "stop history." The immortalizing system insists upon its permanence and immutability. What is proscribed is the very flow and change in collective symbolization that makes man the historical animal he is. His sense of underlying threat—the overwhelming intrusion of various forms of death anxiety—is so great that the symbolizing process itself, the faculty that makes man man, either must be shut down, or radically contained. The "living machine" of individual neurosis is extended to something on the order of a "history machine."[12]

Lethal expressions of totalism can be thought of as an expression of the survivor's terror of annihilation. The characteristics of the survivor syndrome will be examined in some detail here, for the concept of "survivor" is central to Lifton's psychohistorical work and it is difficult to understand his concept of totalism without reference to it. Lifton's most important contributions to psychohistory are all studies of the survivor experience in the face of twentieth-century *death immersions*. Although the concept of historical dislocation is central to Lifton's psychohistorical theory, his central psychohistorical theme is the survivor. The countless small threats, survivals, and transformations in death and life imagery that we experience unavoidably in our growth are the background for our encounters with the historical world. The historical world of the twentieth century has exposed large human collectivities, either directly or indirectly through the mass media, to widely shared experiences. At the center of Lifton's new psychohistorical paradigm (correlative to his new psychological paradigm) is the hypothesis that historical experiences, such as death immersions, yield typical responses, such as the survivor syndrome described in his most widely read book, *Death in Life, Survivors of Hiroshima* (1967). As an investigator, Lifton has sought *shared themes* and imagery induced in a community of sufferers by exposure to an historically momentous trauma. In a sense, he has used extreme cases, such as the survivors of Hiroshima, to argue that all of us share the trauma, all of us are survivors of the death imagery associated with Hiroshima, in some fashion. This speculative diagnosis, like other efforts by psychohistorians to diagnose communal ills, suffers from the usual problems of establishing the scope of communal experiences and the responses to them.

The bulk of Lifton's study of the survivors of the nuclear bombing of Hiroshima is devoted to an analysis of interviews with seventy-five of them, but for our purposes, the chapter entitled "The Survivor," in which Lifton generalizes his findings, is of central significance. He presents an anatomy of the survivor experience: the death imprint, death guilt, psychic numbing, nurturance and contagion, and formulation. The death imprint is the imagery indelibly stamped, as it were, in the human mind by the trauma of the death immersion. The idea of survivor guilt, in traditional psychoanalysis understood as part of the ambivalent response to the death of loved ones, is extended to take into account the human response to any premature and absurd death, in which it is impossible to render any aid. The human sense of responsibility for sustaining life always accompanies feelings of guilt about death, and when death is massively inappropriate and death imagery pervasive, as with nuclear destruction, guilt assumes especially acute and chronic forms. Psychic numbing has been discussed above and need not be rehearsed here. Suffice it to say, the individual who has experienced a death immersion and death imprint defends himself by ceasing to feel and, in some sense, ceasing to live, for feelings are at the core of the experience of vitality. To make things worse, the experience of victimization with concomitant senses of weakness, dependency, and helplessness, coexist with suspicion and resentment toward others who might help, and who are not contaminated by the death immersion. In the case of Hiroshima, of course, there was *real* contamination by nuclear radiation. The sense of victimization may take the acute form of *survivor paranoia*. The paranoid need for power is actually the need for active power over death, and it is an aspect of the survivor's effort to reverse the experience of the death immersion and the sense of helplessness induced by it. The paranoid survivor sometimes becomes an agent and active dispenser of death, because he suspects those whose help he needs (and who indeed offer nurturance) of deadly intentions. Suspicion in the survivor is paralleled by fear of contagion on the part of those who do not have the "death taint." There clings to the survivor the resentment of those around him who sense in him a threat to their own lives.

Lifton's theory of *formulation* is designed to supercede earlier psychiatric explanations of pathologies issuing from impairments of the process of mourning and failures to establish a healthy relationship to an altered reality. Lifton uses the term to describe the process of reasserting, in dialectical fashion, the life-affirming imagery that must succeed death imagery in a healthy process of renewal. By writing the psychohistory of massive death immersions Lifton is not merely providing illustrations of his theory of the formative process, but serving the very process of formulation:

> The survivor cannot formulate from a void. He requires the psychological existence of a past as well as a present, of the dead as well as the living. Without these, neither mastery of his death encounter nor a place in human society is possible. . . . In every age man faces a pervasive theme which defies his engagement and yet must be engaged. In Freud's day it was sexuality and moralism. Now it is unlimited technological violence and absurd death. We do well to name the threat and to analyze its components. But our need is

to go further, to create new psychic and social forms to enable us to reclaim not only our technologies, but our very imaginations, in the service of the continuity of life.[13]

Thus, the writing of psychohistory is for Lifton an act of commitment and a form of advocacy. He asserts that his theme of death imagery and psychic numbing issues from the historical moment—that psychohistory no less than psychology must reflect the challenge of the historical moment—and the challenge of *this* historical moment is the confrontation with death imagery and the acquisition of a new kind of psychohistorical knowledge and awareness. Only with these will we be able to transcend historical dislocation, and renew the inner dialectic of imagery around death and the continuity of life. The psychohistorian, as creative survivor, advocate, and community therapist becomes an agent of the creative formative process which mends the breaks and transforms the experience into renewed vitality. But one of his major tasks is to analyze historically momentous responses to the survivor experience.

The survivor who becomes ideological leader might unconsciously reshape the image of history to fit his own survivor neurosis or psychosis. But, whether as an ideologue fashioning a new image of the historical process or as a political leader of a given community, the obsessional survivor employs a totalistic strategy in dealing with continuity and change. He simply transposes his personal form of psychic numbing to the larger world, which he believes is as subject to threats of disintegration as he is.

> History . . . is looked upon as a large mechanism whose parts must be totally meshed and controlled. As in individual obsessiveness, the collective rituals ward off the horrific temptation toward exactly what is forbidden—alternative images and feelings, especially around ultimate matters. And underlying the totalistic system is the parallel imagery of annihilation, but on a collective rather than individual scale—annihilation of one's nation, culture, religion, or even scientific or intellectual belief system.[14]

The ultimately destructive variation of survivor totalism is expressed by leaders who have acquired total power in technologically developed communities. Survivor-heroes, the most important of whom in the modern world were Hitler, Stalin, and Mao, left heaps of corpses around them, whether in victory or defeat. They did so in the name of past national humiliation and *victimization,* as well as other ideological goals. They sometimes created threats and identified groups against which to defend their followers and upon whom bloody revenge had to be inflicted. From *victims* the survivor-heroes became *victimizers* on a vast scale, destroyers rather than revitalizers. That is not to deny them any positive role. There is still nostalgia for the image of strength and certainty provided by Stalin in the Soviet Union. Mao's evocation of the symbol of revolutionary immortality inspired his society with renewed vitality and probably still does. Even Hitler offered the image of a revitalized and eternal Reich alongside his imagery of death and revenge. One should therefore avoid forming too one-sided a picture of even totalistic leaders, for despite their aberrant ideologies and numbing totalism they give to their communities some measure of revitalization. Indeed, it is no simple matter to recognize even extremely aberrant forms of leadership for what they are in their historical contexts. Identifying survivor paranoia and guarding against its shattering consequences remain two of the great unsolved problems of human history. Both Lifton and Elias Canetti, who, in his own idiom in *Crowds and Power* described the paranoid survivor-ruler as "mankind's worst evil, its curse and perhaps its doom," provide profound insight into the mythology of the survivor and the creative and destructive potentials of the survivor experience.

Anyone writing at the present moment has no difficulty recognizing the problem of the survivor, but the political history of this very moment only confirms the tragically stubborn character of totalistic responses to threats, and the tendency for communities to deliver power into the hands of potentially paranoid survivor-heroes, who beget new victims in a seemingly endless politics of revenge in history. The paranoid survivor seeks not merely revenge, but eternal survival.

Lifton's early interest in totalism brought him near to some of the concerns of mainstream psychohistory. Authority, leadership, and rebellion had always attracted the attention of psychohistorians in the Freudian tradition. Lifton's work on Mao Tse Tung, *Revolutionary Immortality* (1968), carries on the tradition in Lifton's formative idiom. However, aside from the work on Mao, he has characteristically preferred to study survivor groups and psychological syndromes formed by recent historical dislocations, rather than charismatic leaders. There is a very revealing term, *symbol-hunger*, which very nicely shows the centrality of symbols rather than the nexus of leader and led in Lifton's psychohistorical study. One only has to hold it up alongside Erikson's term, *charisma hunger*, to appreciate the difference between the formative idiom and more traditional psychohistorical visions.

Very shortly, alongside the theme of totalism a new theme appeared in Lifton's psychohistorical work, a theme which carried forward his investigation of the response of modern communities to historical dislocation. The new theme was "Proteanism." In an essay first published in 1967, Lifton sketched out a postmodern figure, whose career exhibited a special kind of self-process. He named the figure "Protean Man." Protean Man exists in spite of totalistic efforts to control human responses to historical dislocation. He could be found in such unlikely places as Mao's China, within the interstices of a presumably totalistic culture. It is a bit difficult to talk about Protean Man as a character or personality type, for Lifton denies him the stability associated with "character," "personality," or even Eriksonian "identity." The term "protean" is derived from "Proteus," the figure in Greek mythology who could change his shape at will. The term "self-process" is especially apt when applied to Protean Man, for he experiments with some fragments left over from traditional identities and with others conveyed to him from other cultures and newly emerging styles of life, on a torrent of imagery issuing from modern mass communication. Protean Man does not possess anything like the traditional Freudian superego, which involved the internalization of parental values, yet he suffers from a sense of guilt. In formative theory a sense of guilt "is experienced when one feels responsible, through action or inaction, for separation, stasis, or disintegration."[15]

The emphasis here should be on disintegration, for Protean Man is always seeking connection and can hardly be accused of lack of motion. However, he cannot satisfy his symbol-hunger and is attracted to both open and totalistic solutions to it in a quest for symbolic rebirth. In our era of social and symbolic breakdown, the Protean quest and the sense of guilt associated with it are all-pervasive. Proteanism is an unstable condition. In one of its permutations, it might yield recruits for its seeming antithesis, totalism, although the commitment to totalistic ideologies would be shallow and episodic. The term "ambivalence" seems too weak to capture the spirit of Protean Man in his wanderings. He has no capacity for stable commitment or deep loyalty. The lack of harmony in his values and commitments, and the inability of Protean Man to make meaningful connections with the kaleidoscopic culture swirling around him, yields the post-modern sense of absurdity. Protean Man is out of joint because the symbolic world is disjointed. The dis-ease of Protean Man is akin to that of the survivor, for the death equivalents of separation and disintegration underlie much of his experience.

The survivor theme emerges most strongly in Lifton's discussion of Proteanism in his attribution of a central characteristic of the survivor syndrome, "suspicion of counterfeit nurturance," to Protean Man. Since Lifton believes that all human beings in contemporary culture are exposed to the death imagery that creates Proteanism, it follows that suspicion of counterfeit nurturance touches all of us, and this suspicion is an aspect of survivor paranoia. At its worst, suspicion of counterfeit nurturance renders all institutional and personal relationships problematic; at its best it sensitizes contemporary human beings to the inauthentic. The sense of absurdity and spirit of mockery which often accompany the experience of disintegration and suspicion that all relationships, even seemingly nurturant and protective ones, are somehow life-threatening may be useful in a world whose Gods may indeed at times be life-destroying demons in disguise. Here again, Lifton points out adaptive characteristics of an aberrant self-process.

The Protean spirit in several of its aspects can be seen as an adaptive response to historical dislocation and "to the kinds of technological and cultural holocausts, real and anticipated, that hover over us."[16] Lifton discerns a creative Protean spirit in modern art, literature, and political behavior. Although the experiments of Proteanism are usually associated with youth, they need not be. They may be at the source of *all* authentic creativity in a world threatened with annihilation. It is the Protean experimenter who may be best equipped to break through the psychic numbing of the contemporary survivor experience and create the new symbolic forms necessary for revitalization. In the following passage, it comes clear that Lifton's own advocacy and Proteanism are closely related:

The innovator has always lived in exquisite equilibrium between a refusal to be an adult as ordinarily defined and a burdensome assumption of responsibility for a large segment of adult action and imagination. We sense now a demand that all, whatever their innovative talents, share in this playfulness and Proteneanism until "adulthood" either disappears entirely, or is renewed and transformed. Ultimately, genuine transformation requires that we "experience" our annihilation in order to prevent it, that we confront and conceptualize both our immediate crises and our long-range possibilities for renewal.[17]

Protean Man as creative survivor is therefore a key theme in Lifton's psychohistory of our era. Lifton's own anxious quest in an era of historical dislocation for a new kind of equilibrium in human self-process through a new kind of psychohistorical awareness might explain his attraction to Proteanism, whose aberrant features suggest only pathology to others. For Lifton, the old solutions, whether aesthetic or political, had to be transgressed, and new forms of commitment—indeed new forms of adulthood—invented. Lifton's final paragraph in the book which sums up his paradigm and psychohistorical findings, suggests that he sees Proteanism and Totalism as the two polar aspects of the survivor experience in our century and perhaps in other times and places as well.

Because the impediments are so great the quest becomes confused and takes not one direction but all directions. The self moves about— becomes Protean—in its continuing effort in (Langer's phrase) to "realize the form," to find new and lasting principles of connection. We encounter a back-and-forth movement between Proteanism on the one hand and a seemingly opposite tendency toward finding a single absolute, a safe haven of monolithic belief. We seek a form of awareness that combines immediate and ultimate involvements. Otto Rank spoke of this as "a fusion of the two separate selves, the mortal and the immortal, into one and the same personality." That fusion requires us to confront simultaneously a changing inner landscape of breakdown and revitalization along with our planetary landscape of threat and enlarged connection. We live on images and the images shift. Our increasing capacity for awareness gives direction to our life-symbolizing process and we find a way to begin to understand.[18]

A new equilibrium of self-process must be sought somewhere between the poles of Proteanism and Totalism. But a "planetary landscape of threat" renders any equilibrium problematic. The ordinary human survivor experience of many small threats in one's life and even threats to our ultimate symbols of immortality issuing from cultural transformation is now overshadowed by a vast threat of annihilation. The fateful question is, can human beings respond creatively to imagery of massive death and total annihilation? Here we return to Lifton's dialectical vision, in which new forms can only be generated through a confrontation with negativity. The movement from confrontation to reordering and renewal, a therapeutic process already described in *Thought Reform and the Psychology of Totalism* and a recurring theme in his later work, remains at the therapeutic center of his vision. In the twentieth century, we have no choice but to confront the death imagery of war, genocide, and nuclear holocaust. We must become *creative survivors*.

CHAPTER VII

The Limits of Psychohistory

FREUD'S IMAGE of science and of himself as a scientist encouraged him to search for laws and limits, and it is not surprising that he found them. His followers, inspired by one of the great creative achievements of modern thought, did not always feel constrained by the nineteenth-century vision of science that had nurtured his creative effort. Freud himself had subverted that confident vision, which had traditionally served the natural sciences, by unmasking the relative weakness of the conscious mind and dramatically exposing the power of the unconscious mind. He had hoped to make the inner world available for scientific dissection and manipulation, as part of the real world, and approached the power of the inner world as a realist. It is sometimes difficult to reconcile Freud's realism with his exposure of the unconscious mind's power over the way in which we construct our pictures of reality. However, the position that the human mind actively constructs reality does not betray realism if it contains the assumption that the construction is distinct from the reality. The position that the human mind is of the world and our surest starting point for any systematic investigation of the world does not imply that the mind *is* the world, or that the rest of the world works the way the human mind does. Confusion about the relationship of the mind to the world had affected human world views for millennia, and Freud believed that they still affected modern thought. The tendency to confuse inner and outer becomes especially easy when the inner world is historized—made part of an evolutionary and historical reality. For mental life and its *illusions* are the reality of history. Freud's realism was a kind of faith in the ability of scientists to surmount both the forces within us which distort reality and their cultural products. We should not judge him too harshly if we find that he too transposed his constructed reality of the human mind to history and gave history the structure of a neurosis.

We live amid the detritus of the human mind's efforts to refashion the world in order to satisfy our instinctual drives and to avoid pain and death. Freud tried to show that our efforts at realistic mastery had been limited by the power of unconscious drives, but that education to reality might shift the balance of power. Within the individual psyche he sought to strengthen the ego, and in the larger community, its historical agency, the scientific elite. With the science of psychoanalysis, they can confront the burden of the past and reduce both its pain and its power. As has been noted, this is a more advanced variety of the rationalism of the Enlightenment, a vision which takes into account the power of the irrational and yet pursues the goal of rational control over it.

In this way, Freud created the basis for a psychohistory in which historical actors, groups, institutions, ideologies, and epochs became battlegrounds of endopsychic structures and processes. Agencies in the service of the superego or ego affected the balance of power in the eternal combat of the instincts, themselves representatives of cosmic natural forces. Freud tried to imagine the circumstances in which a scientific elite would be given the chance to mitigate present human misery, but he doubted that psychoanalysis could ally itself with the politics of the larger world. Freud's psychohistorical vision, just as his vision of the individual human psyche, was dominated by a metaphor of conflict or struggle. As has been shown, his vision of eternal struggle can accommodate a wide range of ethical and political positions. One might actively array oneself on the side of Eros or acquiesce in the inevitable victory of Thanatos. For Freud himself, there could be no final victory over the forces of nature. He preferred to know the truth and be damned rather than seek the consolation of illusions. He tried to create an elite movement of men and women of science who were strong enough to face the reality discovered by psychoanalysis. The meaninglessness of life and the inevitability of death and dissolution were part of that reality. One had to enjoy life as one could, sometimes only endure it, with whatever control over the vicissitudes of mental life and the pain inflicted by both the burden of the past and present trials the ego and one's personal gifts might provide.

However, there is no such thing as neutrality in this psychoanalytic vision. Even Freud's minimum program of reducing pain so that individuals might endure life is infused with an activist spirit. The program is therapeutic rather than political. Freud's own profound sense of the limits to the efficacy of individual therapy and to the possibilities of communal therapy should not obscure the Promethean character of his undertaking. Although he was not inclined to console, he did make an effort to heal and to offer his fellow human beings truths that might give them a new weapon in the struggle with disease. Thus, the refrain "unconquerable nature" in Freud's works does not so much imply acquiescence as respect for a powerful foe. The battle had to be joined at the site of the cultural superego, where the death instinct worked as a growing sense of guilt.

The metaphor of conflict or struggle governed Freud's representation of both the unconscious mind and history. Freud showed with great clarity in his own work that psychoanalysts are subject to the limitations of figurative language in their efforts to represent reality, whether inner or outer. It follows that psychohistorians, like all other historians, use figurative language whether they try to represent history as a whole, or only some part of it. We know that representing the past involves selection and construction—that we no more passively record the past than we do present reality. Moreover, we believe (in our guise as realists) that the images and metaphors that we use to represent history are inadequate. In a recent study, *Metaphern für Geschichte,* Alexander Demandt summed up the situation:

> Every image is one-sided, but history is many-sided; every image is a piece cut from the whole of history. . . . We can investigate history and narrate it, we can analyze our subject and describe it, but we cannot represent either the former or the latter.
>
> History is neither a stream, nor a road, nor a book, nor a tragedy. History itself does not grow, and in history nothing grows like a child or a tree. History itself does not move and "within history" nothing moves, whether forward or backward, or upward or downward, or in a straight line or a circle. History is not made like a

house or tapestry, and it is not played like a drama, a chess match, or a symphony. The only thing that we can say about history itself is that it happened. And that is to say nothing.[1]

In short, we are damned if we do and incapacitated for creative work if we don't. Like Freud, we accept damnation in pursuit of our Promethean projects.

Studies of human creativity, of our use of language, metaphor and symbol, of such important mental operations as analysis, synthesis, and pattern recognition, and of the interactions of cognitive and emotional aspects of the mind all suggest that we have not found any way to represent a newly "discovered" piece of reality without reference to some familiar portion of it. When we try to represent the human mind, we do so with cultural materials already at hand. Furthermore, the act of representation often involves anthropomorphism. Freud talked about intrapsychic conflicts as if struggling homunculi were involved. He frequently personified the structures of the psyche. Even more important, he took his metaphor of struggle within the mind and transposed it to history. At first a bloody struggle between real human beings, the conflict was internalized as a species inheritance and fixed into mental structures. Freud then represented history as the battleground of those structures. Thus, the genetic architectonic became crucial to his historical vision. It made the original bloody deed of *Totem and Taboo* more crucial than subsequent events, and emphasized repetition rather than development. In Freud's vision the metaphor of struggle plus the genetic architectonic tended to subvert the more optimistic metaphor of historical development, which he shared with other thinkers in the tradition of the Enlightenment. Both nature and history had set limits. There would be perpetual conflict of homunculi within the mind, of superego, ego, and id in history, and of Eros and Thanatos in the greater scheme of nature, of which the human mind and history were only parts.

Later psychohistorians found ways to transcend those limits. Their theoretical revisions of Freud need not be repeated here. Rather, we will briefly reexamine the strategies of representation that they deployed in order to give Freud's central image of struggle a different meaning and purpose—or, to be more precise *a* meaning and purpose. The dialectical vision of development is, of course, crucial here. It is most useful to think of dialectics as the symbolic juncture of a metaphor-complex. There is a close connection between a metaphor-complex of growth, development, vitality, generativity, and healing and the ideas of creativity and imagination in Erikson, Brown, Marcuse, and Lifton. Wholeness for the individual, unity for the species, the expansion, enrichment, and enjoyment of life—all of these contain the meaning and purpose of the dialectical architectonic. Dialectics has become a symbol of positive change emerging from division and conflict. It is the modern intelligentsia's poetics of hope. The widespread use of dialectics in psychohistory and other intelligentsia doctrines suggests that it is still the most versatile structural principle for bringing together, in one ideological vision, hopeful or positive natural imagery and images of our own most positive dynamic mental features.

Through the use of the metaphor-complex sketched out above in conjunction with dialectics, psychohistorical thinkers developed a wide range of alternatives to Freud's vision of limits. Erikson remained closest of all to Freud. He promoted the integrative and synthetic power of the human ego and its historical agencies, religious and political leaders like Luther and Gandhi who could do for human communities what psychoanalysis had done for individuals. Erikson overcame the grimness of Freud's genetic outlook by placing at the very beginning of his epigenetic process a principle of faith issuing from the experience of the original unity and mutuality of mother and child. He thought of psychoanalysis itself as a maternal therapeutic agency in the service of the healing and rejuvenation of the species, and of the great *homines religiosi* as therapists who might save us from our destructive rages. The great therapists are designed to serve an evolutionary purpose—here too Erikson resembles Freud in his fidelity to a naturalistic framework. The heroes of the inner frontier are "selected" in history; their gifts permit them to cultivate an evolutionary endowment and serve evolutionary goals.

Erikson nests his dialectic within the epigenetic architectonic and the metaphor-complex associated with epigenesis—that of growth and development. However, he avoids a deterministic dialectic and his vision of the ego's powers contains an element of indeterminacy. Powers of integration and synthesis are not always adequate to the task; historical communities often squander the gifts of their creative individuals; creative breakthroughs by individuals and moments of liberation in communities are followed by stagnation and degenerative trends. Conjunctions of inner and outer in an epigenetic process always have an element of risk, of failure. Creativity and development in the individual and progress toward an all-species identity in humanity as a whole are presented by Erikson as existential turning points. The metaphor of history as drama contends with that of history as fitness space in Erikson's psychohistorical vision, for he also pictures history as a stage for creative reenactments of the existential dilemmas of the human species. Thus, Erikson's vision includes religious and existential dimensions that overflow the boundaries set by Freud's obdurate naturalism.

Marcuse and Brown show greater fidelity to intelligentsia traditions quite distinct from the one created by Freud than to Freud's. Marcuse is more a left-Hegelian than a Freudian in his orientation, and in his search for weapons in the struggle against the death instinct, he remained within the broad Marxian tradition. That is, he sought a way out of the limits set by Freud by deploying a traditionally Marxian dialectic of productive and social forces in history. These forces modified the natural forces identified by Freud. Marcuse did not abandon the naturalistic framework completely. As a dialectician, he pictured rational order emerging through moments of negativity, but he also showed the dialectician's sense of original bliss, and nostalgia for an eschatology, in which the original unity is restored at a much enriched, dialectically higher level. The struggle of Eros and Thanatos added a necessary dimension to Marcuse's historical dialectic, for it based the dialectic upon an immutable and distinctively human drive for gratification and wholeness. Marcuse recognized that one could not make history all-powerful, or else there might be nothing to explode the historical structures of domination. However, his dominant metaphors were drawn from the social world and he visualized the unconscious mind as an arena in which both reactionary and revolutionary parties struggled for control. Repressed Eros in the unconscious mind became the representative of the oppressed social groups in history.

Brown's brilliant inversion of Freud cannot be characterized so easily, for Brown ultimately sees through everything, including himself. Brown was well aware of the role of poetics in his construction of history, and knew that what he had to say was, in the end, poetry. However, at least in *Life Against Death,* by far his most widely read and influential work, his strategies are clear enough. Here he took a Romantic viewpoint, in which Nature is benign and healthy (it only made one mistake) and History the landscape of neurosis. The human body before the Fall into History is the end of Brown's eschatology. The resurrection of the human body will put an end to culture as we know it. Culture is for Brown mainly a symbolic structure, or map, which those with psychoanalytic wisdom can read as the map of the repressed body. But later, Brown's program seemed to offer only symbolic consciousness and mysticism. Psychoanalytic realism was somehow transformed into animism.

Brown's references to religion in *Love's Body* made Marcuse nervous, and he also found Brown's quest for wholeness through a total obliteration of boundaries *too* total. When confronting a dialectician of this sort, Marcuse discovered the limits of his own quest for wholeness through dialectics.[2] Marcuse's dialectic of liberation had to take the form of progressive social action, which would not abolish reason but lift it to a higher level. Brown, however, suggested a *return* to the rule of poetry and theurgy. In the end, Brown's dialectic yields word magic—an affirmation of the omnipotence of poetry and a repudiation of rationalism and modern science. It confirms what we know about Romantic visions: They believe in the innocence of the human condition before the Fall and worship the human creative construction of the world. Brown, like all real Romantics, calls for a return to the benign origin.

Lifton's vision of human ontogeny and of history is informed by a more profound sense of negativity and powers of degeneration, stagnation, and disintegration than one finds in dialecticians nourished on Hegelian optimism. His dialectic of individual creativity depends upon an environment which can nourish a sense of continuity. The inner dialectic is fragile, easily broken; the historical world can go out of joint. Lifton's metaphor-complex suggests vulnerability. Although a necessary aspect of development, negativity often exceeds tolerable limits and breaks the dialectic of inner development. These catastrophic moments of discontinuity and distintegration do not occur predictably in an orderly historical process. One cannot prepare for them in the way that one prepares for revolution in some dialectical visions. Rather, we must confront the death imagery. Freud had prescribed death-consciousness as an aspect of his realism and his struggle with the illusions of religion. Lifton does so in the service of human symbols of immortality, for it is a sense of immortality which nourishes vitality. A medical metaphor of homeopathic medicine can be inferred from Lifton's prescription of a confrontation with death. Too much death imagery, like an overdose of drugs, numbs the creative powers of the human imagination; but in order to overcome the numbing and to recover full vitality from death in life, we must confront the very death imagery that numbed us. The only good medicine in an age of death immersions is, paradoxically, death imagery. The psychohistorian, as creative survivor, must therefore practice a homeopathy of death imagery and simultaneously support those creative survivors who struggle to formulate all-species symbols of immortality.

The theories and the psychohistorical corpus created by Erikson, Marcuse, Brown, and Lifton conjoin several great intelligentsia traditions. All four authors showed fidelity to the larger intelligentsia purpose of seeking a unity of theory and practice in the service of human self-fulfillment. Marcuse and Brown, however, achieve their purpose by extending other intelligentsia traditions through Freud, whereas Erikson and Lifton extend the psychoanalytic tradition itself. The reader who seeks deeper knowledge of the rich background to the utopias of Marcuse and Brown can find it in an excellent compendium, Frank and Fritzie Manuel's *Utopian Thought in the Western World*. But it should be clear enough that Freud would not have countenanced the subordination of the therapeutic outlook to revolutionary politics. He accepted inequality as a fact of life and did not embrace radically democratic positions. He was neither a social nor a cultural revolutionary. It is very likely that he would have seen Brown and Marcuse as dangerous heretics, not unlike those whom he opposed during the early years of the psychoanalytic movement. Philip Rieff suggested something like this in *The Triumph of the Therapeutic,* in which the theories of Wilhelm Reich and C. G. Jung might be seen as surrogates for those of Marcuse and Brown.

Readers may find the issue of fidelity to a tradition minor compared to the issue of the value of psychohistory as an instrument for understanding and improving the human condition. However, the practice of appropriating great figures for partisan purposes can lead to confusion, and currently Freud is being pressed into the service of so many causes, that it is easy to lose sight of what he stood for. Erikson and Lifton are surer of their therapeutic genealogy than Marcuse or Brown. Although Erikson is attracted to religious leaders with political and social goals and Lifton to political and social causes, their grounding in psychobiology and therapeutic purposes are never in doubt. They seek to diagnose human ills and mitigate them at both the individual and communal level, and they are more willing to use religious, political, and social agencies in the pursuit of their goals than Freud was. They are alert to the dangers of totalistic interpretations of history (indeed, they have diagnoses for them) and of seeking solutions to human ills through mass violence. They have a sense of limits, but it is informed less by the holocausts of the twentieth century, than by new and more complex visions of continuity and change in the natural and historical worlds, and more complex visions of the mind itself. Furthermore, the intelligentsia always nourish themselves on a deep sense of their own resiliency and inexhaustible creativity in the face of all threats. Erikson and Lifton are confident that limits or boundaries can be extended, if not totally abolished, and that it is possible to create, with whatever evolution, history, and our immediate cultural experience have given us, less destructive solutions to human misery.

Perhaps, in the end, the psychohistorical intelligentsia have been more successful at uncovering the depth and complexity of the problems that face humanity than at providing convincing programs for solving them, but no group of contemporary thinkers has made a better effort at identifying the sources of human division, conflict, violence, and misery. It remains to be seen whether their ideas will win a wide following and in what way therapeutic ideologies can affect the most dangerous communal ills. The question posed by Freud in *Cvilization in Its Discontents* is still the fateful one for the psychohistorical intelligentsia, for it restates the chronic dilemma of all intelligentsias: the dilemma of power.

And as regards the therapeutic application of our knowledge, what would be the use of the most correct analysis of social neuroses, since no one possesses the authority to impose such a therapy upon the group?[3]

Notes

INTRODUCTION

1. This is a short list of some interesting works on the personal, cultural, social, and political background of three of the figures studied here and the psychoanalytic movement: Robert Coles, *Erik H. Erikson, The Growth of His Work* (Boston: Little, Brown, 1970); Peter Gay, *Freud, Jews, and Other Germans* (New York: Oxford University Press, 1978); Russell Jacoby, *The Repression of Psychoanalysis: Otto Fenichel and the Political Freudians* (New York: Basic Books, 1983); Barry Katz, *Herbert Marcuse and the Art of Liberation* (London: Verso, 1981); Paul Roazen, *Freud and His Followers* (New York: Knopf, 1975); Carl Schorske, *Fin-de-siècle Vienna* (New York: Knopf, 1980); Fred Weinstein and Gerald Platt, *The Wish To Be Free* (Berkeley: University of California Press, 1969).

1. THE PSYCHOHISTORICAL INTELLIGENTSIA

1. Julian Jaynes, *The Origin of Consciousness in the Breakdown of the Bicameral Mind* (Boston: Houghton Mifflin, 1982).
2. William H. McNeill, *The Human Condition* (Princeton, N.J.: Princeton University Press, 1980), p. 74.
3. P. A. Kropotkin, *Mutual Aid* (London: William Heinemann, 1910), p. 300.
4. Noam Chomsky, *For Reasons of State* (New York: Pantheon Books, 1970), p. 404.
5. Walter Langer, *The Mind of Adolf Hitler* (New York: Basic Books, 1972).
6. Christopher Lasch, *The Culture of Narcissism* (New York: Norton, 1978).
7. In addition to works already cited, see: David Bakan, *Sigmund Freud and the Jewish Mystical Tradition* (New York: Schocken Books, 1965); Philip Rieff, *Freud: The Mind of the Moralist* (New York: Viking, 1959).
8. The classic modern position is developed by Edward O. Wilson in his works on sociobiology.

9. Stephen J. Gould is a prominent proponent of biological potentialism.

10. For a discussion of the concept of development and its different meanings for the intelligentsia of the nineteenth century, see Maurice Mandelbaum, *History, Man, and Reason* (Baltimore and London: The Johns Hopkins University Press, 1971), pp. 43–49; and Robert A. Nisbet, *Social Change and History* (New York: Oxford University Press, 1969).

2. ARCHITECTONICS OF THE UNCONSCIOUS MIND

1. F. J. Sulloway, *Sigmund Freud: Biologist of the Mind* (New York: Basic Books, 1979).

2. Karl R. Popper, *The Open Society and Its Enemies* (New York: Harper and Row, 1963) 2: 212.

3. Norman O. Brown, *Life Against Death* (Middletown, Conn.: Wesleyan University Press, 1959), p. 321.

4. R. L. Heilbroner, *Marxism: For and Against* (New York: Norton, 1980), pp. 54–55.

5. There is support for this view in the following article: Leon J. Goldstein, "Dialectic and Necessity in Hegel's Philosophy of History," in *Substance and Form in History,* ed. L. Pompa and W. H. Dray (Edinburgh: Edinburgh University Press, 1981), p. 50.

6. Sigmund Freud, *The Standard Edition of the Complete Psychological Works of Sigmund Freud,* trans. and ed. James Strachey, 24 vols. (London: Hogarth Press and the Institute of Psychoanalysis, 1953–   ), 22: 177. Hereinafter cited as *SE,* with volume and page number.

7. Freud used the original English, but his reference is to E. B. Tylor's *Primitive Culture* rather than to Hume's own *Natural History of Religion.* S. Freud, *SE,* 13: 77.

8. Freud, *SE,* 20: 72.

9. Freud, *SE,* 13: 91.

10. Ernest Jones, *The Life and Work of Sigmund Freud,* 3 vols. (New York: Basic Books, 1957), 3: 313–14.

11. Carl Schorske, *Fin-de-siècle Vienna,* p. 203.

12. Mircea Eliade, *Myth and Reality* (New York: Harper and Row, 1963), p. 77.

13. Philip Rieff, "The Meaning of History and Religion in Freud's Thought," in B. Mazlish, ed., *Psychoanalysis and History* (New York: Grosset and Dunlap, 1971), p. 26.

14. G. F. W. Hegel, *The Phenomenology of Mind,* trans. J. B. Baillie (New York: Harper and Row, 1967), p. 75.

15. For example, Norman Cohn, *Warrant for Genocide* (New York: Harper and Row, 1967); Peter Lowenberg, "The Psychohistorical Orgins of the Nazi Youth Cohort," *American Historical Review* (December 1971), 75: 1457–1502; Bruce

Mazlish, *The Revolutionary Ascetic* (New York: Basic Books, 1976); Fred Weinstein, *The Dynamics of Nazism: Leadership, Ideology, and the Holocaust* (New York: Academic Press, 1980).

16. Freud, *SE*, 13: 88.
17. Freud, *SE*, 13: 73.

3. FREUD

1. Bruno Bettelheim, *Freud and Man's Soul* (New York: Alfred A. Knopf, 1983), p. 48.
2. Sigmund Freud, *The Standard Edition of the Complete Psychological Works of Sigmund Freud,* James Strachey, translator and editor. 24 vols. (London: Hogarth Press and the Institute of Psychoanalysis, 1953–   ), 18: 160.
3. Aside from those already mentioned, one should note at least the work of Henri Ellenberger, Robert Holt, and Lancelot Law Whyte.
4. Quoted in E. Jones, *The Life and Work of Sigmund Freud,* 3 vols. (New York: Basic Books, 1957), 3: 312.
5. Freud, *SE*, 19: 36–38.
6. Freud, *SE*, 22: 179.
7. Freud, *SE*, 13: 156–57.
8. Freud, *SE*, 13: 188–89.
9. Freud, *SE*, 20: 72.
10. Freud, *SE*, 18: 116.
11. Freud, *SE*, 21: 53.
12. *Ibid.,* p. 113.
13. *Ibid.,* pp. 141–42.
14. *Ibid.,* p. 144.
15. *Ibid.*
16. Freud and W. C. Bullitt, *Thomas Woodrow Wilson* (Cambridge: Houghton Mifflin, 1967), p. 259.
17. Quoted in Ronald W. Clark, *Freud, the Man and the Cause* (New York: Random House, 1980), p. 491.
18. Freud, *SE*, 22: 211.
19. *Ibid.,* p. 490.
20. Freud, *SE*, 19: 56–57.
21. Freud, *SE*, 18: 38–39.
22. *Ibid.,* pp. 40–41.
23. *Ibid.,* p. 38.
24. *Ibid.*
25. Jones, 3: 280.
26. Freud, *SE*, 21: 145.
27. *Ibid.,* p. 144.

4. ERIKSON

1. E. Erikson, *Insight and Responsibility* (New York: Norton, 1964), p. 164.
2. *Ibid.*, p. 165.
3. *Ibid.*, p. 205.
4. Erikson, *Childhood and Society* (New York: Norton, 1963), p. 271.
5. The chart is taken from *Childhood and Society*, p. 273.
6. *Ibid.*, pp. 261–62.
7. Erikson, *Insight and Responsibility*, p. 92.
8. Erikson, *Childhood and Society*, p. 365.
9. Robert J. Lifton, ed., *Explorations in Psychohistory, the Wellfleet Papers* (New York: Simon and Schuster, 1974), p. 50.
10. Erikson, *Childhood and Society*, p. 400.
11. Erikson, *Young Man Luther* (New York: Norton, 1958), p. 267.
12. Erikson, *Young Man Luther*, p. 231.
13. *Ibid.*, p. 77.
14. Quoted in Robert Coles, *Erik H. Erikson: The Growth of His Work* (Boston: Little, Brown, 1970), p. 351.
15. Sigmund Freud, *The Standard Edition of the Complete Psychological Works of Sigmund Freud*, trans. and ed. James Strachey, 24 vols. (London: Hogarth Press and the Institute of Psychoanalysis, 1953–   ), 21: 144.
16. Erikson, *Young Man Luther*, p. 76.
17. Robert J. Lifton, ed., *Explorations in Psychohistory*, p. 70.
18. Erikson, *Young Man Luther*, p. 22.
19. *Ibid.*, p. 193.
20. *Ibid.*, p. 213.
21. *Ibid.*, pp. 216–17.
22. Erikson, "The Ontogeny of Ritualization in Man," *Philosophical Transactions of the Royal Society of London*, Series B, No. 772, vol. 151 (1966), 338.
23. The chart is duplicated from Erikson, *Toys and Reasons* (New York: Norton, 1977), p. 114.
24. Erikson, *Gandhi's Truth: On the Origins of Militant Non-Violence* (New York: Norton, 1969), p. 433.
25. Erikson, "The Ontogeny of Ritualization in Man," p. 340. Erikson embellished his concept of pseudospeciation in several works, for example, see *Toys and Reasons*, pp. 76–77.
26. Erikson, *Identity: Youth and Crisis* (New York: Norton, 1968), p. 260.
27. *Ibid.*, pp. 293–94.
28. I have cited a reprint in *Explorations in Psychohistory*. The original appeared in *Daedalus* (Summer 1968), 98: 695–730.
29. Erikson, *Gandhi's Truth*, p. 439.
30. Erikson, *Insight and Responsibility*, pp. 220, 242–43.
31. E. Erikson, *Gandhi's Truth*, p. 37.

32. *Ibid.*, p. 395.
33. *Ibid.*, pp. 399–400.
34. *Ibid.*, p. 399.
35. *Ibid.*, p. 413.
36. *Ibid.*, p. 428.
37. *Ibid.*, p. 439.

5. MARCUSE AND BROWN

1. For a good survey of the Frankfurt school see Martin Jay, *The Dialectical Imagination: A History of the Frankfurt School and the Institute of Social Research, 1923–1950* (Boston: Little, Brown, 1973).

2. Two good books on the Freudian left, written from quite different points of view, are Philip Rieff, *The Triumph of the Therapeutic* (New York: Harper and Row, 1966), and Paul A. Robinson, *The Freudian Left* (New York: Harper and Row, 1970).

3. Herbert Marcuse, *Eros and Civilization* (Boston: Beacon Press, 1974), p. 18.
4. *Ibid.*
5. *Ibid.*, p. 35.
6. *Ibid.*, p. 38.
7. *Ibid.*, p. 105.
8. *Ibid.*, p. 143.
9. *Ibid.*, p. 164.
10. *Ibid.*, p. 230.
11. *Ibid.*, p. 235.
12. Norman O. Brown, *Life Against Death* (Middletown, Conn.: Wesleyan University Press, 1970), p. 12.
13. *Ibid.*, p. 82.
14. *Ibid.*, pp. 165, 169.
15. *Ibid.*, pp. 321–22.
16. Norman O. Brown, *Love's Body* (New York: Random House, 1966), p. 161.
17. *Ibid.*, p. 246.
18. Brown, *Love's Body*, p. 254.

6. LIFTON

1. R. J. Lifton, *The Life of the Self* (New York: Simon and Schuster, 1976), pp. 36–37.

2. R. J. Lifton, *The Broken Connection* (New York: Simon and Schuster, 1979), p. 38.

3. *Ibid.*, p. 53.
4. *Ibid.*, p. 55.
5. *Ibid.*, p. 59.

6. *Ibid.* p. 174.
7. *Ibid.*, p. 27.
8. *Ibid.*, p. 122.
9. *Ibid.*, p. 34.
10. *Ibid.*, p. 285.
11. Quoted by Lifton, *ibid.*, p. 393.
12. *Ibid.*, p. 299.
13. R. J. Lifton, *Death in Life, The Survivors of Hiroshima* (New York: Vintage Books, 1969), pp. 539, 541.
14. Lifton, *The Broken Connection*, p. 299.
15. *Ibid.*, p. 137.
16. Lifton, *The Life of the Self*, p. 137.
17. *Ibid.*, p. 149.
18. Lifton, *The Broken Connection*, p. 394.

7. THE LIMITS OF PSYCHOHISTORY

1. Alexander Demandt, *Metaphern für Geschichte* (Munich: C. H. Beck, 1978), p. 453. The translation is mine.
2. H. Marcuse, *Negations,* trans. J. J. Shapiro (Boston: Beacon Press, 1968), pp. 230–42.
3. Freud, *SE,* 21: 144.

Index

Abraham, Karl, 53

Acquired psychological characteristic, *see* Lamarckianism

Actualism, religious, 111

Actuality: Eriksonian, defined 83-84, 87, 112; and mutual activation, 84; historical, and leadership, 85; and religion, 86; and history, 95; of *hominés religiosi*, 104

Aggression, 134, 136, 147; and death instinct, 64-65; historical forms of, 78; Erikson and, 89; *see also* Death instinct; Thanatos

Alienated labor, 122, 125, 128

Anabolism, 78, 82

Analogy, Eriksonian, 100-1

Androgyny, 135, 139

Animism, 59; Freudian theory of, 19, 45-47; in Brown, 140–41, 173; *see also* Anthropomorphism

Anthropomorphism, 59; and constructed unities, 17; and human creativity, 18; endopsychic, 19, 24, 29, 145; and architectonics, 23; Freud on, 28; Hume on, 28; in Freud, 29; in Hegel, 29; in Plato, 29; absence of, in Lifton, 154, 156; and strategies of representation, 170

Anti-Semitism, 118; psychoanalytic explanation of, 71

Anxiety, 134, 135, 148; Lifton's theory of, 150; death, 150, 154; and psychoformative process, 151

Architectonic nesting, 42-44; *see also* Architectonics

Architectonics, 30-44; defined, 22, 25; distinguished from structuralism, 22; Freud and, 22; as metaprinciples, 22-23; and anthropomorphism, 23; and constructed unities, 30; enumerated, 30-31; role of, 30; *see also* Catastrophic principle; Dialectical architectonic; Epigenetic architectonic; Genetic architectonic; Systemic architectonic

Basic trust: sense of, and religion, 89; as foundation of faith, 103-4; and mutuality, 105; compared to inchoate image, 149

Bertalanffy, Ludwig von, 37

Bettelheim, Bruno, 50-51

Beyond the Pleasure Principle (Freud), 49-50, 75-78, 127

Biological determinism, 16-17

Biological potentialism, 16

Biological theories, in Freud, 49-55; *see also* Biology; Psychobiology

Biology: of the mind, xiii, 22; organic repression and, xiv; phylogenetic memory and, xiv; unconscious mind and, xiv; as source of architectonics, 31; in Erikson's theory, 87-88

Bisexuality, 135

Böll, Heinrich, 150

Bolshevism, 95
Broken Connection, The (Lifton), 146-55
Brown, Norman O., xv, 33; as dialectician, 24-25, 30, 171, 173; on psychic system, 38; and genetic architectonic, 44; as utopian, 44; animism in, 45, 173; compared to Freud, 67, 130-31, 134-35, 137, 172; theory of history of, 69, 132, 134; and mystical tradition, 115; and Romantic tradition, 115; as Hegelian, 128; compared to Marcuse, 128, 130-33, 139-40, 173; theory of repression of, 130; theory of sublimation of, 130, 136-38; theory of the instincts of, 131; compared to Erikson, 132-33, 139-40; naturalism in, 133; theory of culture of, 136-37; and poetics of history, 172; and religion, 173; eschatology in, 173
Brücke, Ernst, 52, 81
Bullitt, William C., 67

Campbell, Joseph, 156-57
Camus, Albert, 156-57
Canetti, Elias, 161
Carter, President Jimmy, 12
Catabolism, 78, 82
Catastrophic principle: defined, 40-41; and dialectics, 40-41; negative connotations of, 41-42; and revolutionism, 41; in *Moses and Monotheism*, 68; Freud's use of, 77; Lifton's use of, 150-51, 154
Catholicism, 95
Centering, 152-53
Charisma hunger, 107, 162
Childhood and Society (Erikson), 81, 87, 90, 92, 97, 110
Chomsky, Noam, 8
Christ, Jesus, 103-4
Christianity: the psychohistorical intelligentsia, and, 13; compared to Judaism, 68; therapeutic benefits of, 73; Erikson's attitude toward, 86; Freud's theory of, 95; rejuvenation of, 102-3, 106
Civilization and Its Discontents (Freud), 3, 31, 43, 47, 63-64, 66-67, 79, 81, 96, 99, 100, 115, 123, 175
Closing Time (Brown), 140, 146

Cohn, Norman, 42, 71
Coles, Robert, xv
Confrontation, 165
Connection, 148
Constructed unities: in intelligentsia doctrines, 6, 14; anthropomorphism in, 17; metaphors and, 17, 30; models and, 17; poetics of, 17; morphology of, 22; and architectonics, 30; of psychohistorians, 31; and history, 44
Copernicus, Nicholas, 21
Cosmology, 59, 111; anthropomorphism in, 28; Christian, 111; of death, in Lifton, 150, 155; and historical dislocation, 154
Crowds and Power (Canetti), 161
Cultural superego: theory of, 62; and communal neurosis, 65; origins of, 65; Freud's theory of, 67; power of father in, 68; of Jewish people, 73; and human self-destruction, 78; and death instinct, 169
Culture, 16
Culture of Narcissism, The (Lasch), 12
Cybernetics, 36

Darwin, Charles, 52; and teleology in nature, 14; Freud and, 21; on primal horde, 52-53, 57; *see also* Darwinism
Darwinism: and origin of the human mind, 1; and modern intelligentsia, 6; neo-Darwinian theory, 15; Freudian interpretation of, 32; and epigenesis, 35; Freud and, 52
Death anxiety, *see* Anxiety, death
Death-consciousness, 173
Death equivalents: defined, 148; distinguished from Brown's approach, 149
Death guilt, 158
Death imagery, 148, 151, 155, 160, 163, 173-74
Death immersions, 158-59
Death imprint, 158-59
Death in Life, Survivors of Hiroshima (Lifton), 158
Death instinct, 74, 118, 122-23, 126, 128, 131, 133-34; and human misery, 3; and aggression, 65; and human destructive-

ness, 72; rejected by Erikson, 88-89; and cultural superego, 169; in Marcuse, 172

Death symbols, 155

Decentering, 152-53

Demandt, Alexander, 169

Descent of Man, The (Darwin), 52

Desymbolization, 157

Dharma, 111

Dialetical architectonic, 38-40; and wishes or anxieties, 23; and endopsychic anthropomorphism, 24; as formal expression of spontaneity, 25; and Marx's materialism, 27; defined, 38-39; in Erikson, 44; in Lifton,, 44, 145, 148-49, 150-51, 153, 155-56, 165; in Brown, 69, 128, 130, 134, 138, 141; Freud's rejection of, 77; and ego strength, 103, 105; in Marcuse, 123-24, 141; as symbolic juncture of a metaphor-complex, 170-71; as poetics of hope, 171; *see also* Dialectic; Dialectics

Dialectical integration, 148-49

Dialectic of imagery, 146, 150

Dialaectic of neurosis, 130

Dialectics: as law of development, 6; as guarantee of justice and freedom, 7; as ideology, 9; as serial laws in history, 16-17; psychology behind, 24-26; and epigenesis, 39; and Marxism, 39; and millenarianism, 39; and modern intelligentsia, 39-40; and catastrophic principle, 41; and revolutionism, 41; as all-purpose architectonic, 43

Dimensions of a New Identity (Erikson), 87

Disintegration, 151; as death equivalent, 148, 163

Dislocation: Lifton's theory of, 154-55; historical, 156-58, 160, 162, 163-64; and sense of guilt, 162

"Diver, The" (Schiller), 47

Durkheim, Émile, 53

Ecology, 7

Economic and Philosophical Manuscripts of 1844 (Marx), 49

Ego, the, 123, 131, 168, 170; in structural theory, xiii; unconscious part of, xiii; and history, 29; and the psychic system, 37; and reality principle, 62; rational powers of, 63, 85; as defense, against drives, 74; heroic status of, 83, 106; capacity for faith of, 85, 103-4; and Protestantism, 96; and realism, 103; as agent of unification, 114; in Marcuse, 119, 124-25; and repression, 121; in Brown, 133-35; anxiety of, 134-35; Appolonian, 137, 139; Dionysian, 137, 139, 140; distinguished from self, in Lifton, 145; absence of, in formative theory, 152; in Eriksonian psychohistory, 171

Ego and the Id, The (Freud), 60

Ego-dominance, 105-6, 151; and the idea of freedom, 106; *see also* Ego-strength

Ego-ideal, 60-61; *see also* Superego

Ego psychology, 87, 90

Ego-strength: and ideology, 99; as focus of Erikson's theory, 114

Einstein, Albert, 23, 72

Eliade, Mircea, 33, 43

Emotional valence, 152

Enlightenment, the, 17, 168; and contemporary intelligentsia, xiv; optimism of, and Freud, 43, 73; tradition, rejected by Brown, 136; tradition of, and Freud, 170

Epigenetic architectonic, 34-36, 147; defined, 34-35; and dialectics, 39; optimistic implications of, 81; in Eriksonian psychohistory, 84-85, 93, 153; and ego psychology, 103-6; and psychosocial identity, 107; and psychohistory, 110; and ego-strength, 112-14; in Lifton, 152

Epigenetic chart, 89-91

Epigenetic-dialectical process, 147; in Lifton, 149; in Erikson, 171

Epigenetic landscape, 35

Epigenetic space, 35

Épistème, xiv

Erikson, Erik H., 81-114; biographies of, xv; as critic of originology, 32-33; and epigenetic architectonic, 35-36, 84-85; ecological vision of, 36; and the psychic system, 37; against totalism, 44; and the genetic architectonic, 44; and psycholog-

Erikson, Erik H. (*Continued*)
  ical polarities, 45; compared to Freud,
  81-87; 93-95, 103, 115, 171; and psychoanalytic tradition, 81; concept of mutuality of, 82-83; evolutionary theory in,
  82-83, 171; theory of the instincts in,
  82-83; concept of actuality in, 83-84;
  and religion, 85-87; theory of leadership
  in, 85, 93-95, 171; theory of identity of,
  90-92; and ego-dominance, 151; as dialectician, 171; therapeutic outlook of,
  171; metaphor of drama in, 172
Erikson, Joan, 109
Eros, 75, 115, 123, 125, 127-28, 133,
  135, 145, 168, 172; as agency of unification, 13; and utopian psychohistory,
  13; the psychoanalytic intelligentsia and,
  14; *see also* Libido; Life instinct
Eros and Civilization (Marcuse), 118, 125-
  26
Escape from Freedom (Fromm), 118
Eschatologies, 44
Evolution: of human brain, 3; of human
  species, 74; human, and psychoanalytic
  insight, 113
Evolutionary theory: in Freud, xiii; in Erikson, 82; in Lifton, 148
Existentialism, 112; in Erikson, 86-87,
  172-73; existential curse, 94; and Christianity, 103

Fechner, Gustav, 52, 75, 81, 133
Felt imagery, 149
Feminism, xv
Ferenczi, Sandor, 75
Feudalism, 39
Feuerbach, Ludwig, 123
Formative dialectic, 146
Formative paradigm, 143, 146, 156; com-
  pared to Hegelian dialectic, 149
Formative process, 147, 151, 160; image-
  formation in, 153; symbol-formation in,
  153; *see also* Psychoformative process
Formative theory, 151-52, 162
Formulation, 159-60
Frazer, James G., 53
Frankfurt school, 125

French Revolution, the: and dialectics, 6;
  in Marxism, 39
Freud, Sigmund, 49-80; and modern intelligentsia, xiv; biography of, xv; as diag-
  nostician of communal ills, 3, 11; and
  ethics, 9, 15; and religion, 9; anti-utopi-
  anism of, 9; elitism of, 10, 63, 140,
  168; on group psychology, 10; and socialism, 10; and Marxism, 11, 27, 105;
  pessimism of, 12, 43, 74-80, 83, 122,
  127; and the Nirvana principle, 13; and
  the natural sciences, 15, 21-22, 49-55,
  167; therapeutic outlook of, 15, 169; on
  animism, 19, 28-29; on dialectics, 27-
  28, 44; on Hegel, 27; endopsychic anthropomorphism in, 28-29; and the Enlightenment, 28, 29, 46, 64; theory of
  history of, 28-29; and the genetic architectonic, 30, 33, 43; and the psychic system, 37; realism of, 45-47, 167-68; as
  humanist, 49-51; as psychohistorian, 50-
  51; on figurative language, 50-51; theory of culture of, 57; as therapist, 59;
  and anti-Semitism, 70-71; and Judaism,
  70-71; and Christianity, 71; his identification with Moses, 73; his representation of history, 170
Freud and Man's Soul (Bettelheim), 50
Freudo-Marxism, 5, 116
Fromm, Erich, 118
Future of an Illusion, The (Freud), 63-64

Gandhi, Mohandas: and Freud's Moses,
  87; Erikson's research on, 94
Gandhi's Truth (Erikson), 81, 87, 92, 95,
  106-13
Generativity, crisis of, 106, 111
Genetic architectonic, 147; in Freud, 31-
  32, 93, 116, 170; defined, 34; and primal horde, 61; in *Moses and Monotheism*,
  68; and Freud's theory of the instincts,
  77; and Freud's pessimism, 79; in Marcuse, 119; in Lifton, 149
Genetics: distinguished from genetic point
  of view, 34; Mendelian, 53
Gorky, Maxim, 93
Grounding, 152-53
Group Mind, The (McDougall), 60

Group Psychology and the Analysis of the Ego (Freud), 31, 60–61, 81, 126
Groups: organized, 60; primary, 61
Guilt, *see* Superego

Haeckel, Ernst, 52, 56, 74, 81
Hampden-Turner, Charles, xv
Harvey, William, 34
Hegel, G. W. F., 114, 127, 144; and constructed unities, 14; dialectics of, 19, 23, 43; metaphors in, 19; and the cunning of reason, 25; as forerunner of psychohistorians, 26; psychology of, 26; theodicy of, 26; and individual psychology, 27; endopsychic anthropomorphism of, 29; as catastrophist, 40-42; as systemic-dialectician, 44
Hegelianism, 127, 146; and psychoanalysis, xv, 11; and the modern intelligentsia, 6; as consolatory vision, 45; systemic-dialectical, 94; teleology in, 95; Erikson and, 105, 115; and ego-dominance, 106; left, of Brown, 115; left, of Marcuse, 115; left, of Frankfurt school, 116; left, and permanent revolution, 117; left, and the past, 119; left, and Lifton, 154
Heilbroner, Robert L., 24-25
Hinduism, 86, 106, 110
Hiroshima, 158-59
Historical determinism, 16-17
Historical psychology, xiv
Hitler, Adolph, 161
Holism, 38
Home from the War (Lifton), 144
Homo religiosus, 92; as leader, 86; existential curse of, 94; Luther as, 97; as communal therapist, 99; as saviour pro tem, 104; ideological achievement of, 109; religious actualism in, 111-13
Homo symbolicus, 144, 154
Huizinga, Jan, 99-100
Human mental evolution, 1-3
Human species: self-destructiveness of, 3; biology of, 15-16; flaw of, in Brown, 129
Hume, David, 28

Id, the, 123, 131, 170; in structural theory, xiii; and history, 29; and human prehistory, 59; power of, in psyche, 63; anabolism and catabolism in, 82; instincts, in Brown's theory, 135; absence of, in formative theory, 152
Identification: with leader, in groups, 61; Freudian theory of, 90; and failure of modern revolutions, 123
Identity, 155; role of in Erikson's theory, 83; psychosocial, 85, 89, 92, 107; and Oedipus complex, 90; sense of, in adolescence, 90; Russian, 93; and ideology, 101; negative, Martin Luther's, 101; Christian, 102-3; Protestant, 102; distinguished from self, in Lifton, 145, 153; lack of, in Protean Man, 162
Identity crisis, 92; Martin Luther's, 98-100
Identity diffusion, 92
Identity vacua, 86, 100
Identity: Youth and Crisis (Erikson), 109
Ideology: delusional, 2; extremist, 2; paranoid, 2; defined, 4-5; of historical groups, 5; of intelligentsia, 5; and optimism, 8; and religious revitalization, 8; and secular movements, 8; systemic-dialectical, 38; liberal, and psychoanalysis, 96; Luther's, 96, 99-106; Erikson's definition of, 101; and identity, 109; totalistic, 162
Image-base, 148
Image-feelings, 148
Image-formation, 149
Imagery of immortality, 154; *see also* Symbolic immortality
Imagination, 124, 146-48, 156; dialectical, 142, 145
Inchoate image, 147; compared to basic trust, 149
Industrial Revolution, the, 6
In Search of Common Ground: Conversations with Huey Newton (Erikson), 87
Insight and Responsibility (Erikson), 110-11
Instincts, the: Freudian theory of, 75-80, 116, 118, 146; in Eriksonian theory, 83; mutability of, in Marcuse, 119; Brown's theory of, 131-33; in Lifton, 145

Instincts of the Herd in War and Peace (Trotter), 60
Institute of Social Research, 116, 118
Integrity, 148; *see also* Life equivalents
Integrity crisis, 98
Intelligentsia, the: defined, 5, 17; movements of, 5; psychohistorical, 5, 12-14, 42, 175; modern, and historicity, 6-7, 15, 17; radical, 7-8; voluntarism of, 7; psychoanalytic, 8, 11-12, 79; Hegelian, 11; Marxian, 11; and Freudian pessimism, 12; Christianity and, 13; and constructed unities, 14; and naturalism, 15, 17; limitations on creativity of, 18; and dialectics, 25, 38; and collective heroes, 27; and the architectonics, 31; and the systemic architectonic, 38; revolutionary, and the catastrophic principle, 41; and twentieth-century holocausts, 42; and therapeutic mode, 42
Interpretation of Dreams, The (Freud), 51

Jacoby, Russell, xv
Jaynes, Julian, 1-2
Jones, Ernest, 32, 78
Jonestown, Guyana, 12
Judaeo-Christian culture, 73
Judaism, 68
Jung, Carl Gustav, 143, 174

Kant, Immanuel, 23
Katz, Barry, xv
Kierkegaard, Søren, 86, 95, 97
King, Martin Luther, 109
Koestler, Arthur, 71
Kropotkin, Peter, 8
Kuhn, Thomas, 143

Lamarck, Jean Baptiste, 74; *see also* Lamarckianism
Lamarckianism: psychological, in Freud, 32, 52-55, 82, 130; and genetic approach, 34
Langer, Suzanne, 164
Langer, Walter, 12
Lasch, Christopher, 12
Leadership: and group psychology, 61-63; progressive role of, in Freud, 64; as fo-

cus of Freudian psychohistory, 67; and cultural superego, 73; in Eriksonian psychohistory, 83, 86, 92-95; Gandhi's style of, 109; and mass psychology, 126; totalistic, 161
Le Bon, Gustav, 60
"Legend of Maxim Gorky's Youth, The" (Erikson), 92, 95
Libidinal cathexis, 152
Libido, 60, 122, 128, 131, 133, 147; and group psychology, 61; sublimation and, 74-75; Erikson on, 88; and ego-dominance, 103; narcissistic, 125; *see also* Eros; Life instinct
Life against Death (Brown), 129-39, 146, 172
Life instinct, 3, 122; *see also* Eros; Libido
Lifton, Robert J.: and dialectics, 30, 146; on self-process, 37; and the systemic architectonic, 37, 151; and catastrophic principle, 41; as communal therapist, 42; as epidemiologist, 42; against totalism, 44; and genetic architectonic, 44; and psychological polarities, 45; formative theory of, 143; intellectual biography of, 143-44; compared to Brown, 144-46, 149, 154; compared to Erikson, 144-47, 149, 153, 155-56, compared to Freud, 144, 145-47, 150, 154; compared to Marcuse, 144-46, 154; his emphasis on form, image, and symbol, 144; neo-Kantianism of, 144; research methods of, 144; and psychobiology, 145-47; as psychohistorian, 150, 155-65; compared to systemic-dialecticians, 154; theory of symbolic immortality of, 154-55; as advocate, 160, 163-64; and metaphor-complex of dialectics, 171, 173
Loewenberg, Peter, 42
Logos, see Rationalism
Lorenz, Konrad, 108
Love's Body (Brown), 139-40, 146, 173
Low, Barbara, 75
Luther, Martin: identity crisis of, 97-103; compared to Freud, 101

McDougall, William, 60
Malthusianism, 7

Manuel, Frank and Fritzie, 174

Mao Zedong, 161-62

Maps of the Mind (Hampden-Turner), xv

Marcuse, Herbert, 115-28, 156; biography of, xv; as pioneer of new psychohistorical thought, xv; and dialectical architectonic, 30, 119, 131; and origins, 33; on the psychic system, 38; and the genetic architectonic, 44; as utopian, 44, 126-27; and Freudian psychohistory, 67; and left Hegelianism, 117, 121-25, 172; and the theory of the instincts, 118; theory of repression of, 120-23; his critique of ego psychology, 121; Marxian elements in, 121-22, 124, 129, 172; revolutionism of, 123; compared to Erikson, 124; pessimism of, 126; compared to Brown, 128; compared to Lifton, 144-46; and metaphor-complex of dialectics, 171; naturalism in, 172; nostalgia for eschatology in, 172; social metaphors in, 172

Marx, Karl, 127, 144; as historical determinist, 17; and dialectics, 23; and collective heroes, 27; materialism of, 27; and catastrophic principle, 42; as systemic-dialectical thinker, 44; as humanist, 49; rationalism in, 130

Marxism: and psychoanalysis, xv, 11; and Darwinism, 6; and modern intelligentsia, 6; and psychohistorical intelligentsia, 13; dialectics in, 39; as consolatory vision, 45; Freud on, 56, 117; and ego-dominance, 106; in Marcuse, 115, 118, 121; Wilhelm Reich's, 117; sociological tradition of, 125; as vision of history, 129

Marx's Fate (Seigel), 26

Mazlish, Bruce, 42

Mechanism, 18

Mentalité, xiv

Metaphern für Geschichte (Demandt), 169

Metaphor-complex, 171

Metaphor: use of, by intelligentsia, 18; and architectonics, 23; anthropomorphic, 30; and constructed unities, 17, 30; of conflict, in Freud, 168-69; for history, 169; of drama, in Erikson, 172; social, in Marcuse, 172; of homeopathic medicine, in Lifton, 173-74

Mind of Adolph Hitler, The (Langer), 12

Models: and constructed unities, 17; and architectonics, 23

Morality, Freud's theory of, 58

Morphogenesis, 40, 42

Morphology: of constructed unities, 22; dynamic, von Bertalanffy's, 37

Moses, 87

Moses and Monotheism (Freud), 31, 62, 67-73, 81, 103, 137

Movement, 149; *see also* Life equivalent *Mutual Aid* (Kropotkin)

Mutuality, 82-83; as psychoanalytic Golden Rule, 85; in Erikson, 94; of recognition, and basic trust, 105; as original social experience, 107; as basis for new reality principle, 126

Mysticism, 136; in Brown, 131, 140

Narcissism, 131, 133; and animism, 47; modern theories of, 49; and utopia, in Marcuse, 124-25; in Brown, 136-37, 141

Narcissistic libido, 125, 131

Narcissistic-maternal unity, 125

Naturalism, 118, 171; pessimistic implications of, 7; assailed by radical intelligentsia, 8; Freud's, 9; and the modern intelligentsia, 15; and the question of immortality, 16; and Freudian pessimism, 79; in Marcuse, 116, 123, 172; in Brown, 129, 131, 133

Naturalistic reductionism, 16, 81

Naturphilosophie, 144

Nazi Germany, mass psychology of, 126

Nazism, 71-72

Negative identity, *see* Identity, negative

Neoteny, 131

New Introductory Lectures on Psychoanalysis (Freud), 56

Nietzsche, Friedrich, 97

Nirvana principle, the, 13, 75, 81, 118, 133

Obsessional neurosis: and systemic thinking, 46; and behavior of primitive peoples, 56; and religion, 63, 69; progres-

Obsessional neurosis (*Continued*)
sive role of, in Freud, 69; and Judaism, 73
Oedipal phase, 135-36
Oedipus complex, 128; as nucleus of neurosis, 49, 57; and social science, 53; inheritance of, 56; origin of, in Freud, 58-59; progressive role of, in Freud, 64; and the superego, 78; compared to Eriksonian identity, 83
One-Dimensional Man (Maracuse), 126
"On the Nature of Psychohistorical Evidence" (Erikson), 100, 110
Open systems, 37, 91, 151, 156
Organ modes, 88-89, 102
Originology: Erikson and, 32, 94; in Freud, 58

Panpsychism, 19
Paranoia: and systemic thinking, 46; survivor, 158, 161, 163
Performance principle, the, 120, 122, 123
Phenomenology of Mind, The (Hegel), 29, 40
Plato, 29
Platt, Gerald, xv
Pleasure principle, the, 118, 124, 133
Popper, Karl, 23-25
Poststructuralism, xv
Pre-Oedipal phase, 133
Primal horde, the: Freud's theory of, 61-62, 122; and superego, 63; pattern of, repeated historically, 68-69
Proteanism, 162-65
Protean Man, 162-63
Protestantism: Erikson's attitude toward, 86; generic use of, 95-96; as ideology, 96; and ego-dominance, 106
Pseudospeciation, 108, 113
Psychiatric interview: use of, by Erikson, 144; use of, by Lifton, 144
Psychic numbing: 150, 151, 158, 160, 174
Psychoanalysis: as intelligentsia doctrine, 3-4; and religion, 104-14; and *Satyagraha*, 113; and Brown's theory of culture, 138
Psychoanalytic intelligentsia, the, *see* Intelligentsia, psychoanalytic, the

Psychoanalytic movement, politics of, xv
Psychoanalytic theory of culture, 136-37
Psychoanalytic tradition: Marcuse and Brown and, 174; Erikson and Lifton and, 174-75
Psychobiology: and modern intelligentsia, xiv; and the Freudian unconscious, xv; in Lifton, 149; in Erikson and Lifton, 174
Psychoformative process, 146, 150-51; as dialectic of human development, 41; *see also* Formative process
Psychohistorical intelligentsia, the, *see* Intelligentsia, psychohistorical, the
Psychohistory: intellectual history of, xv; and modern mass movements, 2; utopian, 13, 44; anthropomorphism in, 19; and architectonics, 31; Freudian, 30, 59, 72-74, 168; and counterculture, 116
Psycho-Lamarckianism, *see* Lamarckianism
Psychologie des foules (Le Bon), 60
Psychosexual development: Freudian theory of, 120, 129; Marcuse on, 121; Brown's theory of, 134

"Question of Lay Analysis, The" (Freud), 63

Rage, in Eriksonian theory, 88
Rank, Otto, 5, 143, 164
Rationalism, 169; Freudian, 64; Marcusan, 127; Brown's rejection of, 131, 173
Realism: in Freud, 63, 131; and faith, in Erikson, 103-4; psychoanalytic, inverted, by Brown, 173
Reality principle, the, 123-24; and the ego, 62; in Marcuse, 119, 126, 129; in Freud, 120, 126
Reenactment, 94-95, 172
Reich, Wilhelm, 5, 116-18, 174
Religion: Freudian theory of, 58, 63-64, 69, 79; and actuality, in Erikson, 86; and psychoanalysis, in Erikson, 104-14; in Brown, 139
Renaissance, the: Luther and, 97; ideology of, 102-4; and ego-dominance, 106
Renewal, 165
Reordering, 165

Repetition compulsion, 69-70, and genetic architectonic, 34; and death instinct, 75
Representation, strategies of, 169-70
Repression, 131; individual, xiii; changing forms of, xiv; organic, xiv, 133; as phylogenetic inheritance, 58; theory of, in Marcuse and Brown, 115-16; basic, defined, 120; surplus, defined, 120, 126, 133; in Brown, 128, 130, 136, 138
Repressive desublimation, 126
Republic, The (Plato), 29
Return of the repressed: and the genetic architectonic, 34; in Freudian psychohistory, 58; and the psychohistory of Judaism, 69; in Marcuse, 127; in Brown, 128, 135
Revolutionary Immortality: Mao Tse-Tung and the Chinese Cultural Revolution (Lifton), 161
Rieff, Philip, xv, 174; on the Freudian concept of time, 33
Ritualization, 107-12
Riviere, Joan, 72
Roazen, Paul, xv
Robinson, Paul, xv
Roheim, Geza, 5
Romanticism, 144; in Brown, 115, 141, 172
Russian Revolution, the, 116, 118

St. Francis, 109
Satyagraha, 110-13
Schiller, Johann Christoph Friedrich von, 47
Schizophrenia, 140; and human mental evolution, 1-2
Schopenhauer, Arthur, 79
Schorske, Carl, xv, 32-33
Seigel, Jerrold, 26
Self, the: Lifton's theory of, 145, 152-53; and Eriksonian identity, 153
Self-process, 146, 151, 163-164
Self-symbol, 147
Self-system, 153
Separation: as death equivalent, 148, 151, 163; and sense of guilt, 162
Separation anxiety, 133
Shamanism, 1

Sigmund Freud: Biologist of the Mind (Sulloway), 51
Socialism, 10, 64, 79
Social modalities, 88
Sociobiology, 15
Soviet Union, the, 117, 161
Spencer, Herbert, 53
Stalin, Joseph, 160
Stalinism, 116, 118
Stasis: as death equivalent, 148, 151; and sense of guilt, 162
Strachey, James, 51
Structural principles, *see* Architectonics
Structural theory, Freudian, xiii, 60, 62
Structured imagery, 149; *see also* Image-formation
Structure of Scientific Revolutions, The (Kuhn), 143
Sublimation, 131; and the death instinct, 74-75; rational, in Marcuse, 127; Brown's theory of, 128, 130, 136-38
Sulloway, F.J., 51
Superego, 128, 162, 168, 170; in structural theory, xiii, 60; unconscious part of, xiii; and history, 29; in Freudian psychohistory, 62-64; origin of, in Freudian theory, 66, 122; aggression of, against ego, 75; and the Oedipus complex, 78; in Marcuse, 119; absence of, in formative theory, 152
Survivor paranoia, *see* Paranoia, survivor
Survivor syndrome, 157
Survivor totalism, *see* Totalism
Symbol-hunger, 162
Symbolic immortality, 150; modes of, summarized, 155
Symbolism, 146
Symbolization, 149, 154
Systemic architectonic: defined, 36-37; and dialectics, 38; and holism, 38; and millenerianism, 38; as superordinate principle, 43; and psychosocial identity, 91; in Lifton, 151
Systemic-dialectical vision, 44, 85; Erikson's avoidance of, 94; distinguished from Erikson's, 114; in Marcuse, 124; in Brown, 132, 138; in Brown and Marcuse, 141-42

Thanatos, 115, 127-28, 135, 145, 168, 172; as disintegrative force, 13; the psychoanalytic intelligentsia and, 14; and the Nirvana principle, 75; *see also* Aggression; Death instinct, the
Theodicy, 38
Therapeutic outlook: as a form of moralism, 2; on communal ills, 3; of psychoanalytic intelligentsia, 11, 79-80; of psychohistorical intelligentsia, 11; in Freud, 63, 70-71, 169, 174; in Erikson, 107, 110-11, 175; versus social and political one, 116; in Brown, 136; in Lifton, 165
Thought Reform and the Psychology of Totalism (Lifton), 155, 165
Thomas Woodrow Wilson (Bullitt and Freud), 67
Totalism, 144, 156-58, 164-65; and the systemic architectonic, 44; Erikson and, 93; Frankfurt school and, 125; survivor, 160-61
Totem and Taboo (Freud), 19, 28, 31, 45-46, 53, 56-57, 59-61, 90, 170
Toys and Reasons: Stages in the Ritualization of Experience (Erikson), 107
Transcendence, 153
Traumatic neurosis, 68-70
Traumatic syndrome, 151
Trieb, 51, 120

Triumph of the Therapeutic (Rieff), 174
Trotter, Wilfred, 60

Unconscious, the, *see* Unconscious mind, the
Unconscious mind, the, 167; psychoanalytic conception of, xiii; biological roots of, xiii; dynamic view of, xiii; historical forces and, xiv; cultural basis of, xiv; origins of, xiv; Freudian theory of, 29-30; in psychohistory, 30; in Marcuse, 119; metaphor of conflict in, 169
Utopianism: in Marcuse, 126; in Brown, 131
Utopian Thought in the Western World (Frank and Fritzie Manuel), 174

Von Bertalanffy, Ludwig, *see* Bertalanffy, Ludwig von

Waddington, Conrad, 35-37
Waning of the Middle Ages, The (Huizinga), 99
Weinstein, Fred, xv, 46
"Weltanschauung, A" (Freud), 56
Wilson, President Thomas Woodrow, 62
Winnicott, D. W., 151

Young Man Luther (Erikson), 81, 87, 92, 94-98, 106-7, 110-12